MOZART'S PIANO MUSIC

MOZART'S
PIANO MUSIC

WILLIAM KINDERMAN

OXFORD
UNIVERSITY PRESS
2006

Oxford University Press, Inc., publishes works that further
Oxford University's objective of excellence
in research, scholarship, and education.

Oxford   New York
Auckland   Cape Town   Dar es Salaam   Hong Kong   Karachi
Kuala Lumpur   Madrid   Melbourne   Mexico City   Nairobi
New Delhi   Shanghai   Taipei   Toronto

With offices in
Argentina   Austria   Brazil   Chile   Czech Republic   France   Greece
Guatemala   Hungary   Italy   Japan   Poland   Portugal   Singapore
South Korea   Switzerland   Thailand   Turkey   Ukraine   Vietnam

Copyright © 2006 by Oxford University Press, Inc.

Published by Oxford University Press, Inc.
198 Madison Avenue, New York, New York 10016

www.oup.com

Oxford is a registered trademark of Oxford University Press

Library of Congress Cataloging-in-Publication Data
Kinderman, William.
Mozart's piano music / William Kinderman.
p.   cm.
Includes bibliographical references (p.) and index.
ISBN-13 978–0–19–510067–9

1. Mozart, Wolfgang Amadeus, 1756–1791. Piano music.
2. Piano music—Analysis, appreciation.   I. Title.
MT145.M7K53 2006
786.2092—dc22   2006007861

Printed in the United States of America
on acid-free paper

For Daniel and Laura,
Anna and Marie

ACKNOWLEDGMENTS

Mozart performance and scholarship have never been as vigorous as in the past fifteen years. Some layers of this book reach back to around 1991, the bicentennial of the composer's death. Neal Zaslaw kindly invited me at that time to speak at two conferences about Mozart, which helped inspire ideas for this book. My engagement with Mozart's piano works was deepened by the opportunity to write essays for the Phillips Complete Mozart Edition, featuring performances of solo pieces by Mitsuko Uchida and concertos by Alfred Brendel. Further stimulation came from recent writings on Mozart by scholars including Daniel Heartz, John Irving, Simon P. Keefe, Ulrich Konrad, Siegbert Rampe, Manfred Hermann Schmid, and Maynard Solomon, among others. The following libraries kindly allowed me to examine sources in their rich collections: Biblioteka Jagiellońska, Kraków; Internationale Stiftung Mozarteum, Salzburg/Archiv and Bibliotheca Mozartiana; Staatsbibliothek preussischer Kulturbesitz zu Berlin. The Research Board of the University of Illinois generously supported my study of Mozart's manuscripts. The music examples stem largely from the Neue Mozart Ausgabe with the permission of Bärenreiter Verlag; the remaining examples were prepared by Bradley Decker. Erik Horak-Hult offered valuable assistance in preparing the final typescript for publication. The following individuals made helpful comments, but are in no way responsible for remaining infelicities: Emanuel Ax, Alfred Brendel, Cliff Eisen, Robert Hatten, Robert D. Levin, Nicholas Temperley, and Mitsuko Uchida. Bruno Nettl encouraged the project by facilitating access to the Mozart collection of his late father, the distinguished Mozart scholar Paul Nettl. Material from chapter 6 was presented at the Study Session of the Mozart Society of America, Annual Meeting of the American Musicological Society, Washington DC, October 2005; the discussion of K. 491 in chapter 7 draws on my essay "Dramatic Development and Narrative Design in the First Movement of Mozart's Concerto in C Minor, K. 491" in *Mozart's Piano Concertos: Text, Context, Interpretation,* edited by Neal Zaslaw. My wife, Katherine Syer, supported the project in countless ways; without her vivacious energy it could not have reached publication in this anniversary year, two hundred fifty years after Mozart's birth.

CONTENTS

Photo gallery follows page 94

MOZART'S PIANO MUSIC

For I am a born wood-hitter and all I can do
is to strum a little on the clavier.

Mozart, Mannheim, 22 February 1778

CHAPTER 1

Introduction

THE CHALLENGE OF MOZART'S KEYBOARD MUSIC

Like Bach and Beethoven, Wolfgang Amadé Mozart was a composer of universal scope whose own primary performance medium was the keyboard. During his lifetime the piano became an instrument of choice, responding to demands for a more differentiated expression of feeling. In the 1770s, when Mozart grew to maturity, this new instrument, dubbed *pianoforte* (sound-loud) or *fortepiano* (loud-soft), was replacing both the harpsichord, with its brilliant but fixed levels of sound, and the clavichord, whose quietness lent itself more to private, meditative performance than to the projection of vivid, articulated expression.[1] The flexible tonal range and polyphonic capacity of the piano permitted a kind of musical mimicry, whereby the stylistic idioms from chamber, vocal, or orchestral music could be suggested by a player at the keyboard. Above all, however, it was the potential for conveying nuanced expression in sound that accounted for the growing primacy of the piano. Joseph Haydn alluded to this bonding of sensibility and medium in stating to Albert Christoph Dies that "my imagination [*Phantasie*] plays on me as if I were a keyboard. . . . I am really just a living keyboard."[2]

As a dramatic composer par excellence, Mozart exploited the responsive qualities of the pianos of his day: the instruments he knew, while less robust than their later, iron-framed cousins of the nineteenth century, offered ample resources for dynamic rhetoric and tonal differentiation. The ascendancy of the piano was bound up with a historical shift in taste and sensibility that Mozart helped to shape. His lively, dra-

---

1. Unless otherwise qualified, the common generic term *piano* will be used broadly here to refer to the diverse family of instruments to which both the eighteenth-century fortepiano and the modern Steinway belong. For a colorful survey of the evolution of the piano in its historical and social context, see Arthur Loesser, *Men, Women, and Pianos: A Social History* (New York: Simon and Schuster, 1954).

2. Vernon Gotwals, *Haydn: Two Contemporary Portraits* (Madison: University of Wisconsin Press, 1968), 141. This work contains a full translation of Albert Christoph Dies, *Biographische Nachrichten über Joseph Haydn* (Vienna, 1810).

matic approach to composition predated his discovery of the resources of the piano, and its origins can be discerned at least as early as 1767, when the precocious eleven-year-old, together with his father, Leopold, adapted sonata movements by various composers into pastiche harpsichord concertos by adding ritornello passages. Already from his fifth year, Wolfgang had composed pieces for keyboard. Evidence of this formative creative activity has survived in the *Notenbuch* (music book) that belonged to his sister Maria Anna (Nannerl).[3] Early duet sonatas for Wolfgang's performances with Nannerl were written down out of practical necessity, whereas his first preserved sets of variations on borrowed themes date from 1766. Seven years later, in his first original piano concerto, the work in D major, K. 175, Mozart still often employed keyboard textures more characteristic of harpsichord music. Until the mid-1770s, he was accustomed to use the harpsichord or clavichord rather than the piano.

A major landmark of piano literature is Mozart's first surviving set of six solo sonatas, K. 279–284 (189d–h, 205b), works finished by early 1775 at Munich. In these pieces he first indulged fully in the flexible dynamic qualities of the piano. In the Mozart family correspondence, these works are described as "the difficult sonatas," which may imply that an earlier set of sonatas from this period existed but has been lost.[4] A glance at the dynamic indications alone shows how enthusiastically Mozart engaged with the new and upcoming instrument of preference. Forte and piano markings abound, and there are some unique effects of swelling and receding in dynamics, such as at the beginning of the Andante amoroso of K. 281. It is especially the Sonata in D Major, K. 284 (205b), that marks a brilliant new stage in his evolving treatment of keyboard textures. Thereafter, through works like his masterful "Jenamy" Concerto,[5] K. 271, from 1777 and his many later concertos and solo and duet pieces, Mozart contributed more than any other composer of the day to the growing repertory of the piano.

In October 1777, Mozart encountered the instruments of Johann Andreas Stein, a leading piano builder in Augsburg. A passage from one of Mozart's letters to his father from this time describes the qualities of his playing: "When I told Herr Stein that I should very much like to play on his organ, he was greatly surprised and said: 'What? A man like you, so fine a clavier-player, wants to play on an instrument which has no douceur, no expression, no piano, no forte, but is always the same?'"[6] Two months

3. The fact that his earliest works survive in his father's handwriting indicates that he improvised at the keyboard, with Leopold Mozart writing down what he heard. Wolfgang Mozart's earliest pieces in Nannerl Mozart's *Notenbuch* are discussed in chapter 4.

4. See Wolfgang Plath, "Zur Datierung der Klaviersonaten KV 279–284," *Acta Mozartiana* 21 (1974): 26–30; and Daniel Heartz, *Haydn, Mozart, and the Viennese School, 1740–1780* (New York: Norton, 1995), 586–87.

5. This work was long known as the "Jeunehomme" Concerto, but Michael Lorenz has recently confirmed the name of the pianist who commissioned the work as Louise Victoire Jenamy, as is explained in chapter 7.

6. Emily Anderson, trans. and ed., *The Letters of Mozart and His Family* [hereafter *Letters*] (London: Macmillan, 1985), L. 225. Stein's daughter Nannette married Johann Andreas Streicher and, together with her brother Matthäus Andreas, moved their father's firm to Vienna. In later years she was in close, ongoing contact with Beethoven.

later, Mozart's mother related from Mannheim that "there are pianofortes here, on which he plays so extraordinarily well that people say they have never heard the like."[7] From such reports we can judge that Mozart's emergence as a mature artist coincided with the creation of the piano, an instrument that came alive under his fingers and served as medium for many of his finest compositions.

It is not the aim of this study to champion either historic instruments of the kind Mozart knew and played or the modern instruments that are at home in today's large concert spaces. As the eminent Mozartian Alfred Brendel observed already in 1989, "A coexistence of 'historical' and 'modern' performances is now taken for granted."[8] At the same time, it is surely valuable for all pianists to become acquainted with the sound quality of older instruments, such as the five-octave Anton Walter fortepiano from about 1780 that according to tradition was owned by Mozart and is now held at the Mozarteum in Salzburg. A light action, clear tone, and divided knee pedal, whereby the player can pedal separately for the bass or for the entire keyboard, are features of this fortepiano.[9] In an essay accompanying his recording on this instrument from the Mozartian bicentennial year 1991, András Schiff wrote that "this instrument is capable of covering the full expressive range of Mozart's most mature masterworks, such as the great *Fantasie* K475. . . . One has the sensation of recreating something that goes to the expressive and dynamic limits of the instrument."[10] Some may feel that the music strains the capacity of older instruments, whose shortness of sound in the upper range defies cantabile playing. Mozart himself pushed the limits of his instruments, and for improvisation and concerto playing, he had his Walter fortepiano equipped with a pedal board similar to that of an organ, which presumably enabled him to extend bass passages, while leaving his left hand free to add fullness to the texture.[11]

In approaching Mozart's remarkable legacy from the threshold of the pianistic age, we should reconsider some common assumptions about his life and art. In some ways, the very familiarity of some of these works proves deceptive, posing barriers to understanding and appreciation. For example, the status of Mozart's compositions as influential masterpieces easily distracts attention from their closeness to the performance practice of rhetorical improvisation. In performance, there is much that needs to be

7. *Letters*, L. 267a (28 December 1777).

8. Brendel, *Music Sounded Out: Essays, Lectures, Interviews, Afterthoughts* (New York: Farrar Straus Giroux, 1990), 224.

9. For a detailed description of this instrument, see Richard Maunder, *Keyboard Instruments in Eighteenth-Century Vienna* (Oxford: Clarendon, 1998), 66–69. Maunder observes that Anton Walter did not become fully integrated into the guild system governing instrument-making until 1791; by 1790, he employed fourteen apprentices (*Gesellen*) and claimed to have made 350 instruments, turning Vienna into a net exporter rather than importer of pianos (27).

10. Schiff, "Playing Mozart's Piano," essay accompanying Schiff's compact-disc recording *Mozart: Piano Sonatas K545 and K570, Fantasie K475, Rondos K485 and K511* (Editions de L'Oiseau-Lyre 433 328–2, a coproduction with Internationale Stiftung Mozarteum Salzburg, 1991), 5.

11. See Sandra P. Rosenblum, *Performance Practices in Classic Piano Music: Their Principles and Applications* (Bloomington: Indiana University Press, 1988), 49, 415 n. 9; also see Eva and Paul Badura-Skoda, *Interpreting Mozart on the Piano*, trans. Leo Black (London: Barrie and Rockliff, 1962), 13–14. Mozart's pedal board is no longer extant.

supplied but that may not be indicated in available scores. This gap cannot be filled through devout faithfulness to a fixed musical text. An overly literalistic attitude risks diminishing Mozart's achievement even while it canonizes the texts of his works. As Richard Taruskin put it, "The scholarly project of freezing Mozart in writing and denying the variable aspects of his performance practice has continued apace, even as the dazzling pianistic work of Robert Levin has gone on threatening it."[12] Through his improvised cadenzas and embellishments—and the spontaneous verve of his playing—a performer such as Levin confronts us with a paradox of Mozart performance: an informed historical awareness does not validate fixed rules or constraints so much as underscore the need to go *beyond* the basic musical text. At the same time, those Mozart works that contain detailed performance directions, including K. 271 and K. 475, remind us of the need for caution and restraint in the embellishment and elaboration of the music. The pursuit of embellishment for its own sake can become self-indulgent and blandly conventional.

The relation of musical scores to performances is historically conditioned. By the later nineteenth century, composers tended to incorporate into their printed works detailed indications of expressive nuances to be conveyed in performance. A century earlier, this was not so much the case, but expressive nuance was no less important. In Mozart's day, musical execution tended to take precedence over interpretation: the act of performance was not so clearly separated from the act of composition. Particularly with works that were not published, composers often felt no need to notate fully what was to be played. The cadenzas to some of Mozart's greatest piano concertos have not survived, but they were extemporized by the composer-pianist at each performance.[13] Nor was this situation limited to cadenzas. For some pieces, such as the "Coronation" Concerto, K. 537, the musical text for sections of the solo part was left fragmentary, and it remains to be supplied by the editor or performer. Few of Mozart's piano works were published in his lifetime; for that reason, his scores often contain relatively few expressive indications. Some works that were published, such as the Fantasy and Sonata in C Minor, K. 475 and K. 457, can contain an extraordinary and even bewildering density of performance directions.

A guiding factor in the realization of musical notation in performance is style, and Mozart was undoubtedly one of the greatest masters of stylistic idioms. As is well known, he blended comic and serious—or *buffa* and *seria*—aspects in operatic masterpieces such as *Don Giovanni* or *The Magic Flute*. What is less recognized is that his piano music, too, embodies a considerable diversity of stylistic possibilities. One aspect

---

12. Taruskin, *Text and Act: Essays on Music and Performance* (New York: Oxford University Press, 1995), 286–87. Levin's recordings of many of the Mozart piano concertos with the Academy of Ancient Music, led by Christopher Hogwood, appeared with the Editions de L'Oiseau-Lyre [Decca]. His recording in this series of the Concertos in B-flat Major, K. 450, and in D major, K. 537, was done in Salzburg, on Mozart's own Anton Walter instrument (Editions de L'Oiseau-Lyre [Decca], 455 814–2).

13. For the musical texts of Mozart's concerto cadenzas and "lead-in" passages, see especially the Neue Mozart Ausgabe, Serie X, Supplement 3, ed. Faye Ferguson and Wolfgang Rehm (Kassel: Bärenreiter, 1998).

of this musical context is the distinction between *gebundene* and *freie* arts of improv-isation, corresponding to *strenger Satz* and *freier Satz,* or strict and free styles of mu-sical invention. For Mozart, the strict style was particularly associated with the organ and with fugal playing. He was a highly proficient organist whose extemporizations in that idiom were not confined to the organ. Yet the style of keyboard playing that Mozart regarded as suited to the piano was quite another matter. "Go on practicing and whilst scrambling through scores do not forget your galanterie performance," he cautions his sister from Mannheim, characteristically employing the term *galanterie* to refer to contemporary performance style. As Katalin Komlós states, "In *galanterie* playing, the observance of fine nuances, articulation, precision, differentiation of light and shade, and *Geschmack und Empfindung* (Mozart's favorite expression) were the most important elements."[14] That an insistence on *Geschmack und Empfindung* (taste and sensitivity) remained Mozart's priority is reflected in his damning verdict on so accomplished a player as Muzio Clementi in 1782:

> Now a word about Clementi. He is a fine cembalo player *[ein braver Cembalist]*, but that is all. He has great facility with his right hand. His star passages are thirds. Apart from this, he has not a cent's worth of taste or feeling *[keinen kreutzer geschmack noch empfindung]*; he is a mere *mechanicus*.[15]

Some modern readers may dismiss "good taste" as an arbitrary notion that is shaped by social class and affluence and is hardly viable as a foundation for value. Yet we need to assess this concept sympathetically if we are to do justice to Mozart's aesthetics. The composer who took up Beaumarchais's *Le mariage de Figaro* was no slave to aristo-cratic interests. A basis for Mozart's universal appeal, not only in his Italian comic op-eras and in *The Magic Flute,* but in much of the instrumental music, lies in a con-summate mastery of musical character. Like taste, the notion of *Charakter* assumes a meaning in eighteenth-century aesthetic thought that involves not only a communi-cation of expressive content through gestural and rhetorical means, but also the recog-nition of defining boundaries and an avoidance of elements foreign to the specific music context. Conscious discretion, selectivity, and heightened awareness belong to the over-lapping notions of what Mozart described as taste (*Geschmack*) and sensitivity (*Emp-findung*). Taste is inseparable from the sensitivity (*Empfindung*) of the performer or lis-tener in responding to the musical content. The frequent lack of notational specificity in the eighteenth century underlines the urgency of this bond between style and substance.

The stylistic language of this music is inseparable from its expressive content. And although the aesthetics of Mozart's age have been obscured through the passage of time, its basic principles remain valid. Perhaps most important is the notion of musical ex-perience as a mediation and synthesis between thought and feeling, rationality and sensibility. In the broadest sense, this double image or dialectical tension seems to be

---

14. See Komlós, "'Ich präludirte und spielte Variazionen': Mozart the Fortepianist," in *Perspectives on Mozart Performance,* ed. R. Larry Todd and Peter Williams (Cambridge: Cambridge University Press, 1991), 27–54; quotation from 30.

15. *Letters,* L. 441 (16 January 1782); translation amended.

reflected in the competing historical perspectives that often have been advanced of Mozart as a "Classic" or "Romantic" artist. For early nineteenth-century writers such as E. T. A. Hoffmann, Tieck, and Schlegel, Mozart was the quintessential Romantic composer, whereas for Jean Paul, Schumann, Wagner, and others, he was the Classical composer without peer. Like Beethoven, Mozart represents a figure big enough to encourage fundamental reevaluation. His works—some of which have never required revival—have helped shape some of our most cherished ideas about musical art.

Between Mozart's world and ours lies the ascendancy of what has been termed the "work-concept"—the notion of the autonomous composition, the work regarded apart from its specific performances. Aesthetic and social changes helped to nourish this concept of the autonomous artwork, regarded in the laudatory sense as an original masterpiece. Kantian and post-Kantian aesthetics exalted the idea of originality, envisioning a higher order in nature "giving the law to art" through genius, while the post-Revolutionary era after 1789 encouraged unfettered subjectivity in expression, challenging the rhetorically grounded conventional language of eighteenth-century music. Pragmatic factors reinforced these historical tendencies. For instance, copyright legislation in the mid–nineteenth century enabled composers to regard themselves as the owners of intellectual property, spawning intolerant attitudes toward arrangement and plagiarism. Such attitudes were quite relaxed in the eighteenth century, and composers often borrowed extensively from others and from their own preexisting works. The basic figurative and structural elements of the eighteenth-century musical language were common property, and it was above all the *manner* in which such tropes were employed that manifested originality. As Levin has observed about Mozart, "There is scarcely a musical gesture, from the courtly and martial march to the sighing appoggiatura, that is not related to societal relationships and functions, physical gestures, or emotional archetypes."[16] The successful composer-performer in this era was more analogous to an orator, who possessed the rhetorical skills to spontaneously fashion familiar topics of discourse into an engaging, stirring, persuasive presentation.

It is in this light that the later ideal of authenticity or fidelity—*Werktreue*—rewards reexamination. The emergence of this value-laden concept is connected to the pantheon of musical culture-heros whose busts adorn the large public concert halls of the late nineteenth and early twentieth centuries, from Boston to Moscow. From the outset, Mozart assumed a honoured position in this "Imaginary Museum of Musical Works," since he wrote some of the first musical masterpieces that have remained continuously in the active performance repertory since their inception, seemingly transcending their original time and place.[17] *The Magic Flute* belongs in this category, as do *Don*

---

16. Levin, "Performance Practice in the Music of Mozart," in *The Cambridge Companion to Mozart,* ed. Simon P. Keefe (Cambridge: Cambridge University Press, 2003), 227.

17. See Lydia Goehr, *The Imaginary Museum of Musical Works: An Essay in the Philosophy of Music* (Oxford: Clarendon, 1992), who concludes that "the imaginary museum of musical works may well remain imaginary, as it continues to display the temporal art of music in the plastic terms of works of fine art, but it will never achieve complete transcendence and purity while it allows human beings to enter through its doors" (286).

Giovanni, the "Jupiter" Symphony, and the Piano Concerto in D Minor, K. 466. One early station in the reception history of the D-minor concerto was evidently a performance by Beethoven at Vienna in 1795, four years after Mozart's death, for which the younger composer supplied the cadenzas.

What made the Mozartian achievement possible, emerging as it did out of a transitional period of diverse stylistic possibilities? This brings us to the matter of the so-called High Classical style, forged above all by Haydn and Mozart, a topic that has been explored by various commentators, including Charles Rosen in his insightful study *The Classical Style: Haydn, Mozart, Beethoven*. Rosen did not confine himself to isolating the individual ingredients of Mozart's music, such as rhetorical figures, expressive topics, or formal prototypes. His main interest focused instead on the recipes, that combination of elements that enabled the stylistic synthesis contained in Mozart's finest works. As a platform for criticism, this approach offers advantages in that it fully acknowledges the role of synthesis in Mozart's creativity, without either collapsing his art into preexisting sources and models, on the one hand, or isolating it unduly from its historical context, on the other. The symmetrical resolution of tensions embodied in the Classical style appears as a creative breakthrough, a flexible controlling framework within which convention and innovation could be reconciled.

This achievement occurred at a pivotal moment in the history of music, and it reflects a process of personal development and enlightened striving that repeatedly brought Mozart into conflict with his patrons or public. Born just six years after the death of Johann Sebastian Bach and three years before the death of Georg Frideric Handel, Mozart remained at a distance from the Baroque idioms, for all his knowledge of strict church style and his later assimilation of Bach and Handel in the 1780s, mediated in part through Baron van Swieten. Like other child-prodigies, Mozart was dependent on a selection of contemporary influences and compositional models, starting with those of his own father Leopold. The paternal influence was perhaps most striking in the up-to-date genre of the symphony: Leopold was Salzburg's foremost composer of symphonic music during 1740–60, followed by his son during the 1770s.[18] This concentration on secular music was not appreciated by the Mozarts' employer, Archbishop Colloredo, and it contributed to the mounting tensions that led to Mozart's eventual departure from the archbishop's service in 1781. It is revealing that Colloredo specified of Michael Haydn, Mozart's successor as court and cathedral organist in 1782, that "we accordingly appoint . . . in the same fashion as young Mozart was obligated, with the additional stipulation that he show more diligence . . . and compose more often for our cathedral and chamber music, and, in such cases, himself direct in the cathedral on every occasion."[19]

Mozart's pioneering engagement with the genre of the piano concerto illustrates patterns of assimilation foreshadowing his remarkably productive decade at Vienna

---

18. See Cliff Eisen, "The Salzburg Symphonies: A Biographical Interpretation," in *Wolfgang Amadé Mozart: Essays on His Life and His Music*, ed. Stanley Sadie (Oxford: Clarendon, 1996), 178–212.
19. Cited in Cliff Eisen, "The Salzburg Symphonies," 191.

beginning in 1781. As a child, Mozart absorbed a wide range of musical influences during the years of touring, organized by his father, to Italy, France, Holland, England, and many German-speaking regions of Europe. Some of these influences long remained undetected, due to the widespread uniformity of the fashionable *galant* style at mid-century and a lack of knowledge of contemporary sources. A typical part of the traveling repertoire during the tours of Leopold with Wolfgang and his sister, for instance, consisted of concertos by the Viennese composer Christoph Georg Wagenseil (1715–77). Yet, as Daniel Heartz has observed,[20] it would have been inappropriate for the Mozarts to perform concertos by Wagenseil in 1767 at Vienna, a circumstance that made necessary the arrangement of new concertos for the trip based on recently published music by other composers. The music so arranged stems mainly from four German émigrés residing at Paris: Johann Gottfried Eckard, Leontzi Honauer, Hermann Friedrich Raupach, and Johann Schobert (one movement derives from Carl Philipp Emanuel Bach). The autograph scores of the pieces are in the hand of father and son, and it was for a long time mistakenly assumed that these were original Mozartian works written for the visit to Vienna.[21]

Other influences on Mozart's early keyboard style include the Italian composers Baldassare Galuppi, Giovanni Marco Rutini, Giuseppe Scarlatti, and Giovanni Battista Sammartini, whose works were presumably made accessible to the Mozarts through collections published at Nuremberg by Johann Ulrich Haffner. Further inspiration stemmed from the "London" Bach, Johann Christian, with whom Mozart stood in personal contact and whose sonatas were arranged by Wolfgang into the three concertos K. 107 by 1772. In addition to devising orchestral ritornellos in these arrangements, he sometimes adds and deletes from his models and approximates, in these early works, the general proportions of his later concerto form. The cradle of Mozart's concerto composition thus lay in his transformation of the sonata, a genre associated with private-home performance, into the more public-display genre of the concerto, in which he himself assumed the role of virtuoso.

A decade later at Vienna, the piano concerto was to figure prominently in his success, with a dozen such masterpieces unveiled in the subscription concert series he held until 1786. During these years, Mozart walked a tight line between accessibility and artistry—between the desire to please his audience and the desire to please himself. The need to seek popularity is repeatedly stressed by Leopold in his letters to Mozart, who responded in a famous letter to his father from 1781 that "music . . . must never offend the ear, but must please the listener, or in other words must never cease

20. Heartz, *Haydn, Mozart and the Viennese School*, 511.
21. The identification of most of the movements with sonatas by Eckhardt, Honauer, Raupach, and Schobert was done by Théodore de Wyzewa and Georges de Saint-Foix in *Wolfgang Amadé Mozart: Sa vie musicale et son oeuvre. Essai de biographie*, 5 vols. (1936; reprint, 3rd ed., Bruges: Desclée, De Brouwer et Cie, 1958). Alfred Einstein comments that "the unity of style that prevailed in the galant period is so striking that until the work of discovery by Wyzewa and Saint-Foix it was possible to recognize four concertos (K. 37, 39, 40, 41) as genuine Mozart.'" Einstein, *Mozart, His Character, His Work* (New York: Oxford, 1945), 291.

to be *music.*"[22] After his break with provincial Salzburg and move to independence in Vienna in that year, Mozart experienced initial triumphs but also increasing difficulties with his audiences, and he failed to make success stick during his brief lifetime. The process has been analyzed by Norbert Elias, who shows how Mozart, who developed standards of taste stemming from a courtly, aristocratic environment, lacked the necessary support within his society to enable the transition from skilled craftsman to independent artist—or at least to sustain that transition.[23] Even Beethoven's later success rested crucially on aristocratic patrons and their subsidies rather than on an anonymous public that appreciated artistic worth.

The poignancy of Elias's assessment is deepened in the biography by Maynard Solomon, who reassesses the practical and psychological consequences of Mozart's departure from Salzburg for Vienna. Solomon argues that Mozart was effectively disinherited, materially and spiritually, by the town that now basks proudly in his glory.[24] Ironically, Leopold's actions in withdrawing parental support when he lost control over his son closely paralleled his own disinheritance by his mother at Augsburg, after he moved to Salzburg. Although he habitually pleaded poverty, Leopold earned handsome sums from the early tours with his children. Leopold Mozart played an indispensable role in his son's artistic education, but this gift came at a heavy cost: a manipulative control that Wolfgang could escape only by straining a relationship that he held dear. The repercussions were not confined to Leopold and to Nannerl, with whom Mozart's contact gradually dwindled to nothing. Beginning in 1781, after Mozart left Archbishop Colloredo's service to remain in Vienna, a conspiracy of silence at Salzburg suppressed the living memories of their distinguished citizen. Only much later—in 1842!—was public recognition expressed in the form of a monument to the composer erected at Salzburg. Mozart felt the consequences of his break with Salzburg in financial terms. In 1787, at Leopold's death, virtually the entire family estate passed to his sister.[25] The financial misery of Mozart's final four years, as documented in his series of begging letters to fellow freemason Michael Puchberg, resulted in part from this severed connection to his family and hometown.

To be sure, Mozart's beginning at Vienna was auspicious: the splendid series of piano concertos is a product of the financially successful years up to 1786. For several seasons, he managed to attract the subscribers to support an outpouring of astonishingly innovative works, music in which entertainment and high art values are indivisibly blended. The precarious balancing act that was involved should not be under-

22. *Letters,* L. 426 (26 September 1781).
23. Elias, *Mozart: Portrait of a Genius,* trans. Edmund Jephcott (Berkeley: University of California Press, 1993). This work was originally published as *Mozart. Zur Soziologie eines Genies,* ed. Michael Schröter (Frankfurt: Suhrkamp, 1991).
24. Solomon, *Mozart: A Life* (New York: Harper Collins, 1995).
25. Some scholars have disputed Solomon's views about Leopold Mozart and the settlement of his estate, however. See in this regard Ruth Halliwell, *The Mozart Family: Four Lives in a Social Context* (Oxford: Clarendon, 1998), 545–64, esp. 552 n. 17.

estimated. At the outset of his Vienna residence, for instance, Mozart revived his first original concerto written at Salzburg in 1772, the work in D major, K. 175. Rather than use the original finale in stern fugal style, he substituted an entirely new finale when offering this work to Viennese audiences in 1782. Einstein describes the substitution of the new finale, K. 382, as "the first instance of Mozart's having to write down to the taste of the Vienna public."[26] The movement was enthusiastically applauded, justifying Mozart's calculation, but as Einstein observes, "it does not maintain the style of the earlier movements."[27] In its basic alternation of tonics and dominants and simplified style, sweetened with facile decorative ornaments, the main theme of this "rondo" suggests a children's song. The movement is not actually a rondo at all but a set of variations on this childlike tune.

In contrast to K. 382, Mozart's most challenging works of the following years, such as K. 491, the Concerto in C Minor from March 1786, must have seemed a provocation. Einstein writes that

> it is hard to imagine the expression on the faces of the Viennese public when on 7 April 1786 Mozart played this work at one of his subscription concerts. Perhaps they contented themselves with the Larghetto, which moves in regions of the purest and most moving tranquillity, and has a transcendent simplicity of expression.[28]

The Concerto in C Minor is no isolated achievement. It stands in the company of other passionate pieces in this key, including the Sonata, K. 457; the Fantasy, K. 475; and the Fugue for Two Pianos, K. 426. If Mozart gave his contemporaries a hard aesthetic nut to crack with such compositions, it was through these very works that his impact on Beethoven was most immediate and tangible. In 1799, eight years after Mozart's death, Beethoven is supposed to have commented admiringly about K. 491 that "we shall never be able to do anything like that."[29] Although the proportion of works in minor keys in Mozart's overall output is quite low, his works for solo piano contain several other impressive examples, including the "Paris" Sonata in A Minor, K. 310 (300d), from 1778; the Rondo in A Minor, K. 511, from 1787; and the Adagio in B Minor, K. 540, from 1788.

In the genre of the piano sonata, we can also detect a tensional relationship between Mozart's artistic convictions and his patrons and audience. If his first surviving set of solo sonatas were known as "the difficult sonatas," his now famous, yet posthumously published "small piano sonata for beginners" in C major, K. 545, sports some surprising difficulties, especially in the closing Rondo. It has been suggested that the very last sonata, the work in D major, K. 576, from 1789, possibly represents Mozart's response to a commission for the daughter of King Friedrich Wilhelm II of

26. Einstein, *Mozart, His Character, His Work,* 292. More detailed discussion of K. 382 is offered in chapter 7.
27. Einstein, *Mozart, His Character, His Work,* 292.
28. Einstein, *Mozart, His Character, His Work,* 311.
29. Cited in *Thayer's Life of Beethoven,* ed. Eliot Forbes (Princeton: Princeton University Press, 1970), 1:209—Beethoven's conversation partner was his friend and fellow pianist Johann Baptist Cramer.

Prussia; yet, if so, the formidable technical and stylistic demands of the piece clearly conflicted with the personal needs of the aristocratic dilettante for whom it was ostensibly written. Levin describes Mozart's K. 576 as a work in which "all of the threads of his prior styles reached a synthesis."[30]

The study of Mozart's piano music thus entails consideration not only of a legacy of many individual compositions, but also of a rich stylistic evolution, from childhood assimilation to mature mastery. Since this book considers the compositions according to genre, it will be helpful to summarize in advance some of the chronological tendencies of Mozart's stylistic evolution in his keyboard works. A seminal period was 1775–77. The Concerto in E-flat for piano, K. 271, of 1777 has always been regarded as an astonishing and seemingly isolated achievement, but it was anticipated by the important set of six solo sonatas K. 279–84, completed in early 1775. During 1777–78, Mozart composed three additional solo sonatas, including the weighty and impassioned "Paris" Sonata, K. 310. His last full years at Salzburg, 1779–80, represent a relatively lean period in his output for keyboard; the most notable keyboard work from this time is the Concerto in E-flat for Two Pianos and orchestra, K. 365 (316a). After the production of his opera *Idomeneo* at Munich in January 1781 and his move to Vienna later that year, Mozart focused intensely on keyboard works: many of his finest variation sets, sonatas, and concertos stem from the period 1781–86. In their brilliance and diversity, these works represent the climactic phase in his output for piano. Beginning in 1787, he composed substantially less keyboard music, a circumstance connected to the decline of his soloist activities as well as his shift of focus to other genres, especially opera. Nevertheless, some of Mozart's outstanding individual piano compositions date from these years, including the last two solo sonatas, K. 570 and K. 576, and the "Duport" Variations, K. 573, all three of which date from 1789. These sonatas show contrapuntal and monothematic tendencies that are characteristic of Mozart's last years. Among works completed during his final year, 1791, the Piano Concerto in B-flat Major, K. 595, holds a special place.

What approach can best do justice to this subject? In some recent analytic scholarship, stylistic issues have often been subordinated to the investigation of structure. Yet we need to guard against the risk of excessive abstraction or reductionism in music analysis, if it is to be useful to listeners and performers. The chances for a consensus on this issue may seem remote, in the light of recent controversies concerning the proper role of analysis and its goals and limitations. But a fresh reassessment can be attempted through examination of the interplay of what Richard Kramer once described as "the two classic elements that rub against one another in every work: expressive, fallible substance on the one hand, and determined, inexorable structure on the other."[31] Critics and analysts have often emphasized one or other of these dimensions without savoring the synthesis on which Mozart's art crucially depends.

30. Levin, "Mozart's Solo Keyboard Music," in *Eighteenth-Century Keyboard Music*, ed. Robert L. Marshall (New York: Routledge, 2003), 339.

31. Kramer, "Ambiguities in *La Malinconia:* What the Sketches Say," in *Beethoven Studies* 3, ed. Alan Tyson (Cambridge: Cambridge University Press, 1982), 29.

One might claim that many of the best performances are already fertilized by analysis, and the best analyses already informed by an imagined performance.[32] This touches on aesthetic issues rarely addressed by philosophers of art. A work of musical art is not an abstract entity, but needs to be realized in sound and time. The implications of that fact were probed by Theodor W. Adorno, who regarded the work itself as "a copy of a non-existent original"—for, paradoxically, there is no work as such—it must become.[33] At the same time, in his view, the true performance does not possess the work ontologically—in its essential being—though it must convey it. For, as with any creative act, the product cannot be predicted or fully envisioned in advance, but represents rather an imaginative synthesis comprised of elements that are intimately known.[34] Adorno thus points to one of the pitfalls of analysis—the temptation to reduce the work to a closed matrix of relations; in other words, to downplay or even disavow the "expressive, fallible substance" in favor of the "determined, inexorable structure." Allegations of such reductionism have been leveled at the work of the influential theorist Heinrich Schenker, but these may actually apply less to him than to some of his followers. Kevin Korsyn has pointed out that some of Schenker's terms, such as *synthesis* and *causality*, have often been read without awareness of their full implications and that Schenker's analytical method is more deeply rooted in the immanent temporality of music than many of his adherents or critics have realized.[35] Indeed, the very notion of "reduction" seems to stem not from Schenker directly, but from later scholars, reflecting the positivist intellectual climate of the decades following the Second World War.[36] Nevertheless, an emphasis on serene,

32. For a discussion of the intersection between analysis, criticism, and performance, see Edward T. Cone, "The Authority of Music Criticism," *The Journal of the American Musicological Society* 34 (1981): 5–7.

33. T. W. Adorno, "Aesthetische Theorie," in *Gesammelte Schriften*, ed. Rolf Tiedemann, 20 vols. (Frankfurt am Main: Suhrkamp, 1971–86), 7:32 (my translation). This passage is cited in Jürgen Uhde and Renate Wieland, *Denken und Spielen: Studien zu einer Theorie der musikalischen Darstellung* (Kassel: Barenreiter, 1988), 14.

34. A detailed assessment of Adorno's musical aesthetics is offered in the opening chapters of Uhde and Wieland, *Denken und Spielen*. A discussion of the book in English is contained in my review article in *19th-Century Music* (Summer 1991): 64–68.

35. See Korsyn, "Schenker and Kantian Epistemology," *Theoria: Historical Aspects of Music Theory* 3 (1988): 1–58.

36. A study interpreting Schenker's graphing process as a "technique of reduction" is Allen Forte's article "Schenker's Conception of Musical Structure," first published in the *Journal of Music Theory* (1959) and reprinted in *Readings in Schenker Analysis*, ed. M. Yeston (New Haven: Yale University Press, 1977), 4–37. Forte describes "reduction technique" as follows: "Detail is gradually eliminated in accord with the traditional distinction between dissonant and consonant tones (made with reference to the tonic triad, the elemental consonance) so that the underlying, controlling structure is revealed" (18). He comments in a footnote that "curiously enough, Schenker did not explain in his writings how to carry out a reduction." Schenker's own passing reference to *Abkürzung* (shortening/reduction) in *Der freie Satz* is uncharacteristic and the context ironic: he invites "everyone to take the little trouble to sample" the middleground and background on the basis of "methods taught at schools and well known from instructional books"— sources he otherwise often scorns. This passage might be regarded as Schenker's proleptic critique of subsequent reductionist interpretations of his work. Schenker's enterprise calls for apprehension of a synthesis of relations, and not merely reduction to "ever shorter versions, finally to the shortest: to the *Ursatz*," as he puts it in this passage: *Neue musikalische Theorien und Phantasien, 3: Der freie Satz*, ed. Oswald Jonas

stable, structural features, as Schenker's approach seems to encourage, can limit its relevance to performance, as Adorno once pointed out, claiming that

> relevant analysis [is] not a reduction to some more or less generalized assumption . . .
> but rather the illumination of the special or unique structure of the individual
> work. . . . This new view of analysis has incalculable consequences for the inter-
> pretation of music. To cite a very simple illustration, such thinking leads not to
> suppressing upbeats, other so-called secondary tones, and non-harmonic, espe-
> cially "dissonant" elements, but rather to emphasizing them—in sharp contrast
> to Schenker's approach.[37]

What Adorno describes here is hardly a "new view of analysis," however, but a very
old one surely characteristic of the best performances in Mozart's time. Daniel Gottlob Türk, for instance, in his 1789 treatise on clavier playing, writes that "good taste
has made it a rule that dissonances or dissonant chords must generally be struck with
more force than consonant ones, for the reason that the passions should be generally
aroused by dissonances."[38] The expressive inflections of music tend to be carried precisely by its more unstable, dissonant elements; however, in Mozart these typically
make their mark within a context of impressive structural control, just as his creative
departures in rhythm and phrasing are pitted against the regularity of stylistic norms
treated more predictably by other composers. We cannot dispense here with either
freedom or determination, but clearly need to seek a reconciliation and balance. For
in Mozart, more than most other artists, subjective expression and objective structure
not only rub against one another, but are blended and fused.

The following chapters survey characteristic features of Mozart's style, illustrated
by analytical discussions of selected works. Not all of the pieces are treated in detail,
nor can every work be given attention commensurate to its importance. Only the
piano solo and duo works and concertos are treated here, although certain other compositions including piano, such as the Quintet for Piano and Winds in E-flat Major,
K. 452, and the Quartet for Piano and Strings in G Minor, K. 478, will also receive
mention. Translations in this book are mine unless otherwise indicated. The interested
reader should consult the Selected Bibliography for a list of further sources and readings, including some of the many recent contributions to research. No single study can
be exhaustive—for with Mozart, as with other great artists, the expression attributed
to Hippocrates and echoed in the *Lehrbrief*(letter of apprenticeship) in Goethe's *Wilhelm Meister* well applies: "ars longa, vita brevis" ("art is long, life is short").

(Vienna: Universal, 2nd edition 1956; first published 1935), 58. The translation of this excerpt by Ernst Oster
on p. 26 of *Free Composition,* Vol. 3 of *New Musical Theories and Fantasies* (Hillsdale: Pendragon, 1977), is
not entirely satisfactory.

37. T. W. Adorno, "After Steuermann's Death," trans. G. Schuller, in *The Not Quite Innocent By-
stander: Writings of Edward Steuermann,* ed. C. Steuermann, D. Porter, and G. Schuller (Lincoln: University of Nebraska Press, 1989), 243. This essay—Adorno's obituary for Steuermann—originally appeared in
the *Süddeutsche Zeitung,* 28/29 November 1964.

38. Daniel Gottlob Türk, *School of Piano Playing,* trans. R. H. Haggh (Lincoln: University of Nebraska
Press, 1982), 340.

CHAPTER 2

The Musical Language

THE SONATA IN G MAJOR, K. 283

By his nineteenth year, Mozart had mastered a highly evolved stylistic musical language. Since the discussions of his pieces in this book are necessarily selective, providing an overview of works in various genres, it is appropriate to first examine one of his representative compositions in more detail. The Sonata in G Major, K. 283 (189h), dates from 1774 or early 1775 and was performed repeatedly by Mozart during the following years. The first movement of this piece well illustrates characteristic features of his mature style.

Like all of Mozart's sonatas, K. 283 has three movements. The opening Allegro is followed by an Andante and a Presto. All three movements are in sonata form and display a remarkable formal poise and balance, qualities that are nevertheless compatible with elements of surprise and resourceful ongoing musical development.

The exposition of the first movement of this sonata is shown in example 2.1. A guiding stylistic principle is the thorough attention given to the implications of the thematic material heard at the outset. The movement unfolds in 3/4 meter, and its basic character initially suggests a gracious minuet that soon yields to more vigorous moods. The opening four-measure phrase is built from complementary two-measure units, moving from tonic to dominant seventh and then from the dominant seventh to the tonic, respectively. The treatment of the initial three-note figure with upbeat and the following two-note slurred figure is especially important. Mozart presents these paired motives so that the descending slurred figure triggers the changes in harmony to the dominant and back to the tonic. Noteworthy is the intervallic space that separates each half of these two-measure phrases. The first pairing of figures exposes this gap as a falling fifth, from D to G, whereas the second widens this space to a falling sixth in a higher register, from A to C.

Mozart thus utilizes fundamental aspects of the tonal system in the opening moments, with the flowing, "Alberti" bass accompaniment filling out the harmonies of the tonic and dominant seventh chords. So much is not unusual, but the exploitation of such musical elements in the unfolding musical discourse is impressive. It is as if this music were able to listen to itself, sustaining in the memory those motives that are reshaped in new variations. Sensitivity to such relations is indispensable to appreciative listening and adequate performance, yet seldom are they granted the attention they deserve.

This opening of K. 283 has of course been discussed before, with attention given especially to conventional and structural features that this work shares with many other compositions. Robert O. Gjerdingen, for instance, has reviewed the Schenkerian interpretations of voice-leading offered by other analysts and presented a "network representation" of the first four measures.[1] While appearing comprehensive, however, such an approach remains abstract and even somewhat myopic, inasmuch as the functional and expressive qualities of the short excerpt in its broader musical context are given little attention and issues of aesthetic meaning are scarcely addressed.

The *gestural* aspect of this music is an irreducible part of its content. Consequently, any nuanced attempt at analysis tends to merge with an imagined performance, since it needs to engage with the music as it is heard and experienced. The upbeat character of the initial motive marks the first full measure as metrically strong, whereas the second measure, by contrast, is metrically weak. This effect is reinforced by the registral disposition of the two figures and by the fact that the two-note slur lays stress on the first note, while the articulation of the second note is lightened and shortened. A context of lively, tensional relationships emerges already in the first few seconds of the sonata.

According to the conceptual framework offered in an insightful recent study by Robert Hatten, these paired figures in K. 283 are dialogical gestures, since they "appear to respond to each other, along the lines of a conversation among equals."[2] This sense of gestural meaning is deepened as the movement unfolds. In measure 5, Mozart combines the initial upbeat figure with the slurred descending figure; the dotted rhythm now articulates the falling half-step G–F-sharp. Rhetorically, this arresting idea is underscored in several ways: by the halt in the flowing rhythmic motion of the bass, with half notes placed in the left hand; by the introduction of the new subdominant harmony; and by the dynamic indication *fp*, standing for *forte-piano*. Another implication of this material is explored in the ensuing measures: an extension of the descending linear motion occurs, so that the move from G to F-sharp is continued through E to D in m. 6, with the shift to a G-major chord. At this juncture, Mozart introduces another variant of the upbeat figure to head a new four-bar phrase.

Although the first six measures are piano and the next four measures are forte, Mozart's phrasing actually displays a more complex tensional feature. In some respects, particularly rhythmically, mm. 5–6 are closely associated with the continuation. Al-

1. Gjerdingen, *A Classic Turn of Phrase: Music and the Psychology of Convention* (Philadelphia: University of Pennsylvania Press, 1988), 23–27. Gjerdingen discusses analyses of these opening measures by Felix Salzer and Joel Lester.

2. Hatten, *Interpreting Musical Gestures, Topics, and Tropes: Mozart, Beethoven, Schubert* (Bloomington: Indiana University Press, 2004), 164.

Ex. 2.1 Sonata in G major, K. 283 (189h), I, exposition

though mm. 5–6 derive from the opening gestures, they launch a continuing phrase member.[3] The intensification of the descending "sigh" figure with repeated notes on E in m. 5 and on D in m. 6 prepares the reiterated quarter notes on D in m. 7, even as the stepwise descending thirds in the left hand continues the falling linear pattern initiated in the right hand. The stepwise falling melodic contour G–F-sharp–E–D of mm. 5–6 is carried forth as C–B–A in the tenor voice of m. 7. In turn, the rhythmic

3. In his thoughtful book *Phrase Rhythm in Tonal Music* (New York: Schirmer, 1989), William Rothstein regards "tonal motion" as basic to the definition of a phrase, and he treats smaller units as "segments" or "subphrases" rather than phrases. My discussion does not always follow Rothstein's framework, but his study is a valuable contribution relevant to the study of Mozart's formal procedures.

motive of three even, repeated impulses leading to a downbeat, such as first appears in mm. 7–8, assumes prominence.

Mozart now approaches the cadence of his opening theme. Picking up the cue of the single dotted sixteenth note contained in his upbeat motive, he unleashes two measures of running sixteenths in the right hand. This is the fastest sustained rhythmic motion. Yet the treatment of the bass suggests a *broadening* through the use of a hemiola effect, as the dance-like gait of the triple-time yields to a double-measure in

Ex. 2.2 Sonata in G major, K. 283, I, voice-leading of mm. 7–10

bars 8–9. The quarter-note underpinning of these bars conveys the pre-cadential hemiola, and the distribution of running sixteenth notes outlines a straightforward linear descent along the lines of a progression shown in example 2.2.

Mozart's slightly varied repetition in mm. 11–16 of the six-bar phrase member heard in mm. 5–10 allows him to place the "combined" motivic figure at the head of a formal unit, while recapturing the original register of the G–F-sharp half-step from mm. 1–2. The phrase structure of mm. 5–6 and mm. 11–12 suggests an intensification of the opening bars, whose basic motivic content now takes on a quality of insistence, as is projected through the twofold appoggiatura F-sharp–E. The harmonic dissonance of this F-sharp heard against the perfect fifth C–G in the left hand is what explains the *fp* marking, and it is this F-sharp (and later E), not the notes in the left hand, that need to be played noticeably louder.

If we contemplate the entire opening theme of sixteen measures, a quality of balance amid asymmetry emerges. This is reflected as well in Mozart's dynamic indications. There are precisely eight measures marked "piano" and eight measures marked "forte." However, the disposition is actually four plus two bars of piano material, followed by a four-bar forte cadential phrase; this is followed by just a two-bar piano phrase and then a reiteration of the four-bar cadential unit played forte. The opening of the theme gives emphasis to the expressive character of the initial dialogical gesture. On the other hand, the ending of the theme is rooted in cadential function, firmly grounding the tonic key of G major.

There are important implications here for analysis and performance. For instance, in the theory of formal functions articulated by William E. Caplin, mm. 5–6 are described as having "continuation" function and as "fragmenting" the motivic content of the opening phrases.[4] True as this is, we should not overlook that mm. 5–6 serve a preparatory function as well by acting as a transition and springboard for the ensuing cadential section of the main theme. Another influential approach, promoted by Leonard G. Ratner, stresses "topical" content—those short figures and motives that in an "articulate performance" should be "sharply profiled" and "set against each other in relief by the performer's control of dynamics, tempo, articulation and emphasis to mark critical notes and figures for special attention."[5] There are undoubtedly at least two distinct topics in the first sixteen measures of Mozart's sonata—the initial, graceful minuet *topos* and the more assertive, cadential passages. Yet the challenge of per-

4. Caplin, *Classical Form: A Theory of Formal Functions for the Instrumental Music of Haydn, Mozart, and Beethoven* (New York: Oxford University Press, 1998), 36–37.
5. Ratner, "Topical Content in Mozart's Keyboard Sonatas," *Early Music* 19 (1991): 616.

formance is not merely to set such figures "against each other in relief," but to convey how one gives rise to another in a rich, eventful continuity. As Leopold Mozart wrote to his son on 13 August 1778, "Good composition, sound construction, *il filo* [the thread]—these distinguish the master from the bungler—even in trifles. . . ."[6] This "thread" is indeed an impressive feature of Mozart's style, and it is not confined to direct, sequential connections, but also surfaces in the form of more remote affinities between passages separated from one another. As we shall see, Leopold Mozart's metaphorical concept applies well to that quality of developmental integration that characterizes many of his son's compositions.

Let us now consider the transition in mm. 16–22 (also shown in example 2.1). This passage inverts the stepwise descending linear motion from the end of the cadential phrase. Hence the stepwise fall of a fourth through C–B–A–G in mm. 14–15 is accelerated rhythmically into a pattern of three rising notes serving as upbeat to the quarter note on the downbeat of m. 17. This new motive also relates to the rhythm of mm. 7–8, which it reshapes in diminution; eighth notes replace the quarters of the earlier passage. At the same time, Mozart introduces a new texture through his use of octaves in the bass, while the pattern of sixteenths in the right hand sustains the rapid surface motion from the cadence of the opening theme. Far from bringing relaxation to the musical discourse, this transition actually injects energy, presenting the stepwise motivic contour drawn from the first theme as a series of upward-driving impulses. Pauses punctuate this new form of the motive, which outlines G–C in mm. 16–17, A–D in mm. 17–18, and B–E in mm. 18–19. The figure, which is made up of rising steps, is treated in turn in stepwise rising sequences.

Mozart's goal is the emphatic octave D in m. 22, which opens a gateway to the second subject group. The rising sequences from m. 18 to m. 22 span the octave, and intermittent falling steps connect the rising fourths that represent the backbone of the structure. In performance, it is best to bring out the series of ascending fourths B–E in mm. 18–19, D–G in mm. 19–20, F-sharp–B in mm. 20–21, and A–D in mm. 21–22. The undifferentiated playing of such patterns easily comes across as cluttered or thick. Here, as elsewhere, the figuration is best rendered in the context of an unfolding musical discourse.

The transition in mm. 16–22 not only sets up the second subject group in the dominant key, D major, but a restatement of the identical passage in the recapitulation leads to the resolution of the second group of themes in the tonic, G major. This device is known as a nonmodulating transition, or "bifocal close,"[7] and exploits the inherent ambiguity or multivalent capacity of the Classical tonal system. In this case, the same D octaves can be followed by a continuation in the keys of D or G, with the pivotal juncture facilitated to some extent by the pause that precedes the beginning

---

6. *Letters*, L. 323.
7. Robert Winter describes this procedure as a "bifocal close" and discusses its historical context in "The Bifocal Close and the Evolution of the Viennese Classical Style," *Journal of the American Musicological Society* 42 (1989): 275–337.

of the second subject. In view of the nonmodulating character of the transition—with the dominant D major given minimal emphasis through the C-sharps in m. 21—the smoother continuation is actually the one heard in m. 90 of the recapitulation, in which D, the peak note of the transition, is taken up as the first melodic pitch of the ensuing secondary theme.

The second subject group of the exposition in D major begins on the high A that represented the melodic peak of the opening four-bar phrase of the first theme, and it consistently employs a texture of stepwise falling thirds. The sonority is enriched by an inner pedal point on A. This four-bar unit is varied in turn by a second four-bar phrase that increases the rhythmic motion to steady sixteenth notes in the left hand, with intermittent, and then constant sixteenths in the right hand as well. The outcome of this eight-bar, antecedent-consequent thematic statement is reached by m. 31. Here an event takes place that reminds us quite forcibly of the controlling presence of "*il filo*," in Leopold Mozart's words.

Mozart breaks with the prevailing registral disposition of his theme at the upbeat to this bar, prescribing a hand crossing as a figure of sixteenth notes in forte moves down rapidly to D in the bass, marking a structural downbeat at the outset of m. 31. This gesture assumes weight in the whole larger process of establishing the new contrasting key of D major, and it is revealing in this regard to compare mm. 31–33—with their threefold emphasis on this D on consecutive downbeats—with mm. 51–53, in which the same D appears again on each downbeat as well as on each main beat of the triple meter, seven times in all. These two passages frame off the main body of the second subject group. By contrast, mm. 23–30, the section at the beginning of the second subject area, has the quality of a large-scale upbeat, or anacrusis, which is resolved as the short run in sixteenths reaches the D in the bass at m. 31.

On a detailed motivic level, this short emphatic run spanning A to D is surprisingly meaningful. It is counterpoised, in the lively context of the second subject area, to the gentle, lyric upbeat figure with which the movement had begun; as a descending scalar segment, it seems as if extracted from the cadential portion of the opening theme (mm. 8–9 or mm. 14–15). On the other hand, this forte affirmation of the falling-scale segment audibly recalls the gliding, syncopated piano line with which the second group had begun, in mm. 23–24. There, the falling fifth unfolded over two whole bars (and extended to a sixth, reaching C-sharp), whereas here, by contrast, the motive is compressed into a pair of beats. Nevertheless, the relation is clearly audible, as the relaxed descending contour of the earlier passage is distilled into a highly concentrated gesture.

Despite the difference in key, m. 31 is a kind of variant of m.1 of the movement: D in the treble is followed by G–F-sharp, and that two-note gesture is now reinforced by other voices. The development of the two-note slur in three voices and in rhythmic diminution is underscored by Mozart's forte indication. Beginning at the upbeat to m. 34, he develops this multiple slur motive in an extended forte phrase of five bars leading to a perfect authentic cadence in D major.

The remainder of the second subject group displays another tendency related to our understanding of *il filo*—a predisposition to recall and reshape the textures and events from the first half of the exposition. After the perfect authentic cadence in D major in m. 43, Mozart recalls the motive in sixteenths from the transition, which is now treated in imitation between the hands in mm. 43–44. This passage, in turn, is directly connected to a variant of the smooth, syncopated subject in piano that had opened the second subject group (mm. 45–47), and the further continuation relies— just as had the earlier passage—on figuration involving the introduction of sixteenth notes (mm. 48–50). This reliance of the latter part of the exposition on variation of the material heard earlier goes beyond the merely figurative level, since the entire sequence and juxtaposition of themes is part of this process.

Under such circumstances, it is possible and perhaps even inevitable that seemingly formulaic material—such as the last three cadential bars of the exposition— shows far-reaching affinities to multiple passages. The rhythm of the right hand, with its three eighths leading to a downbeat, recalls the transition as well as the passage later in the second group in which similar chords were heard in the left hand (mm. 40–41). The harmonic conflict between C-natural and C-sharp in mm. 51–52 also parallels the nonmodulating transition, with its belated introduction of C-sharp. As we have seen, the pedal point on D in the bass is a prominent feature of mm. 31–33 as well. Even the vacillation between D and C-sharp heard in the middle voice as the exposition closes corresponds to the two-note figure C-sharp–D in mm. 31–32. It is as if the skeletal framework of the left hand in these earlier measures were bodied out as the exposition reaches its goal.

The beginning of the "second part,"[8] or development section, of the sonata form occupies a distinct expressive space in the first movement of K. 283 and affords Mozart the opportunity to review the events of the exposition. Like certain of the piano concertos, in which the opening solo seems to comment on the orchestral ritornello without just mimicking its materials, this development begins in a reflective, responsive mood. Its first eight measures are marked "piano" and are organized into two four-measure units, with the second statement (mm. 58–61) representing a variation of the first (mm. 54–57). This passage is shown in example 2.3, which includes all of the development section as well as the beginning of the recapitulation.

There is a striking intimacy of voice here, almost suggesting recitative, and this sensitivity of expression is reinforced by the ornaments and appoggiaturas and by the metric position of phrases in the right hand, which begin on downbeats, while the left-hand accompaniment rests on these strong beats. This removes the music from the immediate sphere of the minuet *topos* and suggests that the ornaments should be played lightly and delicately before the beat, while a touch of rubato would not be harmful.[9]

8. Into the nineteenth century, the main divisions of the sonata form were typically designated as *erster Theil* (first part) and *zweiter Theil* (second part), the former referring to the exposition and the latter encompassing the development and recapitulation.

9. Rudolf Steglich discusses nuances of expression in this passage in his essay "Das Auszierungswesen in der Musik W. A. Mozarts," *Mozart-Jahrbuch 1955:* 198–99.

Ex. 2.3 Sonata in G major, K. 283, I, development
and beginning of recapitulation

As we gradually come to expect, the context of Mozart's motivic references can be specified. The first two bars of the development contain an ornamented A followed by a falling scalar figure outlining G to C-sharp. This is precisely the falling stepwise contour from the beginning of the second subject group in the exposition (mm. 23–24, 27–28), and we have already seen how Mozart has decisively reshaped this figure into a short motive already in mm. 30–31 of the exposition. In a network of related passages, he takes this gliding melody from the head of the second group, energetically reinterprets it in the continuation, and finally offers a kind of meditation on the idea in the development, at the very heart of the movement.

Yet one can also sense a relation between this "new" theme that begins the development and the minuet-like idea from the very outset of the movement. Hence the initial A followed by the descending scale figure ending in the semitone D–C-sharp, heard in A major, corresponds to the opening emphasis on D followed by the semitone G–F-sharp, in G major. In this context, it is notable that Mozart's next phrase in mm. 56–57 reproduces the distinctive falling seventh outlined in mm. 3–4, although the pitches are changed. Mozart is clearly concerned here to set up a compelling continuation from the "speaking," recitative-like phrases in mm. 54–61 to the ensuing passage, which is based on a pedal point on D, preparing the recapitulation. For that reason, there is a strong implication that m. 57 be followed by a melodic resolution from E to D, a circumstance reinforced by the A-major harmony on the last beat of this measure. This expectation is delayed by the four-measure phrase in mm. 58–61, but fulfilled by the accented arrival at the D pedal point in m. 62.

The variation of mm. 54–57 in mm. 58–61 deserves detailed attention. The impression of a more direct, spontaneous communication on the part of the performer is enhanced by the elaboration of every gesture in the later phrase. The ornamental G-sharp in m. 54 is replaced by a short trill on G-sharp–A followed by an approach to A through its upper neighbor-note, B; similar treatment decorates the high D in m. 60. The short descending run in m. 55 is enhanced through the addition of an initial pitch A and the employment of an expressive appoggiatura, D–C-sharp. Mozart even emphasizes the wide interval of the seventh in m. 61 by including the high D as a decorative springboard to the E at the outset of m. 61.

Of course, the tendency of mm. 54–61 to move to the ensuing pedal point on D is strongly reinforced by the accompaniment doubled in thirds in the left hand, which moves upward through a fifth to reach the dominant of D major at the end of each four-bar unit. For the second phrase, Mozart broadens the registral distribution, and the accompaniment drops into the bass region. Once the pedal point is reached, however, the figure of stepwise parallel thirds from the left-hand accompaniment does not disappear, though it is radically compressed. This figurative idea—which is spread across four-bar units in mm. 54–61—now appears in inversion in the right hand in mm. 63–64, 65–66, and 67–68. The staccato articulation of these falling parallel thirds in eighth notes redefines the character of the motive, but its derivation from the earlier passage remains audible and bears comparison to Mozart's concentrated reinterpretation in mm. 30–31 of the exposition of the gliding descending contour in thirds from mm. 23–24.

At the same time, each two-measure unit also outlines a pattern of stepwise falling thirds on a larger level of the musical structure. This pattern is outlined in example 2.4. The strong metrical placement of the falling thirds in mm. 64 and 66 as well as the forte indications and use of the lower D in the bass all promote the audibility of this stepwise chain of thirds, which guides the phrasing of this lively passage.

What remains before the onset of the recapitulation is a single dialogical gesture—a pair of rising staccato motives, played forte in octaves, answered by a series of legato

Ex. 2.4 Sonata in G major, K. 283, I, outline of parallel third
progression in the development

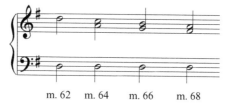

m. 62   m. 64   m. 66   m. 68

motives, played piano in single voice, which descend without accompaniment from
a higher register to connect graciously to the original theme. Significantly, this passage is the only time in the movement in which the left hand is silent for longer than
a single beat. The apparent simplicity of this procedure once more masks the elegance
and subtlety of Mozart's art. The forte motives represent a synthesis of those rising
rhythmic motives from the transition (mm. 16–22) with the staccato articulation from
the immediately preceding passage of the development. At the same time, the ascent
in these bars of a seventh—from D to C—is exactly parallel to the ensuing *descent* in
the gentle piano phrases, which trace the route from high C to the lower D, the initial pitch of the recapitulation. Thus the complementary nature of these two phrases
reveals itself as a near *identity*, in which the same intervallic structure assumes contrasting expressive manifestations.

That this treatment is relevant to an understanding of the style of the entire movement is implied by Mozart's handling of the beginning of the recapitulation. We may
be inclined to regard the recapitulation of a classical sonata form as a vehicle for home-
coming, balance, and resolution, but the beginning of a recapitulation can also reveal
other, more disruptive forces, as is the case in this sonata from 1775. As we have seen,
the basic character of the opening subject suggests a lyrical minuet with a serene, flowing accompaniment in steady eighth notes. Nevertheless, as we have seen, this character does not hold sway over the movement as a whole, which soon makes room for
more vigorous, virtuosic elements. This impulse surfaces already in the opening theme
itself and is also characteristic of extended passages in the transition and second subject group.

It therefore seems fitting that Mozart destabilizes his recapitulation in striking
fashion. The expressive falling half-step C–B in the melody in mm. 74–75 is now suddenly contradicted by an unexpected forte interjection in falling thirds in the left
hand. In terms of motivic derivation, these descending thirds are linked to the falling
staccato thirds heard in the right hand in the development, but their new registral
placement and dynamic emphasis lend profile to the motive. The very notes of the
lyrical melody—C–B—are negated here by the intrusive forte gesture, with the shift
to B reharmonized with a G-sharp, which pushes the music into a new key, A minor.
The fact that the minuet *topos* is now restated in the seemingly alien sphere of the
minor in mm. 76–79 confirms that the dialogical character of the music has become
strained. After a restatement of the intrusive forte gesture in m. 79, a voice of media-

tion seems to be heard in mm. 80–83. The expressive, recitative-like voice from the outset of the development is recalled here, as the music shifts from A minor to C major, the subdominant. Such subdominant coloring placed after a recapitulation, which is characteristic of Mozart, delicately balances the emphasis on the dominant in the first half of the sonata-form design. Rhetorically, at the same time, this passage seems to ward off the looming crisis, with the G-major tonic having been denied stability after the beginning of the recapitulation. As the C-major intervention resolves harmonically to a restatement of the transitional "bifocal close" in G major beginning in m. 83, the movement resumes its normal course, and the remainder of the recapitulation follows the path of the exposition.

In an insightful essay devoted to two of Mozart's later sonatas from the Vienna years, Wye Allanbrook has employed the term "miniature theater of gestures" to describe the aesthetic context of Mozart's style.[10] As we have seen, much the same quality already invests some of his music from earlier years, such as the Sonata in G Major, K. 283. The relevance of this recognition for the analysis and performance of these works is considerable. The gestural meaning of this music is closely bound up with the individuality of its motivic components, but also with the rich web of interrelationships as musical ideas are recalled, combined, transformed, and even placed in conflict with one another.[11]

To what extent are the motivic and harmonic materials in a work like K. 283 conventional features of a common musical language shared by many composers of the day? While there is no doubt about the conventional nature of the language, it is the way these elements are assembled that manifests Mozart's originality. The psychology of this music is rich in *Empfindung* (sensitivity), placing specific demands on the player that are not easily met. In the case of K. 283, the initial minuet *topos* is presented within a tensional field; the piece not only unfolds as a succession of distinct topics, but also involves an active process of integration in which the work seems constantly to be listening to itself. This music requires attentive hearing if its vivid details and its narrative thread—"*il filo*" in Leopold Mozart's words—are to come to life as sound.

---

10. Allanbrook, "Two Threads through the Labyrinth: Topic and Process in the First Movements of K. 332 and K. 333," in *Convention in Eighteenth- and Nineteenth-Century Music: Essays in Honor of Leonard G. Ratner,* ed. Wye Allanbrook, Janet M. Levy, and William P. Mahrt (Stuyvesant, N.Y.: Pendragon Press, 1992), 130. Allanbrook specifically refers here to the opening movement of K. 332.

11. Attention to the articulation of the gestural level of the music also responds to Malcolm Bilson's concern that many performances of Mozart's music on modern instruments are "excessively bland" due to use of a "simple uninflected legato"; see Bilson, "Execution and Expression in the Sonata in E flat, K282," *Early Music* 20 (1992): 237.

CHAPTER 3

An Artistic Microcosm

THE PIANO SONATAS

Mozart's piano sonatas for solo piano fall into several distinct groups according to their dates and circumstances of composition, and they well reflect the evolution of his style even if they do not assume the same importance in his total output as do Beethoven's sonatas. These eighteen works present a microcosm of his art, ranging from youthful stylistic assimilation to the remarkable scope of his mature artistic expression, with its characteristic blending of genres. Aspects of Mozart's orchestral, operatic, and ensemble idioms all surface in the sonatas.

From Salzburg to Munich: The "Difficult Sonatas," K. 279–84

The first five sonatas, K. 279–83, were written at Salzburg during late 1774 or at Munich early in 1775, when Mozart's opera *La finta giardiniera* was produced in the Bavarian capital.[1] A letter from 21 December 1774 from Leopold Mozart to his wife asks Nannerl to bring sonatas by Wolfgang with her on her journey from Salzburg to Munich,[2] which implies that these pieces probably stem from 1774. The sixth and most ambitious work of the series, the "Dürnitz" Sonata in D Major, K. 284, may reflect the influence of music Mozart heard at Munich. The "Dürnitz" Sonata is the only one of the set that was published in Mozart's lifetime. The overall key scheme of the six sonatas outlines a series of three falling fifths (C major, F major, B-flat major, E-flat major) balanced by two ascending fifths from C (G major, D major). The manuscript for all six sonatas has survived, including an extended preliminary draft for the

---

1. See Wolfgang Plath, "Zur Datierung der Klaviersonaten KV 279–284," *Acta Mozartiana* 21 (1974): 26–30.

2. *Letters,* L. 192. Some commentators date the genesis of the sonatas as early 1775; see, for instance, Siegbert Rampe, *Mozarts Claviermusik. Klangwelt und Aufführungspraxis* (Kassel: Bärenreiter, 1995), 228.

first movement of K. 284 that was thoroughly reworked by Mozart. This source, which offers valuable insight into his compositional process, is discussed in detail in chapter 6.

Mozart often performed these six "difficult sonatas" until they were eclipsed by his greater works in this genre in succeeding years. In a letter from 17 October 1777, he relates that he played all six sonatas by memory in Munich and Augsburg; during the following month he performed them in Mannheim. The pianistic demands of these sonatas go beyond those of his earlier keyboard works. In their treatment of character and structural control, these pieces represent a springboard to later works in various genres. Their difficulty is by no means confined merely to playing technique, and the interpretative challenges are easily underestimated. The most brilliant and pianistically challenging is the "Dürnitz" Sonata, which Mozart described as sounding "incomparable" on an instrument by Stein that he played in Munich in late 1777.

The first of the set, the Sonata in C Major, K. 279, has not been a favorite of commentators. Daniel Heartz regards it as the "least interesting" of the set, "filled with minute changes of articulation that seem to belie the opening movement Allegro in common time with mostly sixteenth-note motion."[3] Alfred Einstein writes about K. 279 that "it gives the impression of an improvisation; the tones of the instrument sound in direct response to Mozart's imagination; this is how he must have played when he was in the vein and improvised a sonata."[4] At first glance, the first movement of the C-Major Sonata might seem to be comprised mainly of formulas strung together in an additive, improvisatory series, not welded into the distinctive artistic synthesis characteristic of Mozart's mature music. This impression is to some extent deceptive. On closer examination, the improvisatory character of the piece proves to be shaped by a compelling inner logic.

There is a high degree of motivic integration here—so much as to risk monotony in performances that do not convey the unifying structural forces. How are these relations manifested at the outset of the C-Major Sonata? The forthright opening gesture incorporates a turn figure C–B–C into the left hand at the initial assertion of the tonic triad (example 3.1). This mordent serves as the building-block for an ascending pattern of figuration in the right hand, beginning with C–B and rising diatonically by step to reach the D-minor chord supporting A at the beginning of bar 2. The ensuing balancing phrase descends through the same diatonic scale, reasserting the turn C–B–C with an ornament, and then brings the music back to the C-major harmony and to an exact repetition of the opening two-bar phrase.

The apparently faceless simplicity of this music is misleading; more lurks behind the surface of things than would appear. The arpeggiation of tonic chords at the outset of measures 1 and 3, and of the D-minor supertonic chords at the outset of mm. 2 and 4, polarizes these sonorities and the harmonic-linear elements inherent in them. Noteworthy is the contrast created by the D-minor sixth chord with A, the highest

3. Heartz, *Haydn, Mozart and the Viennese School*, 587.
4. Einstein, *Mozart, His Character, His Work*, 242.

Ex. 3.1 Sonata in C major, K. 279 (189d), I, beginning

Allegro   Entstanden in München, Anfang 1775 9)

tone, placed a major sixth above the C of the initial tonic sonority. An opening of linear space above the tonic, beginning at the rising step from C to D and continuing
upward, is a controlling idea of the passage. Mozart's ornament on C in the middle
of m. 2 is significant, since it marks rhetorically the reassertion of the tonic following
the arpeggiated supertonic chord: each of the arpeggiations or ornaments at the beginning of this sonata underscores this harmonic polarity. Beginning in m. 5, the
sixteenth-note pulse migrates into Alberti-bass figuration, while Mozart reshapes the
turn figure around C and B as a conventionally expressive, *galant* phrase highlighting
the appoggiatura C-sharp–D over a dominant harmony in the left hand. Sequences
in the ensuing bars lift the motive containing the expressive appoggiatura to reach D-
sharp–E and then G-sharp–A, recapturing the pitch level of the contrasting sonority
from m. 2, but with the harmonic support now on the subdominant rather than the
supertonic. In the antecedent and consequent phrases of mm. 9–10 and 11–12, respectively, Mozart reshapes the linear descent from A derived from m. 2 in the same register; the deceptive half-cadence of m. 10, with its use in the bass of the G-sharp–A figure earlier heard in the melody, is balanced and resolved by the tonic cadence in m. 12.
In the following measures, he strongly emphasizes the semitone figure B–C derived
from m. 1, as well as the linear ascent from the tonic, now stressed in forte by ornaments on every strong beat, leading to the half-close on the dominant the marks the
end of the first group of the exposition.

Ex. 3.2 Sonata in A minor, K. 310 (300d), I, beginning

Mozart exploits here the basic tensional conflict of a rising step between the tonic and supertonic, as expressed by harmonic masses of sound as well as motivic and linear means. To appreciate the significance of this compositional strategy, we should glimpse ahead four years in his compositional development to the opening of the celebrated "Paris" Sonata in A Minor, K. 310, from 1778. Like K. 279, the Allegro maestoso of the "Paris" Sonata begins with blocks of tonic and nontonic harmony occupying full measures of the duple meter (example 3.2). The initial change in harmony is to a dominant-seventh rather than supertonic harmony, but the effect of a rising step is similar, with the minor-third B–D in K. 310 corresponding to the third D–F in K. 279. The expressive appoggiaturas in mm. 5–7 of the C-Major Sonata also have a parallel in the appoggiatura thirds of mm. 6–7 of the "Paris" Sonata. Mozart enhances the harmonic juxtaposition in K. 310 by various means, including the use of the fifth A–E as a bass pedal, against which the inner third B–D generates a grating harmonic dissonance. The dotted rhythmic motives heard above pulsing bass chords in K. 310 create a more profiled texture and generate greater rhythmic momentum than does the somewhat mechanical keyboard figuration of K. 279. Nevertheless, the seminal idea that launches Mozart's later masterpiece can be discerned in the earlier work. The opening of the C-Major Sonata, K. 279, resembles a rough sketch for the beginning of the "Paris" Sonata.

Mozart overcomes the uniformity in texture in K. 279 through harmonic polarity and rhythmic control. The notes are not all equal here. Certain events emerge out of the passagework of sixteenth notes to serve as focal points for the unfolding musical discourse. In this process, there is an identification of rhetorical gesture and formal function. The ingenuity of an apparently bland piece like the opening Allegro lies above all in the ways in which basic ideas are elaborated. The opening two measures, shown in example 3.1, can be reduced to the following melodic skeleton outlining a stepwise ascent from the tonic up to the sixth degree followed by the more rapid descent back to the tonic (example 3.3). This framework is filled out in several ways. The C and A at the outset of each measure are reinforced by the bass octaves and longer note values as well as by the arpeggiation of these chords, whereas the flourish on C in the middle of bar 2 marks the symmetrical return to the tonic note. These

Ex. 3.3 Sonata in C major, K. 279, I, outline of melodic
progression in mm. 1–3

gestures take just seconds to play, but their adequate performance is not entirely
straightforward. The melodic shape shown in example 3.3 needs to be rendered with
verve and clarity, and the numerous motivic variants that stem from this energetic beginning demand shaping and emphasis. It is not easy to endow the opening Allegro
of K. 279 with the character this music requires.

Like the outer movements of K. 279, the Andante is full of detailed articulation
signs and dynamic changes between forte and piano. The purpose of these dynamic
indications has been questioned,[5] but some of them underpin larger rhetorical gestures that punctuate or interrupt the otherwise straightforward unfolding of the music.
In the first measure, Mozart lingers melodically on C, intensifying this stationary pitch
with neighbor-note and turn figures, while an accompaniment in triplets is heard in the
left hand (example 3.4). Almost shocking within this placid, flowing context is the upward shift of a seventh to B-flat at the beginning of m. 2, a gesture that is reiterated
with an intensification to forte at the beginning of m. 4. These B-flats are precisely what
enlivens an otherwise static progression, while their conspicuous high register already
anticipates the melodic peak on high C reached in m. 8. The initial sonorities of this
and the preceding bar, with the support of octaves in the bass, anchor the musical
continuity on a level bigger than the basic patterns of figuration in triplets. Some of
the other dynamic shifts create local echo effects in the musical texture, similarly establishing a hierarchy between primary and secondary gestures.

The development section gives attention to the contrasting idea heard in mm. 3–4
of the exposition. Now the placid descending triplets are juxtaposed with a forte reply
in D minor, before a variant of the gesture is answered by another forte statement on
a diminished-seventh chord (mm. 34–38). In the recapitulation of this Andante, as in
the opening Allegro, Mozart delights in reshaping the order of his thematic ideas in the
recapitulation. The second statement of the upward leap to high B-flat in the recapitulation, for example, is now reharmonized, and another repetition of this gesture
leads to material that earlier had been placed near the end of the exposition. The passage indulging in echo effects follows this idea, but Mozart then reverts to the original order of thematic ideas from the exposition.

Concluding K. 279 is a witty Haydnesque finale in sonata form, whose principal
subjects exploit the interval of the ascending fourth. Initially the rising fourth interval is spelled out in long half notes occupying whole measures of the 2/4 meter, but
Mozart reshapes this idea as a series of detached eighth notes in his second subject. In

5. See Heartz, *Haydn, Mozart and the Viennese School,* 587.

Ex. 3.4 Sonata in C major, K. 279, II, beginning of Andante in F major

both cases, the themes begin softly, with the forte dynamic level dominating the later sections of each thematic group. A glimpse of the minor mode in the second subject group is set apart through a contrasting dynamic level of pianissimo. The cadential closing theme, on the other hand, is studded with grace notes and is not untouched by humor: the underlying goal is the attainment of the *descending* fourth C–G, which is avoided several times before its realization closes the exposition. In the recapitulation, Mozart once again alters the order of his themes, but it is the stepwise completion of the falling fourth from F to C that leads to the final cadence.

If the finale of K. 279 seems Haydnesque in its wry humor and almost monothematic concentration on the interval of the fourth, some of the companion sonatas are even more obviously indebted to the older master. Haydn's Sonata in F Major (Hob. XVI:23), published in 1774, may have served as a model for parts of both Mozart's K. 280 in the same key and K. 281 in B-flat major, and Haydn's influence may also have inspired the unusual sequence of movements of K. 282 in E-flat major, as Einstein observed.[6] Already a decade before his "Haydn" Quartets, Mozart had engaged deeply with the music of his older colleague. In his F-Major Sonata, Haydn placed all three movements in the tonic, with a change of mode to minor for the Adagio in 6/8 meter. In his K. 280, Mozart also writes an Adagio in 6/8 in F minor, and he even adopts the siciliano character from his model, although his realization of this slow melancholic dance type is quite different from Haydn's.

Like Haydn, Mozart places the ornamented head of the melody on the fifth degree, followed by a dotted rhythm inflecting the lowered sixth degree of the scale. His continuation introduces new voices in lower registers that echo this opening motive, deepening the mournful, introspective character of the music. Inflection of the lowered sixth step, D-flat, is an obsessive trait of the opening theme. The harmony of the second measure contains D-flat in the tenor voice, as part of the rich sonority of a minor triad with added sixth. In mm. 4 and 6, Mozart emphasizes this scale-step as an oc-

---

6. Einstein, *Mozart, His Character, His Work*, 241.

Ex. 3.5 Sonata in F major, K. 280 (189e), II, cadence theme of slow movement in F minor

tave in the bass, marking each of these dissonances with a forte indication, with a piano marking specified at each resolution to the tonic. Even after the music turns to A-flat major in the second subject, Mozart darkens its character by stressing diminished harmonies played forte, over a chromatically descending bass. An atmosphere of tragic resignation results from the resolution of the second subject into F minor in the recapitulation. But Mozart enhances this effect through added dissonances and chromatics in bars 54–56, leading up to the cadence theme, with its expressive descending motives and silences (example 3.5).

In this extraordinary Adagio, we can discern the origins of Mozart's later use of the tragic siciliano in the minor, as in the F-sharp minor Adagio of the Concerto in A Major, K. 488, from 1786, or the Rondo in A Minor, K. 511, from 1787. As in the concerto, the outer movements of this sonata offer a strong contrast—a radiant, joyous character enclosing the searching melancholy of the slow movement. A striking feature at the outset of the opening Allegro assai is the falling broken chord in the left hand. An *ascending* version of the figure set in forte octaves occurs in the second subject group, where busy figuration in piano provides a witty response. In the Presto finale, Mozart introduces humor through clever use of dynamic and registral contrasts as well as silences. In the opening theme, the second to fourth measures are understated, owing to the soft dynamic level as well as to the prominent use of rests, which tip the balance from sound to silence. The second four-bar phrase, which answers and balances the first phrase, is galvanized through the change to forte, in conjunction with sustained bass notes and continuous sixteenths in the right hand. Such a coy play of conversational phrases enlivened through sharp contrasts recurs in the transition passage to the dominant, where soft harmonized phrases are juxtaposed with comic interjections in the low bass region. Mozart recaptures this quality once more near the end of the exposition and recapitulation, with soft, staccato tiptoeing in the right hand answered by harmonized phrases in the left, before a full-voiced, forte texture brings

Ex. 3.6 Sonata in B flat major, K. 281 (189f), II,
Andante amoroso in E flat major, mm. 16–31

each section to its close. The player should convey here the character of solo passages followed by an orchestral *tutti*. Mozart elongates and reinforces the "orchestral" closing phrases at the end of the sonata, as the curtain closes on this delightful composition.

A striking aspect of the third sonata, K. 281, in B-flat major, lies in its slow movement, carrying the unusual title "Andante amoroso." What precisely is meant by this designation? The title surely has much to do with the coquettish, bashful character that invests the gentle lyric phrases at the beginning of the second group (example 3.6). These phrases convey an intimate conversational dialogue, complete with whispered nothings and meaningful glances; many of the pauses too are made to feel like an intake of breadth, not just a punctuating break between phrases. The term *amoroso* conjures up the idea of a pair of lovers—hence, a pair of musical voices. A venerable rhetorical strategy in such contexts is to employ a lyric doubling involving parallel thirds and sixths, yielding a sweet-sounding, Italianate vocality. In duets celebrating love or conveying amorous seduction, the passages in parallel thirds and sixths can be delayed until the last sections of a piece. Mozart had long been familiar with these techniques. In his little opera *Bastien and Bastienne,* composed when he was twelve for the amateur theater of Dr. Mesmer in Vienna, the duet (no. 15) between the shepherdess and her lover unfolds such parallel thirds to express the tenderness of love. Examples could be multiplied. In a famous piece like "Là ci darem la mano" (There we'll hold hands) from act 1 of *Don Giovanni,* that aria of seduction in which Zerlina yields to

Ex. 3.7 Structural outline of parallel thirds at the beginning
of the Sonata in B flat, K. 281, I

the Don's advances, their passionate singing in thirds is held back until the final section in 6/8: "Andiam, andiam, mio bene" (Let us go, let us go, my beloved).

Hence it comes as no surprise that Mozart's Andante amoroso begins with a gliding descent of thirds in parallel, which are rendered tenderly expressive through the
nuanced swell and hush of *crescendo* and *decrescendo* on the piano. Adequate performance of this theme requires considerable sensitivity and tonal control. The idea of
parallel thirds remains intrinsic to the spirit and the structure of the movement as a
whole; as often in Mozart, the expressive character and formal design are merged. In
the continuation of the second subject group, shown in mm. 28–31 in example 3.6, we
hear a continuation and intensification of the intimate rhetoric in the form of gentle
passages in parallel tenths.[7] This is like a dialogue for soprano and tenor, in precisely
those registers used for Don Giovanni and Zerlina in "Andiam, andiam, mio bene."

The first movement of K. 281 begins with a smooth unfolding of parallel thirds
passing through the interval of a fourth, a progression that is divided between the two
hands of the pianist, with an upward shift of an octave as the subdominant chord is
reached in m. 3 (example 3.7). Against the initial rising thirds, the right hand plays
figuration that sounds like the unraveling of a trill. Characteristically for Mozart,
some of the same basic motivic elements—such as prevalent conjunct motion and an
emphasis on trills—surface in the finale as well. This "Rondeau" opens with an eight-
measure thematic statement: a four-bar piano phrase followed by a four-bar forte
phrase capped by a cadential trill. In the transition and second theme area, the trill
takes on entirely new roles, first initiating a new subject based on a rising broken
chord (mm. 18–20), while later appearing repeatedly as a sustained, syncopated dissonance (mm. 39–42). At the heart of the rondo design is an episode in G minor, full
of chromaticism and agitation. Yet the Rondeau's overall character is joyous, with
touches of humor. The funniest touches relate to the little cadential tag of an ornamented rising fourth F–B-flat, first heard pianissimo at the end of the first theme
group in m. 17. Mozart plays with conventions here with a subtlety rivaling Haydn.[8]
Near the end of the movement, closing phrases with the pianissimo tag are repeated
three times, yet these prove unable to achieve closure, because of the weak rhythmic
position of the rising fourth motive and its character as an understated, whispered

7. This passage also bears comparison with the dialogical phrases in the first movement of K. 280, first
heard in mm. 27–30.
8. For an insightful discussion of closing or "(de)parting gestures" in Haydn's G-Major Quartet, op.
33, no. 5, see Gretchen A. Wheelock, *Haydn's Ingenious Jesting with Art: Contexts of Musical Wit and Humor*
(New York: Schirmer, 1992), 98–101.

gesture. Once before, a forte interjection of this figure had led the music into new keys, as the motive was distorted from F–B-flat to F–A-flat (m. 89). Mozart's "double take" at the very end of K. 281 "corrects" all of these earlier versions in one swoop, trumping surface conventions while reasserting that vein of humor that sustains the whole.

Do these six sonatas represent a cycle rather than merely a loose collection of pieces? The affinity between the slow movement of K. 281 and the first movement of K. 282 lends support to such a claim. Mozart's sonatas normally follow a three-movement scheme, with an opening Allegro followed by a slower lyrical Andante or Adagio movement and a rapid finale in 2/4 or 3/8 time in rondo or sonata form. K. 282 begins however with an expressive Adagio in an idiom somewhat reminiscent of the slow movement of K. 280. Its meditative opening features a stepwise descending bass through an octave to a tonic cadence, whereupon an arpeggiated accompaniment emerges to support paired melodic phrases in the right hand. The second theme in this sonata form design begins with the accompaniment alone, leading to a soft and tentative pattern of similar paired melodic phrases, which seems to mark time before the appearance of the more assertive forte continuation in the dominant key. This subject introduces thirty-second notes, the fastest rate of rhythmic motion, lending momentum to the music at the end of the exposition.

The opening subject of this Adagio suggests a motto that is set off from the continuation by the trill in m. 3 and the sixteenth-note motion in the bass beginning in m. 4. The opening melodic intervals in m. 1—between B-flat and C, and B-flat and E-flat—are sensitively varied in mm. 2–3. This richly expressive passage does not return at the beginning of the recapitulation, but it is restated in varied form at the beginning of the development. Here its recitative-like character is deepened and intensified by rhythmic and harmonic changes, leading through a *crescendo* to an inner climax not untouched by anguish. At the end of the movement, on the other hand, Mozart adds a coda of three bars, in which the opening motto is reshaped once more, leading to a cadence of utmost calmness, marked by the only pianissimo in the entire sonata.

The second movement comprises two minuets, the second of which functions as a trio, although it is longer than the first, fuller in texture and more extroverted in character. Like the spirited finale, these minuets indulge constantly in contrasts between piano and forte, often suggesting the solo and *tutti* alternation of orchestral music. In the second subject group of the finale, Mozart indulges in striking juxtapositions between delicately nuanced piano phrases and robust *tutti* gestures anchored by arpeggiated octave chords, played forte. However, even at these junctures, a larger melodic continuity is carried through the sustained half notes of the chords. The octave registral span of these chords corresponds to the "call" motive at the beginning of the movement, whose figure of repeated notes leaps up an octave. This "call" motive also dominates in the development, where it appears forte and doubled in octaves in the left hand.

The fifth sonata of the series, K. 283, in G major, is stylistically akin to Johann Christian Bach in the gentle lyricism of its opening Allegro. Mozart achieves here a smoothness and breadth while also utilizing the initial upbeat figure in dotted rhythm to trigger more vigorous passages. As we have seen in chapter 2, this upbeat figure leads to the first dynamically emphasized chords in mm. 5 and 6, and it also marks the rhetorically insistent, forte phrases that introduce the first running figuration in sixteenth notes, the second of which connects to the transition to the second theme group. The transition from a gently flowing texture to more animated figuration is largely facilitated by Mozart's economical use of the upbeat motive.

As in the preceding sonata, Mozart places a recitative-like passage at the outset of the development section, whose animated turns and speaking pauses yield after eight bars to a pedal point on the dominant of G major. The ensuing music up to the beginning of the recapitulation assumes a more objective, functional character. Mozart then reinterprets the opening theme to pass abruptly into A minor, incorporating thereby a developmental idea into the recapitulation. As if in response to this dramatic intrusion, he intensifies the lyrical rhetoric of the continuation before leading the music into a transition identical to that of the exposition.

The Andante—"simplicity itself," in Heartz's words[9]—begins with a melodic repetition of the tonic note with a placid accompaniment on a root-position triad. Mozart soon introduces complications into an apparently serene situation. These ensue so gradually that the listener is caught unaware. After a forte restatement of the opening two-measure phrase, a more declamatory rhetoric is introduced, with pauses and dotted rhythms, leading to a new melodic passage employing sixteenth notes with an ascent in register. Starting in m. 9, a more fervent character emerges, and Mozart uses forte-piano alternations and a shortening of phrase lengths to increase the emotional intensity. He breaks off the last forte phrase into silence before thirty-second note figuration leads to the cadence in the dominant.

As the development begins, any remaining pretense of serenity collapses. The stratified texture of melody and accompaniment gives way to a dialogue, as both hands insistently declaim a chromatic figure outlining a diminished-seventh chord. The second of these paired phrases resolves to D minor, a tonal space that Mozart fills with a restatement of the opening placid subject from the beginning of the Andante (example 3.8). The theme now appears in a different metric position, beginning in the middle of the measure. The tonality, moreover, is unstable, and the original theme is restated, forte, in the tonic key of C major. Is this a premature or "false" recapitulation of the main subject? In terms of its character of utmost simplicity, it is much more like a distortion: Mozart breaks off the phrase abruptly, cutting it in half on the knife-like dissonance of another diminished seventh, and allows the shortened, segmented fragment to drop into the left hand. The implied key is A minor, and this tonality exerts sway over the ensuing measures, which contain surprisingly acute dissonances. At the same time, the phrased motive B–F drawn from the original theme—which Mozart has used as trigger for the dissonant interruption in bar 19—is inverted to A–D-sharp as a stretto against the left hand in m. 20 and then expanded to the octave on D in the next bar,

9. Heartz, *Haydn, Mozart, and the Viennese School,* 589.

Ex. 3.8 Sonata in G major, K. 283, II, development to
beginning of recapitulation, mm. 16–26

while the neighbor-note semitone figures are doubled in thirds in the left hand. Then
an augmented sixth F–D-sharp is played twice in the left hand, together with expressive figures in the highest register in the treble, whose peak tone D sounds as an acute
dissonance against the sustained D-sharp.

In keeping with the original character of serene innocence of the main subject of
the Andante, the recapitulation is tonally unprepared. The key of A minor, so clearly
implied at the end of the development, is left hanging, and a simple rising chromatic
scale connects to the return of the original theme in C major. The rest of the recapitulation generally follows the pattern of the exposition with one exception: Mozart caps
the movement by restating the opening two-bar phrase yet again, in a significantly
modified way. The reharmonized phrase, beginning forte, recaptures for a moment

the diminished-seventh sonority on which the theme was broken off in the development. Resolving that chord to an A-minor triad, Mozart reasserts the tonal balance, quietly concluding the movement in the tonic.

We are reminded here again how seeds for greater works to come were sown already in Mozart's sonata cycle of 1775. Maynard Solomon has drawn attention to an archetype in some of Mozart's Adagios and Andantes, in which "a calm, contemplative, or ecstatic condition gives way to a troubled state—it is penetrated by hints of storm, dissonance, anguish, anxiety, danger—and this in turn is succeeded by a restoration of the status quo ante, now suffused with and transformed by the memory of the turbulent interlude." Solomon refers especially to the use of this dramatic compositional pattern in the "Paris" Sonata in A Minor, K. 310, the same piece whose first movement bears comparison to K. 279. Solomon observes that despite

> the striking contrasts, the darkening of mood, the piercing, almost Schubertian dissonances, the brooding intensity, the relentlessness of the rapid modulations through a shifting sequence of major and minor keys, Mozart has not intention of giving way to chaos and disruption. . . . Instead, after this outburst has spent its force, he moves to reinstate the original, Edenic condition, which is now heightened by melodic ornamentation and figurative elaboration.[10]

In the Andante of K. 283, to be sure, only some of these features are present. Nevertheless, the undermining of simplicity is profoundly handled, and the piece consequently displays a fascinating paradox: it contains at once the most naive and unclouded, yet also the most disturbing parts of the sonata. These are two sides of the same coin.

The most brilliant movement of this sonata is the closing 3/8 Presto, which in its resourceful pianistic textures, imitative writing, and richness of contrasts equals the best of Haydn's sonata finales from this period. Its development, which is placed almost entirely in the minor, generates considerable dramatic power that is effectively balanced and resolved in the symmetrical recapitulation. To frame the work and ground its energies, Mozart adds the simplest of codas and labels it as such: a cadence of widely spaced, arpeggiated dominant and tonic chords.

The last sonata, K. 284, in D major, composed for Baron Dürnitz at Munich, is the most virtuosic of the series and marks a new stage in Mozart's writing for piano. The textures in the development section of the opening Allegro are especially brilliant. This passage of twenty measures involves continuous movement in sixteenth notes, with hand crossings and colorful registral contrasts. Mozart foreshortens the musical material to lend forward drive to the music: two-measure units contrasting forte and piano in mm. 60–65 are followed by one-measure units in mm. 65–69, with a further compression to half-bar units in m. 70 and then quarter-bar units in m. 71 leading to the beginning of the recapitulation in m. 72.

French influence may be discerned in the second movement of K. 284, a Rondeau en Polonaise, and in the use here, for the first time in Mozart's sonatas, of a theme

---

10. This and the preceding quotation are drawn from Solomon's *Mozart: A Life*, 187–90.

and variations movement, which forms the finale. (The only other finale in the set that had departed from sonata form was the closing "Rondeau" of K. 281.) This long Andante movement goes beyond Mozart's independent variation sets of these years to incorporate a variation in the minor, no. 7; and the variations that follow are especially inventive and inspired in their contrapuntal writing and in their treatment of the chromatic progression at the beginning of the second half of the theme. In no. 9, Mozart places canonic writing in octaves into each variation half, with imitations in inversion in the second half; no. 10 features rapid octave tremolos whose brilliant effect is heightened by chromaticism and syncopations. On the other hand, no. 6 recalls the brilliant textures and hand crossings of the development of the first movement. The most playfully humorous of the variations is no. 2, in which a short, descending figure in triplets is paired with an even shorter ornamented falling motive, whose rapid motion is dissolved into silence. The duple meter of the theme and variations is eventually succeeded, after the ornate Adagio cantabile (no. 11), by a lively Allegro in triple time, and this dance-like transformation brings the sonata to a jubilant close.

Mozart at Mannheim and Paris: K. 309, K. 311, and K. 310

Mozart's extended journeys during 1777–78 took him for an extended period to Mannheim and to Paris. The Sonatas in C Major, K. 309 (284b), and D Major, K. 311 (384c), were completed at Mannheim during the autumn of 1777; the A-Minor Sonata, K. 310, dates from the grim summer of 1778, which saw the death of Mozart's mother in the French capital. The three pieces were published together as opus 4 by Franz Joseph Heina at Paris in 1782.

Mozart improvised the C-Major Sonata at Augsburg on 22 October 1777, with a different slow movement, and subsequently wrote out the piece at Mannheim. "I then played . . . all of a sudden a magnificent sonata in C major, out of my head, with a rondo at the end—full of din and sound," he wrote. The opening Allegro con spirito opens with a dualistic gesture: the fanfare in unharmonized octaves, played forte, is juxtaposed with a more delicate response, marked "piano" and grazioso in basic character. This contrast generates much of the immense energy that characterizes the movement, an energy expressed in textures and motivic figures reminiscent of the Mannheim orchestral school. For Heartz, the sonata's opening is "orchestrally inspired," foreshadowing the beginning of the "Jupiter" Symphony and especially the overture to the comedy *Der Schauspieldirektor*, K. 486.[11] The irregular phrase lengths of the main subject add to its effectiveness: two measures of the fanfare gesture are pitted against five measures in the more lyrical response. The performer should be alert to motivic reinterpretations of the initial salvo, the falling fourth C–G of m. 1. In mm. 15–16 and 18–19, for example, Mozart enlarges the gesture over the striding bass by repeating each of the notes threefold, while connecting them with a pair of eighth notes. At the transition, in mm. 27–28, the motive of falling fourths is compressed through rhyth-

11. Heartz, *Haydn, Mozart, and the Viennese School,* 591.

mic diminution to sixteenth notes. In between, we hear a series of falling sequences of a rising staccato motive over pulsing thirds in the bass—a passage that recalls the Mannheim symphonists.

In the development, the opening fanfare is restated in G minor, with echoes of its second half carried into the upper register, where a plaintive lyrical phrase emerges. This expressive contrast is then further heightened through reaffirmation of the forceful fanfare in D minor, in a low register, and the tension is sustained through rhythmic intensification in the following passage. In approaching the recapitulation, Mozart places the fanfare in a series of four-bar phrases, which rise in sequences through A minor and G major to reach the C-major tonic. Throughout this movement, Mozart uses a variety of devices to maintain a quality of unpredictability. In the recapitulation, there is a darkening turn to C minor within the first subject group, whereas the angular "Scotch snap" rhythm from the second subject group is initially shifted to the left hand. A triumphant statement of the fanfare ushers in the close.

In the intimate and charming slow movement conceived at Mannheim, marked "Andante un poco Adagio," Mozart claimed to portray the character of Rosa Cannabich, the fifteen-year-old daughter of his friend, the Kapellmeister Christian Cannabich. ("I made it entirely after the *Caractere* of Mlle. Cannabich"). In the same letter of 6 December 1777, Mozart described Rosa as "pretty . . . charming . . . intelligent . . . amiable. . . . She is exactly like the Andante."[12] Of course, the comparison is not to be taken quite literally. Mozart also gave piano lessons to Rosa, and other comments reveal that only through careful practice did she become "exactly like the Andante." On 14 November 1778 he wrote of teaching K. 309 to her that "we finished with the first Allegro today; the Andante will give us the most trouble because it is full of expression and must be played accurately, with the right taste, forte and piano, as it is written." The "portrait" character of this movement surely has to do with a unifying concentration on the main theme of sixteen bars, whose two halves share the same motives and turns of phrase. Mozart develops the theme in a series of ornamental variations, adding episodic material sparingly and in close organic relation to the principal subject. For all its nuances in dynamics, contrast is minimized in this lovely slow movement.

The notion of the Andante as a personal portrait of Rosa Cannabich may have been bound up with the strong association of the opening Allegro con spirito to Mannheim symphonic style and hence to Rosa's father and his orchestral colleagues. If so, the spacious closing "Rondeau" seems to embrace both worlds: the brilliant textures and orchestral feeling of the first movement surface in lively episodes, signaled by rapid tremolos in the right hand, yet the principal character is more intimate and graceful. The main theme of this Allegretto grazioso assumes a gentle, inward quality, and Mozart gives this theme the last word, as the piece ends quietly, with a descent into a lower register, pianissimo.

The Sonata in D Major, K. 311, is a companion piece to K. 309, with which it shares the same elaborate pianistic textures, and even the same designation "Allegro con spir-

12. *Letters,* L. 256.

ito" for the first movement. The vivacious opening is very similar to Mozart's earlier sonata in this key, K. 284. The spacing of the initial arpeggiated tonic chord on the downbeat of the 4/4 meter, set off by a rest and followed by a motivic figure in six-teenths, is virtually identical. In K. 311, however, Mozart separates the opening phrases with further silences, creating a somewhat whimsical effect. A variant of the sixteenth-note figure serves as upbeat to the lyrical theme that heads the second subject group, a tune studded with appoggiaturas. Particularly concerto-like are the passages near the end of the exposition and the coda; but at the last minute Mozart leaves the emphatic rolled chords hanging in the air, recalling thereby the first pause heard at the very out-set of the movement. A sensitive piano phrase of two-note slurred figures then leads to the true cadence—a "feminine" close—whose dying fall enlarges on the appog-giatura motive from the beginning of the second subject.

The Andante con espressione in G major is a piece characterized by warm lyricism and self-possession; like the slow movement of K. 309, it limits contrast to a sensitive play of dialogical gestures. Above an inner pedal point on D, the melody pivots between B and C; a brief tonicization of C major in forte is answered by a soothing response in G major. The main theme consists of a pair of antecedent and consequent phrases followed by a serene postlude in mm. 9–11. The ensuing repetition of the theme is oddly abrupt, giving the effect of a missing measure; although notated in Mozart's au-tograph score, the repetition may have been added later.[13] Some expressive nuance in performance is needed to smooth the transition back to the opening of the theme.

The design of the movement suggests a rondo with elements of sonata and varia-tion form. The threshold to the contrasting area is signaled by a pair of trice-repeated chords (mm. 14–16; 50–52) juxtaposing forte and piano, and involving a delicate shift in voice-leading, as the G-sharp in the middle register of m. 15 is resolved to a gently ringing A in the outer voices of the following sonority. (The analogous gesture in mm. 50–52 intensifies the dissonance to an augmented sixth chord.) The ensuing sec-ondary theme, marked forte, offers a degree of contrast with its expressive appoggiatura gestures, suspensions, and flowing, descending contour; but it soon yields to a deco-rated variant of the main theme, with a trill representing an intensification of the inner pedal point. In the final section, another embellished return of the original subject leads to the serene postlude, which is now expanded, with the continuation doubled in octaves before this rich sonority fades to piano and then pianissimo, in a gentle farewell to the theme. The octave passage in this coda is written in three registers, with sustained bass notes far beneath the accompaniment in the lower middle register; in his Vienna years, Mozart could have performed this passage using the pedal board of his Anton Walter instrument, thereby avoiding a blurring of the texture.

The rondo finale is in the 6/8 meter Mozart favored for concerto finales, and it in-corporates a cadenza that would be at home in a concerto. The opening theme has a

13. See *Klaviermusik,* Neue Mozart Ausgabe Serie IX, 25/1, ed. Wolfgang Plath and Wolfgang Rehm, XVI (Kassel: Bärenreiter, 1986); and the *Critical Report,* Serie X, 25, ed. Wolfgang Rehm, 65 (Kassel: Bären-reiter, 1998).

vivacious, gigue-like character. This movement is full of vividly contrasting and yet complementary phrases, juxtaposing forte and piano, homophony and polyphony, and exploiting disparities in register. Indeed, both of the Mannheim sonatas show Mozart's increasing ability to successfully integrate contrasts of many kinds into a larger whole. In the finale of K. 311, this extends to the imitation at the keyboard of the effect of the orchestral mass, as in the lead-in passage to the cadenza, or the flourishes at the very end. As K. 311 shows, a sonata can pretend to be a concerto.

A key work in Mozart's output for piano is the Sonata in A Minor, K. 310, whose autograph score is dated "Paris 1778." This work stands in splendid isolation among his solo sonatas; its closest companion is the E-Minor Sonata for Piano and Violin, K. 304 (300c). The two pieces were probably written one after the other, during June and July 1778. Mozart's circumstances were anything but auspicious at this time. Reluctantly and unwillingly, he had left Mannheim and his beloved Aloysia Weber at the urging of his father, who demanded, "Off with you to Paris!" Mozart arrived in Paris on 23 March 1778 with his mother, who soon fell seriously ill and died there on July 3. Professionally, the time spent at Paris until September 1778 yielded little. In his own words, Mozart described the situation as follows: "I must now tell you something about my own affairs. You have no idea what a dreadful time I am having here. . . . From my description of the music here you may have gathered that I am not very happy, and that . . . I am trying to get away as quickly as possible. . . ."[14] Mozart was not very productive during his time at Paris, though some works he did write have been lost. Severe disappointments arose from his vain attempts to gain favor among the Parisian aristocracy. In another letter to his father, dated 1 May 1778, he described his futile experience in the unheated rooms of the Duchesse de Chabot: "At last . . . I played on that miserable, wretched pianoforte. . . . Madame and all her gentlemen never interrupted their drawing for a moment, but went on intently, so that I had to play to the chairs, tables, and walls. Under these circumstances I lost my patience."[15]

Mozart's next four sonatas, K. 330–33, had long been assigned to 1778, but manuscript studies by Wolfgang Plath and Alan Tyson have shown that the Sonata in B-flat Major, K. 333 (315c), and probably the other three works as well were actually written out five years later, in 1783. This major revision in dating further underscores the special position of K. 310, Mozart's first sonata in the minor mode. Hanns Dennerlein perceived Mozart trying to overcome his "pain and distress" in this sonata; Einstein described it as a "tragic sonata . . . full of unrelieved darkness."[16] It is delicate matter to assess the relationship between an artist's work and his life. Nevertheless, some connection surely exists between Mozart's precarious path toward independence amid the setbacks of his Paris journey, on the one hand, and the startling artistic power manifested in the "Paris" Sonata, on the other. We have already referred to the "Andante/

14. Cited in Einstein, *Mozart, His Character, His Work,* 47.

15. *Letters,* L. 303.

16. Hanns Dennerlein, *Der unbekannte Mozart: Die Welt seiner Klavierwerke* (Leipzig: Breitkopf and Härtel, 1951), 97; Einstein, *Mozart, His Character, His Work,* 244.

Adagio archetype" proposed by Maynard Solomon; the symbolic depiction of "trouble in paradise" finds an outstanding example in the slow movement of K. 310, the Andante cantabile con espressione. The disturbing intrusion of the uncanny in the development section of this Andante seems bound up with the work as a whole and testifies to a deepened conception of the sonata as an integrated cycle of movements.

The driven, almost fatalistic character of the Allegro maestoso of the "Paris" Sonata is conveyed partly through rhythmic means: repeated chords in the bass and dotted rhythms in the treble dominate at the outset, and large portions of this movement, and the finale as well, are written in an irresistible *perpetuum mobile* (example 3.2). All the more telling, therefore, as Jürgen Uhde has observed, are the poignant piano gestures within the opening theme, with their appoggiaturas and hint of hesitancy, and the related *calando* passage a few moments later.[17] Mozart expands his thematic structure at precisely that moment when the poignant piano gestures are heard; consequently, the tonic cadence, with its vigorous reassertion of the head of the opening theme, is delayed one measure, until bar 9. The continuous driving rhythm of eighth notes connects to this short expressive episode at m. 5, with the ostinato effect curtailed at the sigh-figures in mm. 5–7, as imitations in the left hand mimic the gestures in the right hand. It is as if an implacable external agency embodied in the first measures had yielded momentarily to a personal, subjective presence in the following measures, before collapsing into the irresistible forward momentum. Such passages require nuanced performance if their expressive content is to be conveyed.

Another prominent feature of the work is Mozart's relentless use of adjacent scale-steps as a source of motivic and harmonic tension. The opening blocks of harmony juxtapose and overlap tonic and dominant-seventh harmonies, and Mozart lays stress on a stepwise ascent from A–C to B–D in the left hand while sustaining A as a tonic pedal point. At the same time, the march-like melody in the right hand plunges down the triad to A on the downbeat of bar 2, with this pitch treated as an appoggiatura to G-sharp. When the phrase is repeated, Mozart increases this emphasis on the semitone A–G-sharp by approaching the appoggiatura through a chain of running sixteenth notes. Beginning at the transition, sixteenth-note motion will dominate wide stretches of the form.

In performance, the determined character of these ostinato rhythms and blocks of repeated harmony need to be contested by the side-slipping dissonances and rhythmic hesitations. An attitude of distanced objectivity is not adequate to the aesthetic demands of the work. Dramatic events need to be underscored through expressive means, such as differentiated voicing and the controlled rhythmic placement of points of arrival. One such passage occurs at the beginning of the development, where Mozart destabilizes the tonality of C major by harping on the dominant-seventh chord including B-flat, which soon becomes a German augmented-sixth chord including A-sharp; the third appearance of this sonority in forte marks an acceleration in rhythm to sixteenth notes (example 3.9). The pivotal outcome of this

17. See Uhde and Wieland, *Denken und Spielen,* 259–60.

Ex. 3.9 Sonata in A minor, K. 310, I, development, mm. 54–60

progression is the resolution of the augmented-sixth to B at the fortissimo marking in m. 58. This point of arrival must sound like the decisive intrusion of a powerful force that has dislodged the music from a straightforward continuation. The symbolic overtones of this passage are provocative. What had appeared stable (the march-like theme in C major) is gradually turned into an unstable dissonance (the German augmented-sixth) and resolved into a contrasting neighboring key (B). The harmonic tension investing the main theme is turned inside-out, so that the C-major tonality itself is treated much like the internal dissonances of the theme, requiring resolution to the key a half-step lower. In this music, apparently stable configurations can be engulfed by dramatic impulses that may appear lawless, but which are held in an extreme dialectical tension.

The basic idea of a motion of thirds over a stationary pitch is worked out in many ways in this impressive Allegro maestoso. In the transition, the motion of thirds is between B–D and C–E-flat over the pedal point G. Mozart coordinates the harmonic structure of this passage with the characteristic sound of the whole movement, and he darkens the tonal color by choosing the minor 6/4 chord in preparing the modulation to the relative major key, C major. The second subject is not melodically independent, but is linked to the main subject through its *perpetuum mobile* rhythm and its stepwise descending motion spiked by dissonances between neighboring pitches. Harmonic clashes between adjacent scale-steps are most acute in the development, which begins with the march-like subject in C major. The powerful modulation through the German augmented-sixth chord thrusts the music into B major, fortissimo, but Mozart employs a series of suspensions over the grinding pedal point—a fierce intensification of the opening of the sonata. As this material is transposed to E major, the dynamic level is shifted to pianissimo; but at the following modulation to A major, Mozart reasserts fortissimo. In no earlier sonata had he employed such sharp dynamic contrasts as here.

The slow movement in F major, marked "Andante cantabile con espressione," is in Solomon's words,

> A self-contained, windowless, protected space within which, moving at a measured tempo, we quietly experience sensations of surpassing intensity—oceanic, comforting, and rapturous. These feelings are then reinforced through an unhurried, patient repetition of the entire initial section. But now, without raising his voice or quickening his pace, Mozart opens a trapdoor through which flood disturbing and destabilizing powers, threatening to annihilate what has gone before.[18]

As in the development of the preceding movement, this "trapdoor" opens out of C major. We pass to C minor and enter a labyrinth of shadowy keys that are touched but scarcely entered in an unstable modulatory passage of sixteen measures. The sense of the uncanny evoked here is bound up with the ostinato rhythm of triplets, which rises out of the bass before passing into the right hand, as well as pungent dissonances generated by a suspension series in bars 44–50. The reassuring sanctuary of the Andante is shattered by forces akin to those that had exerted sway in the opening movement.

A disquieting quality also shadows the somber Presto finale, a *perpetuum mobile* in A minor in 2/4 time. The unusual formal design of this movement combines rondo, monothematic sonata form, and a dance form with trio. This Presto may have resonated in Schubert's mind when he wrote his own finales to sonatas in this key, in D. 784 and D. 845, movements containing *perpetuum mobile* passages employing much conjunct melodic movement. Mozart darkens the modulation to the mediant by first moving to C minor, pianissimo (m. 29ff.), and he diverts the cadences to C major by substituting diminished-seventh chords for the tonic (mm. 52, 56). The trio section in A major assumes a musette-like character, as simple consonant phrases are repeated over a pedal point with static accompaniment. The brightness of this trio does not seem quite real. Here, as in the Allegro maestoso, the sway of the minor is irresistible, and the rhythm even more breathless, devoid of those pauses that had marked the hesitating, *calando* phrases in the first movement. The closing cadence in A minor takes on a quality of relentless finality.

The First Vienna Sonatas: K. 330–33

Several years passed before Mozart wrote out four more piano sonatas. In 1781, he left the service of Hieronymus Colloredo, the archbishop of Salzburg, and moved permanently to Vienna. He harbored deep resentments over the insults he was dealt by Colloredo and his employee Count Arco, who ejected Mozart with a kick in the buttocks. Mozart's change of residence was promising. Vienna represented a city with incomparably greater resources than Salzburg, and it was a "Clavierland," in which Mozart's pianistic virtuosity would find abundant expression.

---

18. Solomon, *Mozart: A Life*, 187.

A revised chronology of K. 330–33 has been outlined by the work of Plath and Tyson, as we have seen. According to this redating, the Sonatas in C Major, K. 330, in A Major, K. 331 (300i), and in F Major, K. 332 (300k), all stem from the early 1780s. These three sonatas were composed as a cycle and published together by Artaria in 1784. Since the paper of the autograph scores of these pieces is ruled with ten staves, the standard format for Salzburg paper, Tyson proposed that K. 330–32 could have been composed during Mozart's visit to Salzburg between July and October 1783, whereas the Sonata in B-flat Major, K. 333, might have been written at Linz, on Mozart's return trip to Vienna, as a companion work to the "Linz" Symphony, K. 425.[19] Nevertheless, older commentators, such as Einstein, have remarked on the thematic affinity between the first movement of the C-Major Sonata, K. 330, and the Allegro maestoso of the "Paris" Sonata. Einstein compares "a particle" (m. 27) of the second theme in K. 330 to the opening measure of K. 310, but the point can be expanded.[20] The beginning of the C-Major Sonata, K. 330, seems to transform the basic structure from K. 310, purging its dissonance; both themes share the initial repeated notes and melodic descent from the dominant above a tonic pedal in the left hand.

K. 330 is as optimistic in character as K. 310 is tragic. It exudes an atmosphere of charm and naïveté, yet it is not so naive as it seems. One of the few passages in the minor is the mysterious episode in its noble, slow movement, which is resolved into the major in the final moments of the Andante cantabile. As can be seen in example 3.10, Mozart is concerned to audibly transform the character of the main theme at each juncture between the longer sections in the major and the episode in the minor. When the dolce theme from the outset appears in F minor, he preserves both the upbeat of three even eighth notes and the thematic contour to insure recognition of the melody, while placing the minor third, A-flat, in the uppermost voice, with a soft tonic pedal resonating below, in pianissimo (example 3.10a–b).

Later, at the transition from F minor back to the F major, Mozart retains the fifth degree, C, as the highest voice, underscoring the structural identity of these otherwise sharply contrasting ideas; in m. 39 he even affixes to the F-minor chord the leading-tone E—a piercing dissonance even at this hushed dynamic level (example 3.10c). Finally, in the coda, the voicing from the beginning of the episode in the minor is employed as the theme is resolved into F major (example 3.10d). These nonadjacent connections need to be felt and conveyed in performance, so that the listener perceives how the theme is drawn into the darker sphere of the minor and subsequently reclaimed in the major mode. There is a quality of gigantic simplicity in this Andante cantabile that is bound up with Mozart's ingeniously varied treatments of the opening motive.

19. See Tyson, "The Date of Mozart's Piano Sonata in B flat, KV 333/315c: The 'Linz' Sonata?" in *Musik—Edition—Interpretation. Gedenkschrift Günter Henle,* ed. M. Bente, 447–54 (Munich: Henle, 1980). The music paper Mozart used at Vienna was normally ruled with twelve staves. In view of the redating of these sonatas, their revised Köchel numbers are no longer of value.

20. Einstein, *Mozart, His Character, His Work,* 245.

Ex. 3.10 Sonata in C major, K. 330 (300h), II, variants of head-motive

As Robert Levin has observed, two of the passages that make up this framework of correspondences were added as afterthoughts late in the process of composition.[21] Mozart appended the four-bar postlude to the F-minor section as an addition to the autograph score. He presumably composed the epilogue—the last four measures—still later, since it is missing from the autograph, and must have been added to the piece just before publication.

The 2/4 Allegretto finale of K. 330 invites comparison with the finale of the four-hand sonata in this key, K. 521, from 1787, with which it shares an identical opening melodic figure: a dotted eighth on E followed by two rising thirty-second notes and a fall to the tonic, C. The development section of the finale of K. 330 is poised between reminiscence, improvisation, and a process that we might describe as liquidation, as Mozart creates a gentle path to the recapitulation. The eight-measure phrase that launches the development recalls aspects of the main theme while reshaping these into a new subject with a folk-like aura, while the continuation—a variation employing steady sixteenth notes in the bass—recalls the accompaniment of the restatement of the main theme in mm. 9–14. One textural feature stands out: the presence of pauses setting off expressive, two-note melodic gestures. In the exposition, by contrast, the

21. Levin, "Mozart's Solo Keyboard Music," 321.

sound texture is continuous; there are no pauses in both hands until the very last beat of m. 68, the last bar of the exposition. With exquisite subtlety, Mozart has each two-note figure resolve into a rhythmic augmentation of the same figure, while joining each two-measure unit into a threefold rising sequence in mm. 79–84. By m. 85, he has reached the pitch level and harmony of the recapitulation and signals the nearness of that goal by recalling the opening motive with its characteristic dotted-eighth rhythm. The following passage touches on darker minor harmonies and opens onto the dominant through resolution of an augmented-sixth harmony in mm. 91–92. What remains are a few calm measures in which every two-note figure is set apart by rests, leading to the recapitulation in m. 96, which brings a resumption of the continuous sonorous texture.

Mozart reserves the surprising final twist for the conclusion of the movement, and thereby "corrects" the understated two-bar phrase with which the exposition had ended. That gesture had earlier led into the development, as we have seen, and its introduction of a pause in m. 68 foreshadowed the delightful play with rests that characterizes the development. Now, as the sonata nears its end, Mozart slyly reinterprets this phrase as a deceptive cadence (m. 169). The stage is thus set for three full-voiced chords that firmly shut the door on this captivating work (example 3.11).

In his sonatas up to K. 330, Mozart's treatment of form is generally quite consistent. Most movements are cast in sonata form, and only occasionally, as in the opening Adagio of K. 282 (189g) or the variation finale of K. 284, did he depart from his customary framework. In the Sonata in A Major, K. 331, however, he reshapes the overall design and foregoes any movement in sonata form. The sonata begins not with an Allegro but with a slow movement: six variations on a dignified Andante grazioso theme of "French" character in 6/8 meter, which are followed by a minuet and trio in place of a slow movement.[22] Within this new overall design, the first movement unfolds leisurely, with a gradual introduction of smaller rhythmic units in the opening variations. A distinctive feature of the theme is its concluding melodic extension of two bars, which rises in the treble through the fifth degree, E, to the tonic, A, underscored by octaves in the bass and the indication "forte." Mozart reshapes this gesture in some of his variations, such as in the concluding octaves of the *minore,* no. 3. The return to the major is beautifully embodied in Variation 4, with its hand crossings and its sensuous and almost celestial textures of thirds in the upper registers balanced against pedal tones in the middle register and octaves in the bass. Following the ornate Adagio variation, no. 5, the movement is concluded with a quickening of pace to Allegro and a change from 6/8 to 4/4 meter; in the coda Mozart finally resolves the linear tension of his closing forte gesture through a repeated stepwise melodic descent from dominant to tonic. The lively final variation is pivotal in the sonata as a whole. It caps the series of variations and prepares the finale through its acceleration in tempo

22. Beethoven was probably influenced by K. 331 when he wrote his Piano Sonata in A-flat Major, op. 26, which similarly eschews the use of sonata form, employs a set of variations as the opening movement, and incorporates a "characteristic" piece of a different kind—a funeral march on the death of a hero.

Ex. 3.11 Sonata in C major, K. 330, III, conclusion of finale

and rapid passagework in duple meter and through its prominent use of the turn figure that returns at the outset of the closing Allegretto.

If the theme of the Andante grazioso was demure, the Menuetto has a more assertive character. Its opening motive exactly reproduces the intervals from the beginning of the C-Major "Mannheim" Sonata, K. 309. Mozart retains the tonic key A
major for the minuet, but places the trio in D major. Like the final variation of the
preceding movement, this trio seems to look both forward and back. The sonorous
harmonic textures featuring parallel thirds and hand crossings recall Variation 4 of the
first movement, while the indelicate double octaves, played forte in the second half,
hint at what is to come in the closing Allegretto. Few of Mozart's sonatas show so
many connecting threads between their movements as K. 331.

The redating of this sonata to 1783 makes good sense, since the finale is written
"Alla Turca," in Turkish style. There was a craze for things Turkish in Vienna around
1783 because of the centenary of the lifting of the Turkish siege of the city in 1683.
Mozart's German opera *Die Entführung aus dem Serail* (The abduction from the ser-
aglio) of 1782 is bound up with this fascination with Turkish flair. The key associated
with Osmin's obsessive music of rage and revenge in *Die Entführung*—A minor—is
also the key of the finale of K. 331. Mozart does not reproduce Osmin's rage in this
Allegretto, yet there is more than a bit of obsession in its opening four measures,
which depend upon repetitions on a rising turn figure, and the ensuing phrase contains an clear suggestion of Janizary music. The continuation passes into the "Turkish" key of the opera, C major. The forte sections of the Allegretto in A major convey
the brassy brilliance of a Janizary band through octaves in the right hand supported
by arpeggiated accents in the left. The coda carries the process further, with pompous
military accents. Even without cymbals or triangle, the pianist can bring this sonata
to a rousing conclusion. Mozart's tendency to absorb orchestral textures into his keyboard writing is present in all three movements of K. 331, and no other Mozart sonata
has been arranged so often for different combinations of instruments.

The F-Major Sonata, K. 332, returns to the standard framework of movements,
but is quite as unique in its own way as K. 331. The opening Allegro shows a rich diversity of thematic material that would not be out of place in a concerto or opera, as
Wye Allanbrook and Alfred Brendel have noted (example 3.12).[23] In a confined space,

23. According to Allanbrook, the "Allegro begins as a harlequinade—a miniature theatre of gestures
and styles, which are exposed at first rapidly and without development." See her article, "Two Threads
through the Labyrinth," 130–31. Brendel identifies in the first movement of K. 332 "eight different musical

Ex. 3.12 Sonata in F major, K. 332 (300k), I, beginning

Entstanden in Wien (oder Salzburg), 1783

we hear a lyrical opening suggestive of a vocal duet (mm. 1–12), a comic continuation befitting Papageno (mm. 13–22), and a darkly dramatic, almost orchestral idiom in D minor that turns out to serve as a transition (mm. 26–40). A series of cheerfully naive cadences in F major set up this arresting plunge into the minor, whose beginning is nevertheless structurally linked to the preceding cadences, transforming their rhythm. Mozart prepares the sudden shift to a contrasting theme in a new key and mode through calculated overemphasis on these cadences in mm. 19–22. After three such gestures the trap is set, and the rising semitone C-sharp–D expressed as octaves in forte introduces the plunge into the minor and the distinctive new subject, whose *Sturm und Drang* character is conveyed through accented diminished-seventh chords.

The first theme of the second subject group in C major has a "speaking" quality, and displays the same vivid presence as one of Mozart's operatic characters. This eight-measure theme is treated in variation and resolves into a passage full of syncopations with the darker coloring of the minor mode. In the remainder of the second subject group, Mozart continues to vary and alternate these ideas, while unmistakably evoking the atmosphere of the *opera buffa*. And amid this wealth of material, how does Mozart begin his development but with yet another new theme! Something of this intensely dramatic, quicksilver quality of an opera in miniature also invests the finale of K. 332—perhaps most obviously in the closing moments of the opening the-

---

ideas which appear in quick succession, all of which have their own character. The player must try to orchestrate this amazing variety: the first as a string trio, the second for flutes and horns, the third for full orchestra." (*Me of All People: Alfred Brendel in Conversation with Martin Meyer*, trans. Richard Stokes [Ithaca, N.Y.: Cornell University Press, 2002], 189).

matic group, when a jagged rising chromatic figure twice disrupts attempts of the dolce melody to close serenely in the tonic. Mozart effectively rearranges the order of his themes in the recapitulation, reserving the repetition of this memorable passage to mark the coda and conclusion of the entire sonata. This Allegro assai finale is a movement of considerable brilliance, as is evident at once in the full-voiced tonic chord on the downbeat in the left hand, and the driving, swirling figuration in the right; Mozart effectively uses silence to set off the repetition of the opening gesture beginning in m. 7, and three such pauses soften this second, varied thematic statement, leading to a tonic cadence and then to the dolce melody in m. 15.

Lodged between these lively movements is a lyrical Adagio, which is shaped as a sonata form without development. In the autograph score, the recapitulation closely follows the exposition, involving much literal repetition. That Mozart himself would not have actually performed the sonata that way is implied by the meaningful—and sometimes extravagant—variations and embellishments found in the recapitulation in the first edition of this sonata published by Artaria. At the repetition of the second bar of the theme (m. 26), he lowers the register of the theme by an octave, clearing space for a rapid chromatic scale through one-and-a-half octaves, a gesture that transforms the placid character of the opening of the Adagio.

In *The Masterwork in Music,* Heinrich Schenker gave attention to several passages in the first movement of K. 332, including the opening theme and two themes in the second subject group. In his analysis, the prioritization of a descending linear progression from the half-note C in m. 2 is problematic inasmuch as Schenker urges the suppression of other musical elements, such as the ensuing melodic ascent in register in this opening phrase. He writes: "Should the ear follow the high notes in bars 3–5? Prolongation and Ursatz decide to the contrary."[24] Schenker acknowledges that this "supersession of the Urlinie" creates a more "buoyant" kind of voice-leading and that it "motivates the high register," which becomes the "true register" of the next progression. Our ears should indeed follow this upward melodic path, with the important rising sixth from B-flat reaching G, the highest pitch of the first theme. In his continuation, Mozart has compressed and developed motivic elements from the initial four-measure unit. The melody continues in m. 5 with a descending sixth from F to A, expressed as quarter notes, and this phrase member falls through the pitches of the tonic triad of F major in mm. 6–7, balancing the initial ascent through the same notes in mm. 1–2, where these pitches were expressed as half and quarter notes. The rhythmic foreshortening beginning in m. 5 allows Mozart to imitate the motive in the lowest voice in mm. 7–8, thereby elongating the theme, and this bass voice even incorporates the rising sixth as F to D in m. 9. The contrapuntal dimension of the opening theme becomes prominent as it unfolds.

24. Heinrich Schenker, *The Masterwork in Music. A Yearbook,* 2 vols., ed. and trans. William Drabkin (Cambridge: Cambridge University Press, 1994), p. 106. Originally published as *Das Meisterwerk in der Musik* (Munich, Vienna, and Berlin: Drei Masken Verlag, 1925).

If K. 332 is extravagant in its diversity of themes, the "Linz" Sonata, K. 333, in B-flat major, is more unified in its basic character and extremely economical in its use of motivic material. The opening melody resembles an improvisation on the expressive appoggiatura figure C–B-flat, heard on the downbeat of the first measure. This is approached through an upbeat, so that the entire initial motive outlines a descending sixth, from G to B-flat. In the ensuing bars, the basic appoggiatura figure is stated at different pitch levels (mm. 2–3), doubled in thirds (m. 4), emphasized through twofold and then fourfold repetition (mm. 5, 6), and finally replaced by a straightforward tonic sonority at the cadence (m. 10), following a rhythmic augmentation of the opening motive in the high register. At the restatement of the theme leading into the transition, Mozart continues to vary the appoggiatura figure with single-minded purpose, so that it becomes part of the defining character of the entire opening section of the form. Consequently, the first full-voiced chord on a downbeat (the F-major chord of m. 23) is strongly set into relief. At one stroke, this structural downbeat marks the second subject as an important new event in the unfolding of the work, even while Mozart continues to develop the stepwise descending motive from the beginning of the piece.

In a long-running commentary on Mozart's piano works published in the Vienna *Allgemeine Musikalische Zeitung mit besonderer Rücksicht auf den österreichischen Kaiserstaat* in 1821, Beethoven's friend Friedrich August Kanne sought to explicate their "spiritual threads of connection" (die geistigen Fäden der Verbindung); in the case of the first movement of K. 333, he described its elements as "all arising organically like twigs from a tree" (springen alle organisch gleich Zweigen aus einem Baume hervor).[25] The technical basis for such interconnection can be readily identified in a passage such as this second subject beginning in m. 23, which draws extensively on motivic aspects of the opening theme. These include the melodic descent and subsequent rise through the interval of a sixth, the rhythmic correspondence of m. 25 with m. 5, and the presence of triadic figures in eighth-notes in the left hand that begin on the second eighth of the measure.[26] Kanne's main focus, however, was not to elucidate such details, but to trace an expressive narrative interplay in the predominantly two-voice texture of the Allegro. For him, the beginning of the piece "makes visible a lovely interplay of two beautiful figures [Gestalten], which approach one another with noble grace, whereby the masculine part, the bass, supports with much tenderness but with magnetic strength the gracious movements of the feminine, the soprano melody" ([Hier ist gleichsam] ein

25. "Versuch einer Analyse der Mozartischen Clavierwerke mit einigen Bemerkungen über den Vortrag derselben," *Allgemeine Musikalische Zeitung mit besonderer Rücksicht auf den österreichischen Kaiserstaat* nos. 3–8, 19–20, 22–30, 44–47, 49–50 (1821). The publication appeared twice per week. See in this connection Hartmut Krones, "Rhetorik und rhetorische Symbolik in der Musik um 1800: Vom Weiterleben eines Prinzips," *Musiktheorie* 3 (1988), 125–127, 138 (note 80); and Mark Evan Bonds, "Ästhetische Prämissen der musikalischen Analyse im ersten Viertel des 19. Jahrhunderts, anhand von Friedrich August Kannes 'Versuch einer Analyse der Mozart'schen Clavierwerke' (1821)," in *Mozartanalyse im 19. und frühen 20. Jahrhundert*, ed. Gernot Gruber and Siegfried Mauser (Laaber: Laaber, 1999), pp. 70–71.

26. See Mark Evan Bonds, "Ästhetische Prämissen der musikalischen Analyse im ersten Viertel des 19. Jahrhunderts," 71–72.

liebevolles Umschlingen zweyer schöner Gestalten sichtbar, die sich in holder Anmuth einander nähern, und wo der männliche Theil, der Bass, die graziösen Bewegungen des weiblichen, der Sopranmelodie, mit aller Zartheit, und dennoch mit anziehender Stärke unterstützt).[27] Such an interpretation may seem fanciful, but it raises the issue of metaphorical meaning as lodged in musical dialogue, a matter of significant concern especially in relation to the genre of the concerto.

Even in this graceful, Apollonian work, Mozart occasionally unveils expressive regions of surprising turbulence and drama. Such a passage is the F-minor episode in the development of the opening Allegro, whose striking upward leaps and syncopated falling lines are a transformation and intensification of the descending scalar figure and appoggiatura from the very outset of the movement. (For Kanne, this passage suggested an eruption of anger, which was only gradually stilled, with a reconciliation effected by the outset of the recapitulation.)[28] Thus even here, in one of the most decorous of all Mozart's sonata movements, there arise moments that challenge the decorum of the age while exposing the dramatic potential of the most basic musical elements. Einstein suggested that this movement showed the influence of Johann Christian Bach, and Wye Allanbrook and Siegbert Rampe have identified the first movement of Bach's Sonata in G Major, op. 17, no. 4, as a possible source of inspiration for the texture of Mozart's Allegro, including the prominent emphasis on appoggiatura figures.[29] In its rhythm, meter, and pattern of motivic repetitions, this Allegro by Bach indeed shows an affinity to Mozart's work.[30] However, Bach's movement lacks anything resembling the dramatic plunge into the minor in Mozart's development.

The development of the Andante cantabile, too, harbors passages of probing and even disturbing import, again in the key of F minor, although the tonic of this movement is E-flat major. The original theme contained a turn to the supertonic harmony of F minor in its third bar, and Mozart reinterprets and magnifies this inflection through chromaticization of the theme modulating to that key (mm. 32–35). After the cadence in F minor in m. 35, he sounds a figure of repeated notes on F in the low bass register, opening a mysterious gulf between the cavernous sound of the chromatically ascending bass and the motives in the right hand that descend out of the high register to alight on diminished and minor harmonies. Even after the music reaches A-flat major in m. 43, sequences of the repeated-note upbeat figure leading to expressive appoggiatura chords dominate the music. The development section is highly unified and deepens the expressive potential of the motivic figure with an upbeat of

---

27. The score excerpt with Kanne's annotations is reproduced in Bonds, "Ästhetische Prämissen der musikalischen Analyse," 76–80.

28. Bonds, "Ästhetische Prämissen der musikalischen Analyse," 79.

29. Einstein, *Mozart, His Character, His Work,* 246; Allanbrook, "Two Threads Through the Labyrinth," 146–47; Rampe, *Mozarts Claviermusik,* 262. The chronological arguments adduced by Einstein are no longer plausible, but this does not undermine the case for J. C. Bach's sonata as a source of influence on Mozart. Allanbrook also draws attention to the possible influence of the second movement of Haydn's Piano Sonata in B Minor (Hob. XVI: 32, mm. 1–4) ("Two Threads Through the Labyrinth," 147).

30. The piece has been published in vol. 42 of *The Collected Works of Johann Christian Bach 1735–1782,* ed. Stephen Roe (New York: Garland, 1989).

Ex. 3.13 Sonata in B flat major, K. 333 (315c), II, motivic variants

a)

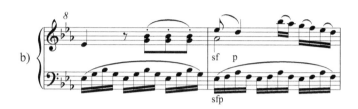

b)

c)

three eighth notes that featured prominently in the second subject area of the exposition. In turn, this figure is audibly derived from the second and third measures of
the main theme, where the motive appears in quarter notes instead of eighth notes.
Already in m. 8, Mozart treats this original idea in rhythmic diminution, in eighth
notes heard over a flowing Alberti bass pattern. In mm. 12–13, this rhythmic variant
appears at the half-cadence to the dominant, B-flat major.

A comparison of these motives from the original theme and the transition is shown
in example 3.13a–c. As this comparison implies, the Adagio cantabile is a largely
monothematic piece, in which even seemingly conventional gestures are strictly derived from basic thematic ideas. The dissonant inflection to the F-minor harmony in
m. 3 provides a springboard for the far-reaching reinterpretation contained in the development, in which the tonality and basic character of the music are fundamentally
altered. In its structure and expression, this Adagio cantabile is an ingeniously concentrated work. In another telling gesture in the coda, Mozart concludes the movement in pianissimo with a deliciously understated reiteration of the basic idea, with
the appoggiatura figure enlarged through rhythmic augmentation.

The finale of K. 333 is a rondo, whose main theme shares motivic features with the
opening Allegro: the appoggiatura figures (mm. 3–4) and the stepwise fall from dominant to tonic (m. 5). This Allegretto grazioso begins piano, in a restrained texture in
two voices, but the varied repetition of the eight-bar theme in forte brings more en-

ergetic figuration, which is succeeded by concerto-like passagework in the ensuing first episode of the rondo form. When this episode returns near the end of the rondo, it indeed leads to an "orchestral" lead-in to a cadenza, as in the finale of K. 311. Unlike the earlier sonata, this is an extended solo cadenza, which includes its own lead-in to the head of the theme, dolce, a turn to the minor mode serving as a platform for dramatic development, and finally a series of ad libitum flourishes leading to the coda and full return of the main theme. This cadenza supplies an exciting climax to the finale and lends an end-weighted quality to the work as a whole. The sonata concludes with a series of cadences suggesting a gentle farewell to the theme, but the final forte chords belong to the imaginary orchestra that had ushered in the cadenza.

The redating of K. 333 to the fall of 1783 makes much sense in relation to Mozart's concentration during the ensuing months at Vienna on keyboard works, particularly concertos. This sonata shows some conspicuous similarities to his landmark concerto in this key, K. 450, from March 1784. Both pieces display an unusually tight network of motivic relations in their opening movements, with the initial material reappearing in ingenious, ongoing variations; in each case, Mozart intensifies the development sections with a driving, dramatic turn to the minor with sustained sixteenth-note motion in the piano. Extraordinary are the concerto-like features in the finale of the sonata, especially the big cadenza *in tempo* preceding the final appearance of the main rondo theme. In this passage, as in the finale of K. 311, the sonata strives to become like a concerto.

Fantasia in C Minor, K. 475, and Sonata in C Minor, K. 457

This Fantasy and Sonata in C Minor, published by Artaria as op. 11 in late 1785, represent Mozart's most celebrated solo works for keyboard. He dedicated this opus to his pupil Therese von Trattner, wife of his publisher friend Johann Thomas von Trattner. Detailed letters that once existed from Mozart to Therese Trattner concerning the interpretation of these pieces have unfortunately not survived. In the catalogue he kept of his own works, Mozart dated the Fantasy as "20 [May 1785]" and the Sonata as "14 October [1784]."[31] Although composed at separate times, the two works share the same autograph score, a manuscript that was long presumed lost but which resurfaced in 1990 at Philadelphia and is now housed at the Mozarteum in Salzburg.[32]

It is a matter of debate whether the Fantasy and Sonata should be performed together. Alfred Brendel has asserted, "I maintain, as Artur Schnabel did, that it is a mis-

31. This catalogue has been published in facsimile as *Mozart—Eigenhändiges Werkverzeichnis Faksimile,* intro. and ed. Albi Rosenthal and Alan Tyson, British Library, Stefan Zweig MS 63 (Kassel: Bärenreiter, 1991).

32. The manuscript has been published in facsimile as *Wolfgang Amadeus Mozart: Fantasie und Sonate c-Moll für Klavier, KV 475 + 457. Faksimile nach dem Autograph in der Bibliotheca Mozartiana Salzburg,* intro. Wolfgang Plath and Wolfgang Rehm (Salzburg: Internationale Stiftung Mozarteum, 1991). Also see Eugene K. Wolf, "The Rediscovered Autograph of Mozart's Fantasy and Sonata in C minor, K. 475/457," *The Journal of Musicology* 10 (1992): 3–47.

take to connect in performance Mozart's C minor Fantasy K. 475 with the C minor Sonata K. 457. The fact that they were published in one volume proves nothing. Each of these works is an autonomous masterpiece; together, they cancel each other out."[33] On the other hand, Mozart's handling of the C-minor tonal idiom in the Fantasy and the opening Molto allegro of the Sonata is distinct, and there were historical precedents for such a pairing of fantasy and sonata in works by Georg Simon Löhlein and Johann Wilhelm Häßler, as Katalin Komlós observed.[34] The end of the Fantasy contains restless gestures that might be heard as destabilizing the conclusion and preparing a sequel, namely the two deceptive cadences in mm. 178–79 and the vehement rising C-minor scales through three octaves played forte in the final bar. Supporters of the pairing of Fantasy and Sonata, such as Robert Levin, have offered substantial arguments without insisting that the pieces must be so performed.[35]

The Fantasy and Sonata rank among the greatest achievements in Mozart's piano music. The dissonant chromaticism of both pieces looks back to J. S. Bach's *Musikalisches Opfer* (Musical offering), while in their dramatic concentration they strongly prefigure Beethoven's famous "C-minor mood." An impressive feature of the Fantasy is the way Mozart unifies the form of the whole, with its several sharply contrasting episodes, through a varied return of the opening Adagio at the conclusion. The bare unison octaves of this opening seem to embody an inevitably objective, immovable, even alien reality confronting the player and listener, a sense heightened here by Mozart's motivic chromaticism, the descent by semitone governing the initial phrases, and his effective use of silence as a rapport of sound with the void (example 3.14). As Uhde observes, this is the musical *topos* of "der alte starre Fels, das Schicksal" (the old rigid rock, fate), in Hölderlin's words, in relation to which the following harmonized phrases and echoes in the upper register take on a feeling of helplessness.[36] Revealingly, Mozart originally notated a key signature of three flats in the first systems of the autograph score of the Fantasy, implying C minor, but then erased this key signature. The guiding structural aspect in the opening Adagio section is the chromatic motion of the bass, which connects the opening C minor with the tonal goal of B minor, as is shown in example 3.15.

Hence the mysterious opening phrase in unison octaves rises from C and falls back to that pitch, preceding the semitone descent to B at the outset of m. 2; further drooping half-steps carry the music through B-flat to A in mm. 3–4 and to A-flat in m. 6. Eventually, an extension of this chromatically descending motion occurs when an octave G is sounded in m. 14; another descent reaches G-flat in m. 15, with this point of

33. "On Recitals and Programmes," in *Alfred Brendel on Music: Collected Essays* (Chicago: A Capella, 2001), 353.

34. "Fantasia and Sonata K. 475/457 in Contemporary Context," in *Mozart-Jahrbuch 1991: Bericht über den Internationalen Mozart-Kongress 1991*, vol. 2, ed. Rudolph Angermüller, Dietrich Berke, Ulrike Hofmann, and Wolfgang Rehm (Kassel: Bärenreiter, 1992), 816–23.

35. See the discussion following Komlós's article "Fantasia and Sonata K. 475/457 in Contemporary Context," 820–21.

36. Uhde and Wieland, *Denken und Spielen*, 372.

Ex. 3.14 Fantasy in C minor, K. 475, beginning

Datiert: Wien, 20. Mai 1785

furthest remove from the original C reinterpreted enharmonically as F-sharp in the following measures. Within this overall framework, the G-major area in mm. 18–20 is unstable, and the German augmented-sixth chord on G in m. 21 serves as pivot to the dominant of B minor.

The ensuing, internal sections of the Fantasy explore a range of expressive contexts. Mozart first reinterprets the repeated F-sharps at the end of the first section as the third of D major, and a spacious period unfolds in this key. A later episode begins in F major before shifting to minor and modulating to other keys, whereas the Andante beginning at m. 91 is set in B-flat major with a change in meter to 3/4. None of these episodes achieves closure; all remain open-ended. A notable destabilizing aspect in this scheme is the presence of chromatic octaves in the bass, such as surface in the Allegro beginning in m. 42 and again starting in m. 79. The efforts to sustain music of a lyric or dance-like quality in the major mode are unsuccessful; these episodes lack staying-power. On the other hand, the original uncanny music in C minor seems to lurk behind and ground the whole design, with tragic implications.

Toward the end of the Fantasy, immediately preceding the return of this Adagio (Tempo primo), a searching, mysterious passage penetrates the highest register, effectively setting into relief the stark octaves from the outset of the work. These octaves are already clearly foreshadowed in the immediately preceding transition (mm. 157–61), with its extended *rallentando,* which restores the slow tempo. The chromatically descending voice-leading of the continuation is then altered by Mozart to keep the music within the orbit of C minor, and the cadences that follow have the same quiet inevitability as in his remarkable Rondo in A Minor, K. 511, from 1787. Also striking is Mozart's masterful control of pitch registers, as embodied in the soft, harmonized echoes of the bare unison octaves or in the free melodic inversion of that motive arising out of the high register (mm. 170–71). The tension is sustained until the end, as

Ex. 3.15 Chromatic bass line at the beginning
of the Fantasy in C minor, K. 475

Measure(s) 1 2 3 4 5-7 8 9 10 11 12 13 14 15-17 18-21 22-25

Mozart fittingly expands the final emphatic tonic sonority over the entire keyboard in a poetic gesture of resolution and summation.

The C-Minor Fantasy offers precious insight into Mozart's powers of invention in an improvisatory style, a spontaneous artistry at the keyboard that much impressed his contemporaries. In his 1866 study *W.A. Mozart als Clavier-Componist,* Franz Lorenz expressed regret that Mozart only rarely reproduced on paper his "moments of ecstatic rapture in a half-conscious state," continuing that "of the few remnants of this kind that we possess . . . the marvellous C-minor Fantasy offers at best some notion of these remarkable, yet irretrievably lost tonal creations."[37] At the same time, both the Fantasy and Sonata show how Mozart strove to integrate the mysterious opening music of K. 475 into a musical design conceived on a grand scale.

The C-Minor Sonata, K. 457, is a counterpart to Mozart's concerto in this key, K. 491, and, like the concerto, it exerted a potent influence on Beethoven. The middle episode of Mozart's Adagio, beginning of A-flat major (mm. 24 ff.), for example, unmistakably resembles the beginning of the Adagio cantabile in Beethoven's "Sonate Pathètique"—even beginning in the same register. Mozart's Adagio contains a series of elaborate melodic variations of the main theme, which in his autograph score are designated as "no. 1," "no. 2," and "no. 3," corresponding to the passages found in the finished work beginning in mm. 17, 41, and 49, respectively.

Mozart's characteristic contrasts between an objective, detached expression and a more inward, personal response—as embodied at the outset of K. 457 in the rising staccato forte octaves and the harmonized piano phrases that follow—tend to be subsumed by Beethoven into an all-encompassing subjective dynamic. This accounts, at least in part, for the greater sense of despair or fatalistic resignation in some of Mozart's C-minor works. The vehement outbursts in the first movement of K. 457 dissolve at times into mysterious, muted gestures, such as the pianissimo passages that close the development and the entire movement.

The beginning of the opening Molto allegro parallels the Fantasy in its use of a head motive in unison octaves moving from C to E-flat and in the dialogic opposition between this unison gesture and soft, harmonized sigh-figures in a higher register. In its forte-piano alternation, rhythm, and dialogic character, the prominent theme in the second subject group that first appears in mm. 44–48 represents a variant of this idea. Mozart marks the threshold of the coda, in mm. 168–72, with a series of robust imitations of the head motive, divided between the hands of the pianist, with this passage leading to a tonic cadence and the hushed, dissolving coda.

37. Lorenz, *Mozart als Clavier-Componist* (Breslau: Leuckart, 1866), 26.

The Allegro assai finale is racked by extreme contrasts, more so than any other sonata movement by Mozart. Its opening theme is characterized by sigh-figures, insistent syncopations, and dissonant suspensions. The phrase members ending on B-natural (mm. 2, 10) and E-flat (mm. 4, 12) need to be set apart as discrete gestures, as Mozart's slurs prescribe. This opening theme reaches a quiet, firm cadence at the downbeat of m. 16 in the middle register. The fanfares that follow contradict this cadence while returning to the higher register of the outset of the movement: strident octaves are played on the dominant above the texture of thirds that connects this theme with the preceding phrase. The theme pushes into the highest register with loud arpeggiated chords, but it remains open and unresolved, breaking off into silence on the dominant. Mozart alternates these two opposing ideas, so that the first subject group seems to be made up largely of a collision between incompatible forces. There is a distinct suggestion here of a tutti-solo alternation, with the insistent forte fanfares in mm. 17–24 and mm. 31–38 enclosing the expressive piano statement in mm. 26–30.

At the last return of the main theme in this rondo-sonata movement, Mozart sets off each phrase in turn, with fermatas and rests, while instructing the player through the indication *a piacere* to employ his or her own discretion as to nuances of tempo and rhythm. These rhetorical pauses prolong the subject, lending emphasis to its sigh-figures and to the ensuing cadence in C minor *in tempo*. Then, following the fanfares, contrasting cadential phrases, and an abbreviated appearance of the main theme of the second group in the subdominant, we reach one of Mozart's most extraordinary codas. The drive to the powerful final cadence is prepared here by extreme registral contrasts involving unusual hand crossings. It is here that the recovery of the autograph score of the work has proved most revelatory. As the manuscript shows, the last nineteen measures of the work as we know it were an afterthought. The original final cadence at m. 301 was turned into a deceptive cadence, leading to an astonishing gapped thematic presentation that soars to high C and E-flat before plunging five octaves to F-sharp in the lowest possible register.[38] In the first edition of the sonata, the low F-sharp and the five following notes were raised up an octave; there are other divergences as well, as are shown in example 3.16. The deep, coiling line played three octaves *under* the accompaniment reaches a tonic cadence five measures later, and another eight measures of cadential flourishes across all these pitch registers prepare the final framing chords.

Mozart sought a culminating gesture here, and the fanfare passages that had been interrupted earlier find an outcome in this decisive breakthrough. Furthermore, as Rampe has observed, the added passage offers evidence of Mozart's attitude toward the pairing of Fantasy and Sonata.[39] The melody of the added passage—C–E-flat–F-sharp–G–A-flat—reshapes the crucial chromatic motive from the beginning and end of the Fantasy and then grounds it in the strongest possible way in C minor. The five-

38. One is reminded here of the extreme contrasts in register in the first movement of Beethoven's C-Minor Sonata, op. III (mm. 48–49, 114–15).
39. Rampe, *Mozarts Claviermusik,* 270–71.

Ex. 3.16 Sonata in C minor, K. 457, III, conclusion. The upper staves
show the reading in the first edition, the lower staves the reading in
the autograph manuscript.

octave plunge from high E-flat to low F-sharp splits the motive through drastic registral opposition, with its aspiring beginning contradicted and completed in the dark
continuation. Hatten writes that "gesturally, although the same hand performs the
'line,' the extravagant cross-hand move marks another voice—fateful in response to
the more pleading high register, and implacable as it takes over for an inexorable cadence in the lowest register."[40] One original voice is virtually bifurcated into two in
this majestic and radical reassertion of the motive that had begun the Fantasy. Even
the understated close of the first movement—tonic chords in the low register set off
by rests—seems to be recalled and resolved here, in the powerful conclusion of K.
457. It is unlikely that these correspondences could be accidental. Since the Sonata
was composed before the Fantasy, it seems likely that the expansion of the coda to the
finale of K. 457 occurred in response to his subsequent pairing of these remarkable
works; his addition begins precisely at the recall of the seminal motive from the Fan-

40. Hatten, *Interpreting Musical Gestures, Topics, and Tropes,* 164.

Ex. 3.17 Sonata in F major, K. 533, I, beginning

tasy. We catch Mozart's musical mind in action here, casting audible connecting threads across one of his most imaginative and innovative works.

The Last Sonatas: K. 533, K. 545, K. 570, and K. 576

The four sonatas from 1788 and 1789 share certain stylistic features, such as Mozart's keen interest in two-voice invertible counterpoint. According to his catalogue of works, Mozart finished the Sonata in F Major, K. 533, by 3 January 1788; in so doing, he wedded two newly composed movements to a rondo (K. 494) that he had written two years earlier. In view of the substantial changes made to the rondo when it became part of the sonata—including a change in tempo from Andante to Allegretto and the addition of an extended and weighty new passage—it is best to avoid use of the double Köchel number 533/494 in referring to this impressive but still somewhat underestimated composition.

The opening Allegro of K. 533 is characterized by transparent textures evocative of chamber music, which unfold with considerable contrapuntal complexity. The psychology of the beginning of this sonata is insightfully described by Levin, who observes that instead of depicting a settled character, the composer gives us "the impression of watching a sculptor mold the clay: Mozart seems to pause in mid-air right away (m. 2) ponders (thus the half-note upbeat rather than the original quarter), apparently finds his original idea satisfactory after all, and only then does the left hand enter to confirm that the decision has been made"[41] (example 3.17). Even minute details of this music, such as the curious absence of accompaniment at the outset, can be rich in gestural significance. Particularly outstanding is the Andante, a seemingly abstract piece characterized by calm breadth, but also by poignant dissonances. There

41. Levin, "Mozart's Solo Keyboard Music," 333.

is a delicate balance here between repose and tension. At the beginning of the second measure the melody falls a tritone, while another tritone is heard between tenor and bass; dissonant suspensions are prominent throughout. As Edward Lowinsky once pointed out, Mozart's flexible treatment of rhythm and phrasing sustains the intensity throughout the opening passages;[42] later, in the development, a shattering climax will be built out of these materials, unleashing their dramatic power. Striking as well is Mozart's sensitive use of an isolated high A in the right hand at the end of the exposition, which appears like a ray of light emerging out of the darkness of the minor; this crucial pitch later becomes the starting point for the chain of sequences that initiate the forceful development.

The finale is more naive than its companion movements and more restricted in its treatment of register, but Mozart's substantial revisions forged links to the rest of the piece, even while risking stylistic discontinuities in this rather innocent rondo. Originally, m. 142 resolved directly to m. 170; the twenty-seven intervening measures were added when Mozart joined the Rondo to the sonata. The added passage includes an astonishing contrapuntal development of the head of the Rondo theme (mm. 152 ff.), which rises through the entire tonal space before leading to a trill and cadence into the original coda, with its quiet conclusion in the lower register.

The most familiar of all Mozart's sonatas is his "short piano sonata for beginners" in C major, K. 545, from June 1788, and it is surprising that, unlike many of his other works in this form, it was not published during his lifetime. This piece is not so easy to play well and is less simple than it appears; the motivic relations—with an inverted variant of the opening broken chord used as the head of the second subject and employed subsequently in double diminution spread between the hands—are not lacking in subtlety. The cadence theme after the resolution of the trill in the dominant continues the process of motivic development by incorporating the broken chord in sixteenth notes from the earlier double-diminution passage, and the development begins by restating this idea in G minor. This is the only sonata with a subdominant recapitulation; and like the first movement of K. 283, it contains a bifocal close at the threshold to the second theme group—a transition that can be followed by either the dominant or the tonic, which therefore requires no transposition in the recapitulation.

The opening of the charming slow movement is somewhat reminiscent of Don Ottavio's soothing "Dalla sua pace la mia depende" (On her peace depends mine, too) from act 1 of the Viennese production of *Don Giovanni,* which Mozart had written shortly before. Ottavio's piece shares the same key of G major, and it is marked "Andantino sostenuto" rather than andante, as in K. 545, and it is written in 2/4 rather than in the 3/4 meter of the sonata. A still closer thematic relationship connects Mozart's Andante from K. 545 with another piece from *Don Giovanni:* the beginning of the Andante con moto of Leporello's "Catalogue" Aria in act 1.[43] This part of Leporello's piece is in 3/4 meter, and although its key is D major, the melodic outline and rhythm

42. Lowinsky, "On Mozart's Rhythm," *The Musical Quarterly* 42 (1956): 180–82.
43. This point was drawn to my attention by Mitsuko Uchida, personal communication.

Ex. 3.18a Mozart, Sonata in C major, K. 545, II

Ex. 3.18b Beethoven, Sonata in G minor, Op. 49 No. 1, II

are extremely similar to K. 545. The text of Leporello's passage is "Nella bionda egli ha l'usanza/Di lodar la gentilezza" (With blondes he usually praises their courtesy).

Unlike Leporello's comic piece and more than Ottavio's aria, the episode in minor in the Andante of K. 545 embarks, in Solomon's words, "upon a voyage into a troubled *Innerlichkeit* ('inwardness')." Solomon continues that "when the trapdoor opens, Mozart ironically undermines the rococo surface as though to subvert not only the vision of tranquillity, but the aristocratic order it is customarily intended to validate."[44] The core of this disquieting episode (example 3.18a) left its impress on a passage in the G-minor Andante that forms the first movement of Beethoven's sonata op. 49, no.1, composed about a decade later. The musical rhetoric, transparent textures, and balanced repose of the phrasing in op. 49, no. 1, are all reminiscent of Mozart, as are the chromatic inflections in Beethoven's Andante. Beethoven extends his theme upward in register to a forte climax on the very same sonority that had served Mozart (example 3.18b). The comparison shows both composers as critical heirs of the cultural tradition that sustained and challenged them.

In the rondo finale of K. 545, Mozart employs canonic exchanges between the hands such as are common in his other later piano sonatas. He resourcefully varies the opening pattern of falling thirds to trigger modulations and contrasting episodes. Much happens in a small space. The rondo is a delightful miniature, but surprisingly difficult to play for a work described as a "sonata for beginners." The form of the movement can be construed in three main sections: mm. 1–20, involving a move to the dominant; mm. 21–52, with a return of the rondo subject in the tonic followed by varied statements of the head motive in A minor; and mm. 53–73, beginning with the last statement of the rondo theme. Within this design, the tonal contrast of the first section is resolved in the last part, while the middle section acts like a developmental episode. Characteristically, Mozart absorbs aspects of sonata procedure and variation into this compact rondo design.

Within each of these sections, the music progresses to an animated texture with steady sixteenth-notes in both hands; the middle episode, in A minor, unfolds broadly

44. Solomon, *Mozart: A Life,* 205 (preceding quotation on 204).

enough to accommodate a statement of the theme with the voices inverted in mm. 41–44, whereupon the turn-figure in sixteenths is developed into descending two-note slurred figures in the following bars. The last of the lively sixteenth-note passages culminates in thirds tracing a twofold descent from dominant to tonic in mm. 69 and 71. These closing gestures combine the stepwise falling motive first heard in m. 4 with the texture of parallel thirds from the main theme itself. To the end, the piece remains true to its emphasis on triadic fundamentals: thus the bass octaves in the last measure recall, in a symmetrical gesture, the melodic outline from the very beginning of the *first* movement.

Einstein described Mozart's Sonata in B-flat Major, K. 570, from 1789, as "perhaps the most completely rounded of them all, the ideal of his piano sonata."[45] This work was nevertheless neglected in earlier times by pianists, since it first appeared with violin accompaniment in an edition by Artaria in 1796. The arrangement was almost certainly spurious; Mozart refers to the piece in his catalogue as a sonata for solo piano. The broad, leisurely opening theme of the Allegro, with its repeated, almost suspiciously tranquil cadences in B-flat, is calculated to withstand the shock of an abrupt turn to the relative minor and subdominant; later, a variant of the same shift plunges the music into D-flat major at the beginning of the development. The thematic material is highly concentrated, with figures drawn from the opening theme serving as contrapuntal motives of the second subject. Another subtle motivic feature is the turn figure first heard in m. 7, which reappears in the exposition several times, in the passages beginning in mm. 12, 23, 35, and 57. In its ordering of thematic ideas, the development section resembles the exposition, with a deepening in character achieved through Mozart's resourceful use of invertible counterpoint.

The slow movement is an Adagio in E-flat major whose textures suggest the character of wind instruments; this impression is confirmed by the ensuing episode in C minor, which bears an intimate resemblance to the first wind interlude in this key in the Larghetto of Mozart's concerto K. 491, a movement also in E-flat major. There is something haunting about this episode; one can understand why Mozart felt compelled to reuse its content in his great concerto in this key. In the concerto, the episode's opening motives in parallel thirds are varied somewhat and assigned to a pair of oboes. Here, in the sonata, these gestures are heard above a throbbing accompaniment of repeated sixteenth notes in the left hand. As the episode unfolds, Mozart distributes between the hands of the pianist a particularly sensitive dialogue of voices — a texture that lends itself well to articulation by a chamber ensemble of separate players.

The charming and vivacious Allegretto finale is in an unconventional rondo design, in which the apparent episode in mm. 9–14 remains in the tonic key, forming the middle section of a ternary form embracing the restatement of the opening theme in mm. 15–22. The contrapuntal theme in E-flat major with prominent repeated tones beginning in m. 45 is somewhat reminiscent of *The Magic Flute* overture, in the same key. Further contrapuntal combinations involving these repeated detached notes domi-

45. Einstein, *Mozart, His Character, His Work,* 249–50.

Ex. 3.19 Sonata in D major, K. 576, I, beginning

Allegro

Datiert: Wien, Juli 1789

nate the coda, which unfolds in an atmosphere of exquisite grace and high comedy[46] and closes with a witty allusion to the head of the main theme, with its initial rising third and pattern of eighth notes set off by eighth rests. The movement as a whole well illustrates the innovative spirit of Mozart's treatment of the rondo form. It may be true, as Charles Rosen has stated, that "rondos are defined as much by the characters of their themes as by the structure,"[47] yet Mozartian rondos often resist those elements of predictability that stem from the periodic return of the main theme in the tonic key. Mozart is especially prone to depart from the expected path in the second half of a rondo; and in this case, he achieves a kind of thematic role reversal, with the contrapuntal subject becoming the dominant idea in the latter stages. The lively unpredictability of the form as a whole mirrors the playfully humorous rhetoric of the details. In retrospect, we can recognize that the motivic seeds of the crucial contrapuntal idea with repeated notes were already planted in m. 7 of the original opening theme.

Mozart's very last sonata, K. 576, in D major, from 1789, has often been associated with his reference in a letter to Michael Puchberg to writing "easy sonatas" for Frederike, the Prussian princess. This seems doubtful in view of the treacherous performance demands of the piece. More than any other of the sonatas, K. 576 displays an intense cohesiveness and motivic unity. The work begins with a theme featuring rising arpeggios in octaves in 6/8 meter—a gesture evocative of a "hunting" *topos*—but there is otherwise no suggestion here of a pastoral or rustic character. The call-motive of the first two measures is answered by harmonized phrases marked by trills in mm. 3–4, thereby pairing the arpeggios with gestures sweeping upward by step. A repetition of the arpeggiated idea on the supertonic E-minor harmony and a varied yet framing unit of two bars closes the theme on the tonic (example 3.19).

This eight-bar theme is pervasive throughout. Mozart repeats the idea in mm. 9–16, transferring the original melodic progression primarily to the left hand, while intro-

46. For a sensitive discussion of the musical rhetoric of this movement that explores its "ludic perspective" and "mysterious discontinuities," see Peter Pesic, "The Child and the Daemon: Mozart and Deep Play," *19th-Century Music* 25 (2001–02): 100–104.

47. Rosen, *Sonata Forms* (New York: Norton, 1988), 124.

Ex. 3.20a Sonata in D major, K. 576, II, beginning

Ex. 3.20b Sonata in D major, K. 576, II, mm. 17–19

ducing a quasi-canonic counterpoint in the treble that breaks into running sixteenth notes. These imitative entries draw emphasis to the head motive outlining broken chords, which on the strong beats of the 6/8 meter initially outline D–F-sharp–A. Consequently, the left-hand accompaniment beginning in m. 16 sounds like a distillation of this triadic structure into three-note legato phrases in each half-measure. The apparently commonplace ostinato accompaniment can be heard as a kind of rhythmic diminution of the opening idea. This illustrates the deceptive simplicity of Mozart's ripe style, in which seemingly conventional elements prove to have deeper resonance and significance.

At the outset of the second subject group, the opening tradic figure appears in a six-measure passage of strict canonic writing, with the lower voice in close, hectic pursuit of the right hand. At the end of the exposition, on the other hand, the figure assumes like a motto-like character, and it then becomes the basis for the development section, which is spiked with dazzling canonic episodes beginning in B-flat major and then G minor. The virtual saturation of the movement with the opening triadic motive reaches yet another climax in long series of close canonic exchanges heard after the beginning of the recapitulation.

One theme stands apart. Marked "dolce," this idea in the second group is prepared by a cadence and begins without accompaniment in a mood of reflection. Yet it too is audibly connected to the second phrase of the opening theme, whose ascending line—C-sharp–D–E–F-sharp—it reproduces in the same register (mm. 41–42). The role of such nonadjacent connections in this sonata emerges clearly if we examine Mozart's chromatic reinterpretation of this motive toward the end of the exposition and recapitulation, as well as a network of related passages. Between the E of m. 49 and the F-sharp of m. 50 he has inserted an E-sharp, supported by a diminished harmony in the left hand. The E-sharp–F-sharp half-step is echoed in the following gesture in sixteenth notes. For the corresponding passage of the recapitulation, Mozart devises an ingenious passage that peaks on F (the enharmonic equivalent of E-sharp), which for Levin is "capped by the crash of the diminished seventh chord at m. 152 and

Mozart's nonchalantly dusting off his pants, smiling ingenuously, and continuing straight on into the coda."[48] In the development, on the other hand, Mozart coordinates motivic stress on the crucial E-sharp–F-sharp half-step with emphasis on F-sharp as the dominant of B minor. The augmented-sixth harmony on m. 76 incorporates the E-sharp–F-sharp semitone, and in mm. 79–83 the main motive is sounded on harmonies of F-sharp major and minor, initiating the passage leading to the recapitulation.

These motivic elements from the first movement are conspicuous as well in the finale, whose main theme displays the rising steps C-sharp–D and E–F-sharp that were highlighted by trills at the outset in the first movement. Here, the rising line outlines first C-sharp–D and D-sharp-E (mm.1–2) and then E-sharp–F-sharp (m. 4). With the same single-minded intensity as the first movement, this rondo-sonata finale explores the chromatic space between tonic and mediant.

The center of gravity in Mozart's last sonata rests in its fascinating Adagio in A major. This movement involves an extended meditation on the sustained pitches highlighted in the opening theme, particularly the very first note, C-sharp, as well as the melodic crux of E that is heard as a tied half-note in m. 2 (example 3.20a). This melodic crux is replaced by other pitches each time the two-bar phrase is restated: in m. 6 it becomes E-sharp, and in m. 14, G. The resulting tension between E and E-sharp, in particular, is reflected in m. 3, m. 15, and elsewhere, but most remarkable is the expressive transformation that leads into the middle section of the large ternary form, beginning in m. 17 (example 3.20b).

That section is set in one of Mozart's rarest keys—F-sharp minor—and its reharmonization of the movement's initial C-sharp becomes prominent since this pitch, in its original register, occupies the downbeats of mm. 17 and 18 and of subsequent phrases as well. An uncanny agitation is conveyed through the repeated dyads in sixteenth notes, while the sinuous contour of the melodic phrases absorbs the telltale stress on the half-step E-sharp–F-sharp. An effect is created of the F-sharp minor episode *transforming* the bright serenity of the opening theme, revealing the darker potential behind its surface, while exposing an expressive sphere that also lurks behind the gaiety of the outer movements.

---

48. Levin, "Mozart's Solo Keyboard Music," 337.

CHAPTER 4

Variations and Miscellaneous Works

Variation Sets

Mozart's numerous sets of variations for piano solo span his entire career and well illustrate his reception of contemporary musical currents. Nearly all of the themes chosen were drawn from familiar songs, dances, or opera arias by other composers, and the variation techniques employed consist largely of melodic and figurative decoration. Variation sets of this kind were more easily published than works in most other genres.

In most cases, the themes Mozart chose had already been used for variations by other composers.[1] His prowess as a keyboard virtuoso and improviser found a natural outlet in such variations, as he himself related to his father after his successful concert appearance at Vienna on 23 March 1783 in the presence of Emperor Joseph II: "I played variations on an air from an opera called 'Die Philosophen' which were encored. So I played variations on the air 'Unser dummer Pöbel meint,' from Gluck's 'Pilgrimme von Mekka.'"[2] Gluck, the composer of *The Pilgrims* (Les hommes pieusement), was in the audience and must have listened with pleasure and astonishment to the improvisations on his theme by the younger master, which Mozart wrote out the following year, in August 1784 (these are presently catalogued as K. 455). The comic spirit of this aria on "the stupid man in the street" is reflected for instance in Mozart's reharmonizations of the initial gesture in octaves in Variation 4, whereas in other variations the melody is transformed in pianistic textures reminiscent of Mozart's great piano concertos from these years.

The very first preserved variation sets date from Mozart's stay in Holland in 1766, at the age of ten, when he wrote Eight Variations on the Dutch song "Laat ons Juichen"

---

1. A comparative study of Mozart's keyboard variations in relation to other composers of his time is offered by Paul Willem van Reijen, *Vergleichende Studien zur Klaviervariationstechnik von Mozart und seinen Zeitgenossen* (Buren: Frits Knuf, 1988).

2. *Letters*, L. 484 (29 March 1783).

by C. E. Graaf, K. 24, and Seven Variations on the Dutch national song "Willem van Nassau," K. 25. There are few hints of Mozart's mature artistry in these early pieces, but the structural layout of the variations, especially in K. 24, already shows features characteristic of most of his later sets. The initial variations follow the traditional practice of employing increasing subdivisions in the rhythmic values of the theme; and the penultimate variation is an Adagio followed by a return to a faster tempo in the final variation.

Such subdivisions in rhythm, proceeding from eighth notes to eighth-note triplets and sixteenths, also shape the opening three variations of Mozart's next set, on "Mio caro Adone" from Antonio Salieri's *La Fiera di Venezia* (The fair of Venice), K. 180 (173c), from 1773, but here the variations are much more vividly characterized. In Variation 4, he introduces a brilliant trill figure and elaborate textures, including a passage in double octaves. An ornate Adagio follows, with thirty-second note motion in the accompaniment as well as in the decorative melodic writing for the right hand.[3] In his closing variation, Mozart changes the meter, replacing the 3/4 time of the minuet theme by a 2/4 Allegretto, and he appends a coda with broken chords in forte to cap the work.

The potential of the variation set for brilliant display is more fully realized in the Twelve Variations in C Major on the Minuet from Johann Christian Fischer's Oboe Concerto no. 1, K. 179 (189a), a work Mozart composed the following year at the age of eighteen and which long served as a showcase for his virtuosity. Variation 1 already transforms the texture largely into running sixteenth notes, with the notable exception of the initial half note of the melody, G. This sustained opening note becomes a series of four persistent staccato eighths in Variation 2, and that motive in turn is treated in imitation, lending much emphasis to the motive, with humorous effect. The next four variations are grouped into pairs: the figuration of nos. 3 and 4 involves triplet eighths and then sixteenths in the right hand, while a similar progression from triplet eighths to sixteenths animates the left hand in nos. 5 and 6. The next four variations are more characteristic than figurative in their handling of the theme. In no. 7, a turn and upward-striving melodic motive are prominent; no. 8 involves a texture of syncopation between the hands of the pianist; no. 9 establishes three distinct regions of sonority, as an expressive dialogue between treble and bass unfolds around an accompaniment of broken chords in the middle register; and no. 10 creates the most massive sonorities of the set, as forte octaves appear in each hand in turn and then in both together, in the form of slurred sixteenth-note parallel broken octaves at the distance of a tenth.

The virtuosity of Variation 10 sets up the utmost contrast to the ensuing Adagio variation, marked "dolce." In this ornate transformation of the minuet—and unlike the other variations—Mozart rewrites each of the repeated sections of the theme,

---

3. Another, even more extravagant example of Mozart's ornamentation of a given theme in Adagio tempo from the early 1770s is offered by his Adagio in F major, K. Anh. 206a=65, which has been edited by Neal Zaslaw. See Zaslaw, "The Adagio in F Major, K3 Anhang 206a=A65," in *Haydn, Mozart, & Beethoven: Studies in the Music of the Classical Period,* ed. Sieghard Brandenburg (Oxford: Clarendon, 1998), 101–113.

eliminating all literal repetitions. The opening melodic phrases in the right hand, which contain expressive breathing pauses, for instance, are replaced at the repetition by a syncopated chromatic line. The most elaborate ornamentation of all is heard near the end of the Adagio variation, before a boisterous, assertive recapitulation of the minuet tune, realized in chords and running sixteenths, closes the work.

While at Paris during 1778 Mozart wrote two sets on French themes: Twelve Variations in E-flat Major on the romance "Je suis Lindor" (a favorite song in Beaumarchais's *Le barbier de Séville* [*The Barber of Seville*] by A. L. Baudron), K. 354 (299a); and Nine Variations in C Major on the popular arietta "Lison dormait" by N. Dezède, K. 264 (315d). These works show a new resourcefulness in their pianistic textures, devices for linking adjacent variations, and variety of figuration. Yet the individual character of the variations is always paramount, especially in the "Je suis Lindor" set, with its tenderly expressive theme. At the heart of K. 354, Mozart places an imposing Maestoso variation, no. 7, followed by a *minore* featuring imitative echoes and expressive turn figures. The return to *maggiore* is marked by a pair of spirited variations sporting octave tremolos, followed by an ornate Molto Adagio and a Tempo di Menuetto. Surprisingly, this closing variation leads into a short, capricious Presto in duple meter, and the set closes with improvisatory flourishes across the keyboard followed by a serene cadence.

The charming "Lison dormait" Variations are perhaps the more brilliant of the two Parisian sets, with a spirited final Allegro variation culminating in a cadenza and capped by a wistful reminiscence of the original melody. Mozart follows a similar recipe here, inasmuch as his *minore* (Variation 5) is followed by a linked pair of energetic variations in the major, with the broken-octave figuration in the right hand of no. 6 passing into the left hand of no. 7. The ensuing Adagio is especially elaborate, and as in K. 354, the final variation in triple time—here a 3/8 Allegro—is not yet the end. Mozart's cadenza is particularly concerto-like, and leads at the resolution of its trill to the brief recall of the original Andante theme followed by a registral descent to the quiet ending.

Soon after his move to Vienna in 1781, Mozart wrote out two further variation sets on French themes. The Twelve Variations in C Major, K. 265 (300e) are written on "Ah, vous dirai-je, Maman," a very familiar song known in English-speaking countries as "Twinkle, Twinkle, Little Star," the "Alphabet Song," or in slightly altered form as "Baa, Baa, Black Sheep." Mozart presents the tune simply, with the accompaniment moving in step with the melody, but his variations effectively intensify the descending melodic patterns from the theme as dissonant suspensions, which are further developed in the poignant chromaticism of the *minore,* Variation 8. Mozart's variations in the minor often involve a more far-reaching transformation of the character and structure of the theme. This *minore* is deepened as well by a series of polyphonic entries of voices two measures apart, which appears in a descending pattern, three times in all (example 4.1). The ternary structure of this theme consists of eight measures in the tonic, which is repeated, followed by an eight-bar continuation on the dominant and a nearly literal reprise of the first eight bars, both of which are repeated together as a unit. In Variation 8, the unfolding polyphony brings about an impressive inten-

Ex. 4.1 12 Variations on "Ah, vous dirai-je Maman," K. 265 (300e), Variation 7

sification in each of these three sections of the theme, while in sections 1 and 3 the original contour of the falling sixth derived from the theme—A-flat–G–F–E-flat–D–C—is retained as a *cantus firmus* in the highest voice. A registral development of the overall descending contour is carried furthest in the chromatic middle section, as the third voice entry sinks in octaves into the depths of the bass; in the closing reprise section, Mozart varies the peak of the melody with expressive sigh-figures containing chromatic neighbor-notes. Following the very serious tone of this *minore*—the dark center of this delightful work—the ensuing *maggiore* indulges in playful reminiscence of the original innocent tune, before Variation 10 introduces new virtuosic textures with hand crossings and octaves in the bass. Mozart's Variations on "Ah, vous dirai-je, Maman" show an especially sensitive and controlled ordering of the successive variations, which strive to overcome the essentially loose and additive nature of the form.

The interplay in this set between quietly expressive and brilliantly figurative variations is also characteristic of the set of twelve in E-flat Major on "La belle Françoise," K. 353 (300f). The opening variations of K. 353 employ striking rhythmic motives to adorn the melody or surround it as a sonorous background in various registers, whereas the fourth variation delicately reshapes the thematic structure. Following the penultimate Adagio, the final Presto variation departs from the 6/8 meter of the theme and the basic character of the whole; but Mozart closes with an abbreviated and varied restatement of the original melody.

The Eight Variations in F Major, K. 352 (374c), also from 1781, are based on the march from A. E. M. Grétry's "Dieu d'amour" in his *Les mariages samnites* (The Samnite marriages). It is a dignified, noble theme, showing structural similarities to the subject of Mozart's variations beginning his Sonata in A Major, K. 331—at least two of the present variations (nos. 1 and 6) remind us strongly of that movement. At the heart of the set is the *minore,* Variation 5, whose poignant dissonances are enhanced through syncopation, contrapuntal imitations, and a sensitive exploitation of pitch registers. The serious tone of this work is maintained throughout, and the set closes plainly, without any cadenza or concluding flourishes.

As we have noted, Mozart performed his Six Variations on an aria from *I Filosofi Immaginarii* (The imaginary philosophers), K. 398 (416e), in March 1783; the opera is by Giovanni Paisiello, and the theme in question from the chorus "Salve tu, Domine." William Glock has pointed out that some of the patterns in these variations, such as nos. 2 and 6, "still preserve the theatrical excitement of a great occasion."[4] The first part of Variation 2 ingeniously combines a tricky pattern of syncopations between the hands with allusion to the melody of the original theme in the high register, whereas Variation 6 builds up rich textures of sound through rapid triplet sixteenth notes played simultaneously in contrary motion in both hands.[5] So climactic is the virtuosic flair of no. 6, in fact, that this variation breaks out of its formal self-containment: following a pause on a tonic 6/4 chord, a full-blown cadenza ensues, as Mozart first composes out the 6/4 chord horizontally to reach high F and then accelerates the motion downward to reach low C, the deepest pitch of the sustained chord that launched the cadenza (example 4.2). The continuation of the cadenza is notated without bar-lines, complete with swooping runs, pregnant pauses, and chains of turns and trills. After these fireworks, Mozart finds a magnificently *understated* close by resolving the cadenza's final trill into the middle of the theme, and he gradually dissipates the remaining energy through silences and a process of gravitational inertia, as sinking thematic fragments come to rest above several low tonic octaves sounded in the bass.

Another striking improvisatory passage in these "Paisiello" Variations comes at the end of the *minore,* Variation 4, which reaches an Adagio written without bar-lines. There is no cadence to this variation either; instead, Mozart leads the music into a reprise of the theme in the major in the left hand, played under sustained trills in the right hand such as he loved to employ in this period. As this fifth variation proceeds, the prolonged trills migrate to the low bass before dissolving into yet another passage of improvisatory fancy. No other set of variations captures the spirit of Mozart's extempore playing so well as K. 398.

The Eight Variations in A Major on "Come un agnello" from the opera *Fra I Due Litiganti* (When two quarrel, the third profits) by Giuseppe Sarti, K. 460 (454a), from 1783 or somewhat later, raise provocative issues of style and authenticity. Listeners fa-

---

4. Glock, program notes to the recordings *Mozart: The Complete Music for Piano Solo,* by Walter Gieseking, vol. 2 (Seraphim ID-6048).

5. This idea is derived from the pattern of repeated eighth notes in the left hand of the original theme, whereby Mozart builds a triplet group upon each of these notes.

Ex. 4.2 6 Variations on an aria from *I Filosofi Immaginarii* by Giovanni
Paisiello, K. 398 (416e), cadenza following Variation 6

miliar with *Don Giovanni* will recognize the tune from the beginning of Mozart's second finale, where it is performed as incidental music during the Don's supper, immediately preceding Mozart's humorous self-quotation from *Figaro*. A striking feature of
this set is the departure from the 3/4 meter of the Allegretto theme in all of the later
variations. Variation 7 first shifts into a meter of 4/4, and it is connected through a
cadenza to a pair of slow variations also in duple time, the second of which is more
ornate and placed in the minor. The ensuing final Allegro variation initially restores
the audible melodic contour of the original theme but declines to restore its meter,
continuing instead in 4/4, in a flowing, robust texture of triplet eighth notes.

The surviving autograph manuscript of the "Sarti" Variations in Mozart's hand contains only the theme and two variations; in 1958, Kurt von Fischer, editor of the variations for the Neue Mozart Ausgabe, proposed on the basis of the primary sources and
stylistic evidence that the more extended version of the "Sarti" set is not by Mozart.[6]
A vigorous debate ensued between von Fischer and Paul and Eva Badura-Skoda, who
sought to defend Mozart's authorship.[7] Returning to the matter two decades later,
von Fischer suggested that the composition is Sarti's, though written on the basis of
a performance by Mozart.[8] It appeared that some kind of joint authorship was involved, with Sarti creating a pasticcio composition based on a working-out and completion of a Mozartian improvisation. However, further research by Richard Am-

6. Fischer, "Sind die Klaviervariationen über Sartis 'Come un'agnello' von Mozart?" *Mozart-Jahrbuch*
1958: 18–29.

7. Paul and Eva Badura-Skoda, "Zur Echtheit von Mozarts Sarti-Variationen KV 460." *Mozart-Jahrbuch*
1959: 127–39; Kurt von Fischer, "Sind die Klaviervariationen KV 460 von Mozart?" *Mozart-Jahrbuch 1959:*
140–45.

8. Fischer, "COME UN'AGNELLO—Aria del SIG'SARTI con Variazioni," *Mozart-Jahrbuch 1978/79:*
112–21.

bruster has clarified the mystery. The composer of the Eight Variations on "Come un agnello" was evidently a different and little-known Viennese composer named Joseph, or Giuseppe, Sardi.[9] The close resemblance of his name to Giuseppe Sarti has long acted to obscure his identity to scholars.

The theme as well as the Twelve Variations in B-flat Major, K. 500, from 1786, apparently stem from Mozart himself. This Allegretto subject features motives with trills and two-note sigh-figures over an Alberti-type bass. Hermann Abert has drawn attention to the presence in this set of keyboard figuration suggesting an influence of Muzio Clementi, a composer Mozart had dismissed rather scornfully a few years earlier.[10] The textures of certain variations, such as the severe contrapuntal density of the *minore*, Variation 7, also show a certain kinship with the finale of Mozart's great Piano Concerto in C Minor from the same year, as William Glock has observed.[11] In K. 500, a direct interconnection of variations takes place between no. 10, which ends with a cadenza emerging out of the lowest register, and no. 11, a stately Adagio. By contrast, the final variation is a nimble Allegro in 3/8 time with a swaying, syncopated accompaniment. This lively Allegro contains its own varied repetitions and ends (like no. 8) in a short cadenza, before a literal da capo of the original theme closes the work.

The Nine Variations in D Major on a Minuet by Duport, K. 573, represent one of Mozart's finest works in this form. He conceived this piece while in Potsdam, Prussia, in April 1789, during an extended journey that had also taken him through Prague, Dresden, and Leipzig. In Potsdam, Mozart met the celebrated cellist and composer Jean-Pierre Duport. He then selected a charming *menuetto* theme from Duport's Cello Sonata Op. 4 No. 6 as the basis for six variations. After returning home to Vienna, Mozart expanded his work with three additional variations.

Duport's minuet has a dignified character and features a main motive consisting of descending broken chords on the tonic D major. This is a well-worn conventional formula whose solid structure lends itself particularly well to variation. In its motivic structure, the theme is not lacking in subtlety. There are initially three levels of texture in the minuet, including sustained pedal notes in the lowest voice and an inner voice in flowing eighth-notes. In the middle section (mm. 9–12), a rising arpeggiated figure appears in the left hand; this motive is then asserted in the treble, and proves to be an elaboration of the original triadic figure from the beginning of the theme. The repetition of the opening eight-bar period in mm. 17–24 brings rhythmic variants of the falling triadic motive, with this figure expressed in sixteenths in the last four bars. Thus some elements of figurative variation are already present in the theme.

9. Ambruster, "Joseph Sardi—Autor der Klaviervariationen KV 460 (454a) Zum Schaffen eines unbekannt gebliebenen Komponisten in Wien zur Zeit Mozarts," *Mozart-Jahrbuch 1997:* 225–48.

10. For Abert, the treatment of triplets in the opening variations, the bass figuration in Variation 4, and the chordal configuration in Variation 8 suggest Clementi's influence (Abert, *W. A. Mozart* [Leipzig: Breitkopf and Härtel, 1921], 2: 373). In letters to his father from 1782 and 1783, Mozart wrote dismissively about Clementi's piano playing as well as his compositions.

11. Glock, program notes to the recordings *Mozart: The Complete Music for Piano Solo,* by Walter Gieseking, vol. 2 (Seraphim ID-6048).

In K. 573, Mozart not only effectively embroiders this structure through flowing figuration, as in Variations 1–4, but discovers unsuspected depths of character in the transformations that follow. Variation 5 replaces the sustained half notes from the head of Duport's Allegretto theme with witty staccato repetitions, while subtly varying the static tonic harmony of the theme. At the beginning of the second section, on the other hand, Mozart replaces Duport's fourfold repeated chords on dominant and tonic with a more dynamic progression, in which the reiterated chords expand upward chromatically to reach a new goal.

The *minore,* Variation 6, conveys a character of bleak despair, particularly in its repeated melodic ascents to high F, whereupon the music falls earthward in a series of expressive appoggiaturas (example 4.3). This variation shows special subtlety in its treatment of the thematic structure, which consists of eight bars in the tonic, which are repeated, followed by eight bars on the dominant and a nearly literal reprise of the eight opening bars, both of which are repeated together as a unit. Particularly in his minor variation, Mozart is disinclined to maintain this close parallelism of the outer sections. Hence in the reprise section, he compresses the two-bar ascent to the high F (mm. 4–5) into a single bar (m. 20), shifting the moment of arrival at the high F into a more prominent position in the overall metrical framework, at the beginning of the last four-measure unit. This structural compression also clears the way for a surprising new event: the melodic descent converges onto a startling Neapolitan sonority of E-flat major before a dry cadence in D minor closes the variation with an air of resignation.

A moment later, however, the ensuing Variation 7 restores the major mode with an irresistible gaiety, with broken octaves heard above the harmonic support of the left hand (this is also shown in example 4.3). Following the elaborate Adagio variation, Mozart quickens the pace with the swinging 2/4 meter of Variation 9, which is joined through a cadenza to an exquisitely varied closing da capo of the theme. At the conclusion, Duport's original descending motive is replaced by increasingly rapid falling scales, leading to an emphatic cadence reaffirming the joyous character of the seventh variation.

The "Duport" Variations impressively shape the successive variations into a larger progression. Variation 1 initially remains close to the register and textures of the theme while introducing continuous motion in sixteenths, which shifts in Variation 2 predominantly to the left hand. An emphasis on parallel thirds in the middle sections of Variation 2 and especially Variation 3 anticipates the continuous texture of thirds and sixths in triplets in Variation 4. The delicacy of Variation 5 prepares for the thoughtful melancholy of the *minore,* Variation 6, which is complemented in turn by the celebration of the brighter major mode in No. 7. By juxtaposing the intricate decorative passagework of the Adagio, Variation 8, with the metrically foreshortened pace of the ensuing Allegro in 2/4 time, Mozart heightens the sense of contrast as the work moves into its final stages.

In this context, there is something delicious about the nostalgic abbreviated recall of the original minuet at the end. This is no literal return. In their high register, spare

Ex. 4.3 Duport Variations, K. 573, Variation 6, beginning of Variation 7

texture and melodic articulation, mm. 5–6 of the Tempo primo recall the *minore,* Variation 6. The repeated cadential gestures in the final bars recall of course the end of the theme, but with a new twist. Already in his "coda" in 2/4 time following Variation 9, Mozart had stated this cadential gesture from the minuet on shifting levels of harmony, which dissolved in turn into a vigorous passage on the dominant of D major, leading through a brilliant fantasy-like transition without bar lines to the Tempo primo. Now, in the last moments of K. 573, Mozart moves beyond the rather hackneyed cadential formula to recapture the highest pitch D from Duport's minuet, which becomes the melodic focus and then the goal of the emphatic closing chords.

Mozart's final contribution to this genre are the Eight Variations in F major on "Ein Weib ist das herrlichste Ding auf der Welt" (A woman is the most marvelous thing in the world), K. 613. This set is based on an Allegretto theme drawn from the operetta *Der dumme Gärtner* (The foolish gardener) by Benedikt Schack,[12] which Emmanuel Schikaneder produced at the Theater an der Wieden at Vienna in 1789. In the performances, Schickaneder himself played Anton, the "dumb gardener." The variations date from March 1791, during the last year of Mozart's life. A noteworthy feature of this set consists in the distinct function of the first eight measures, which stand apart from the continuation, since they represent the instrumental introduction to the song. Here again, as so often in Mozart's variations, the initial sections bring a gradual acceleration in rhythmic values. The theme is not thoroughly transformed, but Mozart's treatment is full of subtleties, such as the contrapuntal combinations in the coda that finally merge the introduction with the melody proper. Most impressive is the Adagio (no. 6), with its trills, syncopated textures, and chromaticism. Saint-Foix likens the introduction of this variation to the accompaniment of the trio of the three boys ("Seid uns zum zweiten Mal willkommen" [A second welcome from us]) in *The Magic Flute*,[13] and the variations as a whole have an atmosphere of somewhat naive yet noble simplicity akin to that work.

In this instance, the context sheds considerable light on the musical work. As David Buch has observed, these variations confirm Mozart's ongoing involvement with the troupe of actors, singers, and musicians at the Theater auf der Wieden. He had contributed music to their heroic-comic opera *Der Stein der Weisen oder die Zauberinsel* (The philosopher's stone or the enchanted island) in September 1790; a year later, and sixth months after writing K. 613, his famous collaboration with Schikaneder, *The Magic Flute,* would be brought to the stage, with Benedikt Schack singing the role of Tamino. The improvisatory spirit of K. 613 undoubtedly owes much to this theatrical environment, and Buch has shown how Schickaneder in his performances interpolated new texts to follow the refrain, which always ended with the word "Welt."[14] One variant was "Ich bin wohl der glücklichste Mann auf der Welt" (I am surely the luckiest man in the world); another was "All' Augenblick erfährt man was Neus in der Welt" (Every moment one learns of new things in the world), which offered Schickaneder the pretext to make references to current affairs, such as Austria's recent victo-

12. The full title of Schikaneder's two-act comic opera is *Die verdeckten Sachen, oder der dummer Gärtner aus dem Gebürge, zweiter Theil* (The Hidden Things, or the Dumb Gardener from the Mountains, Part 2). David J. Buch observes that the attribution of the music to Schack is speculative, and other composers may have contributed as well, including Schikaneder. See Buch, "On the Context of Mozart's Variations to the Aria, 'Ein Weib ist das herrlichste Ding auf der Welt,' K. 613," *Mozart-Jahrbuch 1999: 71–80.*

13. See Wyzewa and Saint-Foix, *W. A. Mozart. Sa Vie Musicale et Son Oeuvre,* vol. 5 (Bruges: Desclée, De Brouwer et Cie, 1946), 197.

14. See Buch, "On the Context of Mozart's Variations," esp. 73–80.

Ex. 4.4 Eight Variations on "Ein Weib ist das herrlichste Ding auf der Welt,"
K. 613, first measures of the theme with the words of the refrain.

ries in the Turkish War. Thus it is not surprising that Mozart retains such framing devices in composing his variations or that he showcases the opening phrases of the vocal theme in his coda. The first four measures of the theme following the instrumental introduction fit precisely to the words of this refrain (example 4.4).

Miscellaneous Works

Mozart's other works for solo piano apart from sonatas fall roughly into three categories: childhood pieces, especially minuets, some of which date already from his fifth to seventh years; pieces in Baroque idioms, such as fugues and suite movements stemming from all periods of his career; and finally the fantasies, rondos, and other individual pieces, among which the Rondo in A Minor, K. 511, and Adagio in B Minor, K. 540, are undoubtedly the most important.

Our knowledge of Mozart's early musical education is considerable, thanks to Leopold Mozart's diligent and even indefatigable efforts on behalf of his two surviving children. On 21 November 1747 Leopold married Maria Anna Pertl, and the couple took up residence in the Getreidegasse in Salzburg, an address they were to occupy for sixteen years. Of their seven children, five did not long survive. Mozart's sister Marianne, known familiarly as Nannerl, was born at the end of July 1751. In 1756, the year Wolfgang was born, Leopold published his *Versuch einer gründlichen Violinschule* (A treatise on the fundamental principles of violin playing), a distinguished and enduring contribution to musical performance practice.

By 1759, when Marianne was eight years old and Wolfgang three, Leopold devoted himself to the musical education of his daughter and, in the process, soon became aware of his son's extraordinary talent. The surviving document that records his efforts assumes unusual importance, since it opens a window on Wolfgang's earliest creative activities in music. This source is known as Nannerl Mozart's *Notenbuch* (music book); it remained in her possession until her death in 1829 and is now held at the library of the Internationale Stiftung Mozarteum in Salzburg.

Until relatively recently, the content of Nannerl's *Notenbuch* as it relates to her brother was imperfectly understood. During the long period of her life following Wolfgang's death in 1791, some of the choice pages of the *Notenbuch* that record his first compositional efforts were removed; in all, about a dozen leaves are missing from the original total of approximately forty-eight leaves. By the 1980s, a detailed source reconstruction was undertaken by Alan Tyson, whereby leaves that once belonged to the *Notenbuch* but are now held in other collections were conceptually restored to their original place in this document.[15]

Especially significant is the recognition that two leaves in Leopold Mozart's handwriting, now held at the Pierpont Morgan Library in New York City, represent Wolfgang's earliest surviving compositional efforts, as is confirmed by their original position in the *Notenbuch,* preceding those childhood pieces that previously had been given the lowest Köchel catalogue numbers. Consequently, these earliest pieces have been designated K. 1a, 1b, etc., with the original K. 1 relabeled as K. 1e. Leopold Mozart's comments on many of the entries in the *Notenbuch* enable us to construe in some detail the situation in early 1761, when the precocious five-year-old youngster took his first steps into uncharted territory.[16]

Mozart's first compositional efforts were intimately connected with his growing practical proficiency at the keyboard. Following a series of eight minuets written into the *Notenbuch* as keyboard practice, Leopold observes, "Diese vorgehende 8 *Menuet* hat d. Wolfgangerl im 4t Jahr gelernet" [These preceding 8 minuets were learned by Wolfgangerl in his 4th year]. An even more detailed comment accompanies the transcription of a scherzo by Georg Christoph Wagenseil: "Dieß Stück hat der Wolfgangerl den 24t *Januarij* 1761, 3 Täge vor seinem 5t Jahr nachts um 9 uhr bis halb 10 uhr gelernet" [Wolfgangerl learned this piece on the 24th of January 1761, 3 days before his fifth birthday, in the evening from 9 until 9:30].

Shortly thereafter, as we know from the conceptual reconstruction of the placement of the two leaves from the Morgan Library into the *Notenbuch,* Leopold started to write out his son's improvisations. The very first preserved piece is an Andante in C Major in 3/4 time, which switches after a few measures into 2/4 meter (example 4.5). Leopold's comment on the pieces beginning with this Andante, "Des Wolfgangerl Compositiones in den ersten 3 Monaten nach seinem 5ten Jahre" [Wolfgangerl's compositions in the first 3 months after his 5th birthday], attests to this as Wolfgangerl's initial compositional effort, written a few weeks after his learning of Wagenseil's scherzo in late January and preceding by some margin the famous Minuet in G Major that

15. See the chapter "A Reconstruction of Nannerl Mozart's Music Book (Notenbuch)," in Tyson, *Mozart: Studies of the Autograph Scores* (Cambridge, Mass.: Harvard University Press, 1987), 61–72.

16. Writings on Mozart are especially imprecise in discussing his earliest compositions. Arthur Hutchings states inaccurately that "the first of Mozart's surviving keyboard pieces were written down in a notebook to occupy his time in London . . . during the winter months of 1764–65" ("The Keyboard Music" in *The Mozart Companion,* ed. H. C. Robbins Landon and Donald Mitchell [London: Faber and Faber, 1956], 38), and this claim is echoed by Patrick Gale, that "the first series of short pieces (the London Sketchbook, K. Anh. 109b [151a–ss]) was set down on paper during a visit to England in 1764–5" (*The Mozart Compendium: A Guide to Mozart's Life and Music,* ed. H. C. Robbins Landon [London: Thames and Hudson, 1990], 301). In his biography, *Mozart: A Cultural Biography* (New York: Harcout Brace, 1999), 57, Robert W. Gutman writes that "Leopold began writing down Wolfgang's compositions at the beginning of his sixth year, putting to use blank pages in Nannerl's exercise book. It thus sheltered Mozart's earliest surviving work, an Andante for piano (K. 1a) in C of 1761. With these six measures began the suite of creations that would end thirty-one years later with the transcendent D-minor Requiem." Mozart was at the beginning of his fifth year, and the Andante in C is ten, not six, measures long.

Ex. 4.5 Andante in C major, K. 1a

Des Wolfgangerl Compositiones in den ersten 3 Monaten nahc seinem 5ten Jahre.

Wolfgang wrote out in his own childish hand and that long carried the special distinction of being number one in the Köchel catalogue. Among Wolfgang's earliest pieces are a number of minuets, some of which have virtually the same bass. This circumstance suggests that his father may have set him the task of inventing different minuets on this common foundation.[17]

Hermann Abert's observation that "there is an extraordinarily clear and intelligible form common to all of these first pieces"[18] indeed applies to the G-major piece, KV 1e, and to others, such as many pieces in the so-called London Sketchbook used by Mozart in London in 1764–65, yet it fits less well to the C-Major Andante, K. 1a. This piece is closer to spontaneous improvisation, and it lacks the sense of poise and symmetry that characterizes the G-Major Minuet. Yet a distinctive quality of K. 1a that invites attention is its spontaneous momentum or directional thrust, a feature already evident in the opening measures. Each of the first four measures moves in its three beats from tonic to dominant to dominant seventh, respectively, with a melodic drop from G to F marking the move to the dominant-seventh chord. This descending scalar motion is carried forth with a sense of acceleration into the section of the piece in 2/4.[19] Measure 5 contains two stepwise falling fourths spanning F–C and E–B, whereas mm. 6 and 8 both spell out the descending melodic fourth spanning B-flat–F in the lower octave, beneath middle C. This linear descent leads in turn to the cadence in the last two measures, which recalls the descending pattern of the opening 3/4 section, but now proceeds from the third degree to the tonic, or E to C. Thus despite the

17. The minuets K. 4, K. 5, and another that became part of the violin sonata, K. 6, all have virtually the same bass, as was pointed out by Wyzewa and Saint-Foix, *Wolfgang Amadé Mozart,* 1:16–18.

18. "Allen diesen Erstlingen ist eine außerordentlich klare und übersichtliche Form gemein" (Abert, *W. A. Mozart,* 1:37).

19. Konrad Küster is surely right in assuming that "the time signatures were of course contributed by Leopold Mozart," but we need not accept his explanation for the change of meter—"that Mozart had not yet learnt how to distribute the stresses within longer stretches of music." (Küster, *Mozart: A Musical Biography,* trans. Mary Whitall [Oxford: Clarendon, 1996], 4.)

change of meter, an impression is conveyed that this cadence resolves the whole short composition, all the more in view of the pervasive descending motion that brings about this close in a register noticeably lower than the one in which the piece had begun.

Another short piece in binary form in Nannerl's *Notenbuch* from Wolfgang's fifth year carries the following inscription from Leopold: "Sgr. Wolfgango Mozart 11ten Decembris 1761" [Mr. Wolfgang Mozart 11 December 1761]. This Allegro in 2/4 time shows a solid sense of form, with a reprise of the opening four-measure phrase rounding off the second part after four intervening bars poised on the dominant. A startling feature of the melody is its strong similarity to Papageno's song as he plays the Glockenspiel in Act II of *The Magic Flute:* "Ein Mädchen oder Weibchen wünscht Papageno sich!" (example 4.6a–b). Even the key of F major is identical. The melodic similarity must be attributed to the folk-song character of Papageno's music, already so vividly captured by the five-year-old.[20]

Alongside the compositional diet of minuets and other binary forms and sonatas[21] that sustained the young Mozart, he undoubtedly cultivated his improvisational abilities, even if such activities were much less readily committed to paper. The spontaneous currents in Mozart's art still require more recognition and are often compatible with and balanced against his penchant for symmetrical forms and deterministic construction. That Mozart's creativity was rooted from an early age in intense powers of imagination is emphasized as well in the perceptive account of his sister Nannerl, given after his death:

> Mozart's over-rich imagination was so lively and so vivid, even in childhood, at a time when it still lies dormant in ordinary men, and perfected that which it had once taken hold of, to such an extent, that one cannot imagine anything more extraordinary and in some respects more moving than its enthusiastic creation; which, because the little man still knew so little of the real world, were as far removed from it as the heavens themselves. Just one illustration: As the journeys which we used to make (he and I, his sister) took him to different lands, he would think out a kingdom for himself as we traveled from one place to another, and this he called the Kingdom of Back [Rücken]—why by this name, I can no longer recall. This kingdom and its inhabitants were endowed with everything that could make of them good and happy children. He was the King of this land—and this notion became so rooted within him, and he carried it so far, that our servant, who could draw a little, had to make a chart of it, and he would dictate the names of the cities, market-towns and villages to him.[22]

20. For a discussion of this type of melody in relation to the "Lied im Volkston," see Erich Valentin, "Zu Mozarts frühesten Werken. Die Klavierstücke von 1761," in *Mozart-Jahrbuch 1955:* 238–42.

21. In addition to writing minuets and binary miniatures, the young Mozart also composed keyboard sonatas with violin accompaniment (K. 6–9 and K. 26–31) as well as sonatas with ad libitum parts for violin or flute and cello (K. 10–15).

22. See Otto Erich Deutsch, ed., *Mozart: A Documentary Biography*, trans. Eric Blom, Peter Branscombe, and Jeremy Noble (London: Black, 1965), 493; originally published as *Mozart: Die Dokumente seines Lebens* (Kassel: Bärenreiter, 1961).

Ex. 4.6a Allegro in F major, K. 1c

Sgr: Wolfgango Mozart 11ten Decembris 1761

Ex. 4.6b Papageno's "Ein Mädchen oder Weibchen" from *The Magic Flute*

Ein Mädchen o-der Weib -chen wünscht Pa-pa-ge-no___ sich!

Mozart's desire to create an alternative kingdom of pleasure beyond the constraints of the real world was more than childhood fantasy. As late as 1786, when writing to Sebastian Winter, his family's servant and mapmaker of "Back" from those early days, Mozart declared that "I have often been in Rücken during these many years." While real-life disappointments drew clear limits to wish fulfillment—the termination in 1777–78 of his love experiences with his cousin, the "Bäsle," and with Aloysia Weber and the terrible journey to Paris come to mind—Mozart's artistic preoccupations offered a seemingly unlimited source of fulfillment, an apotheosis of play, which reached a climax in *The Magic Flute* of 1791, the work that would have alleviated his real-world problems, if only he had lived to see it.

There were many stages on this creative path, but an especially revealing glimpse into Mozart's evolving improvisational skill at the piano is offered by the modulating preludes that he wrote out in 1777, at the urging of his sister. The beginning of one of these "free fantasies," as they would have been called by C. P. E. Bach, is shown in example 4.7. The overall tonal trajectory of this prelude involves a move from F major to E minor, and a prime controlling element of the musical unfolding is the bass. The sustained low F at the outset is reaffirmed following the first wave of figuration as an F octave, whereupon this bass-line soon drops by step to E and then to D, just as another high peak in the figuration is reached in the right hand. The importance of the stepwise falling bass becomes even plainer in the continuation, which reaches C as part of an A-minor 6/3 chord before Mozart spells out the falling fourth C–B–A–G, utilizing shorter note values until the arrival of a sustained G. That G supports figurative elabo-

Entstanden wahrscheinlich Salzburg, 1776/77

ration of E minor, allowing the preceding D-sharps to be heard as resolving to E, and Mozart thereby signals his ultimate tonal goal at about the midpoint of the prelude. In retrospect, the initial mixing of F-major and A-minor triads and the apparently rhapsodic D-sharps and G-sharps that pepper the opening figuration already point toward the emphasis to be placed on E minor and A minor and already shape the directional quality of the music. Hence even here, where Mozart would seem to be at his freest and most whimsical, one can perceive the presence of a logical discourse in the progression of unfolding musical ideas.

On 7 February 1778 Mozart wrote to his father, "As you know, I can more or less adopt or imitate any kind and any style of composition,"[23] a claim that is vividly illustrated in his Fantasy, or Capriccio, in C Major, K. 395 (300g), from 1777. Like the modulating preludes, this piece reminds us most of all of C. P. E. Bach in its rambling and rhapsodic unfolding, with extended improvisatory passages devoted to the composing-out of diminished-seventh chords in rapid figuration. Also reminiscent of C. P. E. Bach are the sudden shifts in affect at the center of the work, where Mozart

23. *Letters,* L. 283a.

writes the succession of indications "Andantino–Presto–Adagio–Andantino–Allegro–
Cantabile–Allegro assai" within only thirteen measures.

Yet another work that suggests the influence of C. P. E. Bach is Mozart's "Fantasie"
in C Minor, K. 396, an outstanding composition whose genesis is shrouded in mystery.
The surviving autograph score, which once belonged in Goethe's manuscript collection,
is a fragment with a subsidary part for violin. This Adagio apparently dates from about
1782; it was published in 1802 after Mozart's death, in a solo piano version completed
by Maximilian Stadler, who may have had access to additional original material. In its
rhetoric and ornamental figuration, the Adagio shows a stylistic affinity with the piano
fantasies of C. P. E. Bach, yet the title "Fantasie" does not stem from Mozart and is somewhat misleading. In its design, this is a slow movement in sonata form, whose second
subject is marked by patterns of rising thirds in the right hand. A speaking, recitative-
like quality invests the opening material, and brilliant embellishments and expressive
harmonies add to the fascination of this music, which deserves to be better known.

Mozart wrote quite a number of works, on the other hand, evoking the style of J. S.
Bach, especially around 1782, soon after the beginning of his residence at Vienna. A good
example is the Prelude and Fugue in C Major, K. 394 (383a), from April of that year. The
fugue, marked "Andante maestoso," reminds us of Bach's fugues in this key in *Das Wohl-
temperierte Clavier.* Another work in an earlier style is the incomplete Suite, K. 399 (385i),
also from 1782, consisting of an overture, allemande, and courante, the sarabande having
been left unfinished. The overture is Handelian in style, but differs from Baroque precedent in that the final cadence is left unresolved on the dominant and is only granted at the
beginning of the ensuing allemande, in C minor; Mozart also departs from Baroque tradition in placing the following courante in the relative major, E-flat, instead of the tonic key.

The Fantasy in D Minor, K. 397 (385g), which presumably also dates from about
1782, shows Mozart writing in a more individual style than K. 395 and places him well
on the way to his great Fantasy in C Minor, K. 475, from 1785. The main body of the
D-Minor Fantasy is formed by three varied appearances of an Adagio theme, interspersed with contrasting improvisatory gestures and vivid, almost theatrical touches
often based on falling chromatic progressions. The introductory Andante section presents a descending bass pattern sustained in long notes, on the one hand, and arpeggios in triplets that drift up from this cavernous foundation, on the other. Its seventh
and eighth measures contain two-note descending motives that roughly anticipate the
falling melodic outline of the expressive Adagio to follow.

This is followed by a resolving Allegretto section in D major, which is characterized by an atmosphere of lyric warmth and grace. This Allegretto has been regarded
as too brief to complete the work, although it displays audible motivic parallels to earlier sections, notably to the Andante.[24] Mozart evidently interrupted work on the Fan-

24. For Otto Jahn, the close of the work is "not satisfactory and so the whole is only preparatory for
something larger" (*W. A. Mozart,* vol. 2, ed. Hermann Deiters [1859; reprint, Leipzig: Breitkopf und Härtel, 1907], 166); this opinion echoes the original 1804 first edition of K. 397, in which the last ten measures
were lacking and the work was given the title "Fantasie d'introduction." Einstein similarly regards the Al-

tasy without supplying a conclusion, and the version published by Breitkopf and Härtel finished the piece, extending the Allegretto to an affirmative end in D major by adding a further ten measures. These ten bars probably stem from August Eberhard Müller rather than Mozart.[25] In any case, this solution is by no means the only possible one, and the relatively low registral position of the final chord notated by Mozart and the fermata over the following rest in this measure suggest another possibility: a return to the opening section of arpeggios in the minor, which thereby frames the entire Fantasy in a manner foreshadowing Mozart's later Fantasy in C Minor, K. 475.[26]

Among the works in the Classical sonata style from the early Vienna years is an incomplete Allegro movement in B-flat major, K. 400 (372a). The manuscript is undated: but in the development, shortly before Mozart broke off work on the fragment, he wrote the names "Sophie" and "Co[n]stanze" above sequences of an expressive phrase employing appoggiaturas. This strongly suggests a date of summer 1781, when Mozart stayed with the Weber family in Vienna and "fooled about and had fun" in the company of the Weber daughters, much to the consternation of his father in Salzburg. The movement was completed by the Abbé Stadler, who similarly finished the last few measures of Mozart's impressive Fugue in G Minor, K. 401 (375e), yet another of his archaising compositions from 1782.

Mozart's sense of humor surfaces in an unusual work that probably dates from 1784, a processional march in C minor, K. 453a, a piece that is serious enough in its musical tone but is titled "Marche funebre del Signor Maestro Contrapunto" (Funeral march of Sir Master Counterpoint). Mozart's autograph score of this short piece in binary form was preserved in the personal album of his student Barbara von Ployer, for whom he wrote two of his concertos in 1784: K. 449, in E-flat major, and K. 453, in G major. As Einstein wrote, Mozart's jokes "are always to be taken half seriously and . . . always possess artistic form."[27] This Lento has little counterpoint, but it is imbued with a strongly orchestral character, suggesting that the piano phrases in parallel sixths that answer the lugubrious opening tutti gestures would be given a lighter, more transparent setting in the strings or woodwinds. At the beginning of the second half, heavy tutti gestures in the first two measures are balanced against a poignant chromatic descent suggesting an oboe; another characteristic touch is the inflection to a Neapolitan D-flat harmony as the expressive parallel sixths are recalled, three bars before the close. Despite Mozart's irony, this is a masterful miniature, unique among his compositions for keyboard.

---

legretto as "far too short" (*Mozart, His Character, His Work*, 248). On the other hand, Rudolf Steglich regards the Allegretto melody as a *Zielthema* (goal theme) and discusses motivic connections in "Über das melodische Motiv in der Musik Mozarts. Eine Analyse der d-moll-Phantasie für Klavier," *Mozart-Jahrbuch 1953:* 128–42, esp. 137.

25. See Paul Hirsch, "A Mozart Problem," in *Music and Letters* 25 (1944): 209. Steglich, in "Über das melodische Motiv in der Musik Mozarts," 140, finds the suggestion of Müller's authorship less than completely convincing.

26. This is how Mitsuko Uchida chooses to end the Fantasy in her fine recording (Philips 412 123–2).

27. Einstein, *Mozart, His Character, His Work*, 246.

Highly serious, on the other hand, is the undated Allegro in G Minor, K. 312 (590d), which is written in a lean but intense *Sturm und Drang* idiom. Saint-Foix considered it early Mozart and assigned it to 1774, but this was mistaken. There are significant musical affinities between this G-Minor Allegro and Mozart's penultimate piano sonata, K. 570, from 1789, as Glock has observed—not only in the broad linear continuity of its phrasing, but in the sense of sovereign freedom and plasticity that informs the whole and seems to guide the transformations from one musical texture to another.[28]

The first of Mozart's three independent "rondos," the lively Allegro in D Major, K. 485, from 1786, hardly seems to be a rondo at all: it lacks independent episodes and employs a monothematic design in which the principal subject appears in a wide range of keys. The first section, moreover, is repeated in the manner of a sonata exposition, and the recapitulation also follows the basic principles of sonata procedure, resolving material previously heard in the dominant into the tonic. For Mozart, this is an unusually consistent monothematic movement, and perhaps its very lack of thematic contrast and many appearances of the main subject may have prompted him or the publisher to call it a "rondo."[29] The theme of this piece was taken from the Rondo of Mozart's Piano Quartet in G Minor, K. 478, which was probably composed in 1785 and was published around the beginning of 1786.

The Rondo in F Major, K. 494, also dates from 1786; Mozart entered it into his thematic catalogue on 10 June 1786 under the title "Ein kleines Rondo für das Klavier allein" [A small rondo for solo piano]. This version of the rondo as a separate piece was published in April 1787, about a year before Mozart revised it and joined it to the two sonata movements K. 533. As we saw in discussing that sonata, Mozart added a twenty-seven-measure cadenza to the Rondo movement (after m. 142) when he revised it as the sonata's finale; he also changed the tempo indication from Andante to Allegretto. The movement in question thus enjoys a double life as an independent piece and as a sonata finale, yet it is rarely performed as a separate composition.

At the beginning of 1787, Mozart was at Prague, where his "Prague" Symphony, K. 504, was first performed on 19 January. Soon after his return to Vienna, Mozart composed the Rondo in A Minor, K. 511, which he entered in his work catalogue on 11 March and described as "Ein Rondò für das klavier allein" [A rondo for solo piano]. There are parallels between the slow movement of the "Prague" Symphony and this profound rondo. Both are Andante movements in 6/8 meter, tinged with expressive chromaticism and lilting melancholy. The post-Prague timing of the composition of this unusual rondo seems scarcely accidental, but other factors played a role as well.

28. Glock, program notes to the recordings *Mozart: The Complete Music for Piano Solo,* by Walter Gieseking, vol. 2 (Seraphim ID-6048). Also see John Irving, "A Fresh Look at Mozart's 'Sonatensatz', K. 312 (590d)," *Mozart Jahrbuch 1995:* 79–94, and Irving's *Mozart's Piano Sonatas: Context, Sources, Style* (Cambridge: Cambridge University Press, 1997), 95–96. As Irving notes, Alan Tyson confirmed a date of 1790 for K. 312 based on study of the paper of the autograph manuscript.

29. The designation "Rondo trés facile" supposedly stems from the publisher Hoffmeister in Vienna, though no copy of the 1786 edition is extant.

The Rondo in A Minor is the last of several Mozartian piano works to draw on the "siciliano" dance type. Through works of Handel and J. S. Bach, Mozart would have been familiar with this old Italian dance, whose elegiac sensuousness is often conveyed in the minor mode.[30] Mozart's use of the siciliano includes the slow movements in minor of his Sonata in F Major, K. 280, and Concerto in A Major, K. 488, but K. 511 is a particularly fascinating example, a profound work of compact dimensions and yet vast scope. Unlike the "small rondo" in F, K. 494, which Mozart later joined to a sonata, the rondo K. 511 seems too weighty to easily serve as part of a sonata. This piece transcends the typically light genre of conventional rondo form, becoming a work sui generis.[31] At the same time, as Charles Rosen has written, "Rondos are defined as much by the characters of their themes as by the structure."[32] Since Mozart chose in this instance to base a rondo on a slow melancholic siciliano theme of chromatic cast, it is not surprising that the resulting work took on a highly individual character.

The main theme displays the siciliano character at once through its dotted rhythmic figures in 6/8 time and its somber, lamenting, yet graceful quality (example 4.8). The melody rises with a crescendo through all of the chromatic steps from tonic to dominant in the second and third measures. As is typical of Mozart, this highly expressive idiom, whose fervent character is later intensified through elaborate melodic variations, is enclosed within an absolutely objective structural framework on which it is wholly dependent and from which it cannot escape. The sustained tonic pedal heard beneath the chromatic ascent—or the dry, understated cadences in the tonic—have a quality of inevitability, and the merging here of subjective expression with objective determination produces an effect of tragic resignation.

Mozart's impressive control of the musical structure in K. 511 provides modes of transformation between contrasting and seemingly incompatible affects. The opening turn on the dominant, for example, is no mere ornament, for its lays bare the chromatic relations that are crucial throughout; so important are the semitones adjacent to the dominant, F and D-sharp, that Mozart incorporates this turn motive into the triplet figuration of his coda, repeating the figure over and over, whereupon the bass echoes, in slower note values, an analogous chromatic figure on the tonic in the closing moments, and the work ends with a reiteration of the original chromatic ornament in the treble.

The two episodes, in F major and A major, are to be understood as optimistic and yet ultimately unsustainable transformations of the main theme. The F-major section beginning at m. 31 has the same upbeat and turn on the dominant above a pedal as

---

30. István Kecskeméti discusses this legacy in his article "Barock-Elemente in den langsamen Instrumentalsätzen Mozarts" (*Mozart Jahrbuch 1967*: 185–86), citing as an example the slow movement of J. S. Bach's E-flat Major Sonata for Flute and Cembalo, BWV 1031.

31. See in this regard Glenn Stanley, "Einzelwerk als Gattungskritik. Mozarts Klavierrondo in A-Moll KV 511," *Mozart Jahrbuch 2001*: 257–71.

32. Rosen, *Sonata Forms*, 124.

Ex. 4.8 Rondo in A minor, K. 511, beginning

the main theme, whereas the A-major episode at m. 89 opens with a cheerful transformation of the cadence. Yet neither of these complexes can resist the chromaticism
drawn from the main theme, a chromaticism that eventually invades their textures
and exposes their essential fragility.

In a study of "generative chromaticism" in the rondo, Allen Forte has stressed the
close relation of the first episode to the main theme or refrain, claiming that this episode is "not at all 'detached' or 'contrasting' except in the most superficial sense."[33]
This interpretation surely goes too far, since a distinct effect of contrast is created
through the diatonicism and the thicker, more vigorous texture at the beginning of
the F-major episode. Nevertheless, quite apart from its reuse of the opening turn figure, the episode soon introduces chromatic figures in sixteenth notes combined with
a swaying upbeat rhythm of two eighth notes—motivic elements unmistakably recalling the siciliano refrain. The F-major tonic of this episode is denied strong articulation, but much weight is placed on the lengthy transition back to the main theme
(example 4.9).

The expressive design of the A-Minor Rondo allows us to respond to an interpretative challenge posed by Wolfgang Hildesheimer in his Mozart biography of 1977.
For Hildesheimer,

> Mozart's works in the minor are so rare that when we do suddenly come upon them
> we prick up our ears and search for a particular motivation: why here, precisely?
> Let it be understood that we seek, not an occasion, not an external cause, but the
> determining factor within the sequence of his works. Of course, we seek in vain.
> Is it really a decision for "the tragic"? Since we have no definition for a musical
> equivalent of what we call in words "the tragic," the question cannot be answered.[34]

33. Forte, "Generative Chromaticism in Mozart's Music: The Rondo in A minor, K. 511," *Musical Quarterly* 66 (1980): 466.
34. Hildesheimer, *Mozart,* trans. Marion Faber (New York: Farrar, Straus and Giroux, 1982), 163; originally published, 1977.

Characteristic of Mozart's works in the minor is the presence of chromaticism, a phenomenon closely bound up with the inherently unstable nature of the minor mode. Side-slipping semitones and dissonant harmonies serve in K. 511 as an allusive force, a siren call of the mournful refrain. How does Mozart foreshadow this return to the siciliano theme? By introducing chromatic elements that destabilize the preceding episode, he causes the music to float or wander—it is cast adrift. Beginning in m. 69, the melody pivots around the half-steps adjacent to A, outlining a turn figure on that pitch: B-flat–A–G-sharp–A. This represents a rhythmic augmentation of the familiar turn at the head of the siciliano itself, and the downward drift of the transition soon allows these dissonant pitches to sound at their original pitch level, as D-sharp and F, the half-steps that surround the dominant note, E. But if Mozart uses rhythmic augmentation to anticipate the telltale turn at the head of the siciliano, he employs the inverse procedure—rhythmic diminution—to signal the chain of rising half-steps that forms the melodic spine of the refrain. Hence the transition becomes saturated with descending and then ascending groups of chromatic sixteenth notes in mm. 76–80, leading directly into the reprise of the original siciliano in m. 81.

This passage is thus less a transition as such than a kind of relapse, whereby the normality of the episode—its stable, diatonic setting of F major—proves to be less autonomous and self-sufficient than might be expected. Yet even the siciliano theme

Ex. 4.10 Rondo in A minor, K. 511, conclusion

itself proves to be remarkably unstable. This malleability is by no means limited to the changing melodic surface of the theme—which becomes a chain of trills at one point. In the closing stages, the main theme itself is virtually transformed, its static bass-line replaced by a sinuous pattern of sixteenth notes, which is carried upward in an exchange of parts to the treble, then connecting to the passage in which Mozart hauntingly stresses that chromatic turn figure with which the rondo had begun (example 4.10).

The dissolving effect of the first episode into the thematic reprise, or of the final thematic statement into the hushed, understated close, may not be a musical equivalent for "the tragic," but nonetheless points strangely toward a kind of oblivion, akin perhaps to the proverbial path, "from which no one has ever returned."[35]

35. As in the song "Wegweiser" in Schubert's song cycle *Winterreise,* set to poetry by Wilhelm Müller.

Ex. 4.11 Adagio in B minor, K. 540, beginning

Datiert Wien, 19. März 1788

About a year after writing the rondo, on 19 March 1788, Mozart completed another splendid solo piano work in the minor, the Adagio in B Minor, K. 540. This
work goes still further in exploiting the tension between a lyric, often almost recitative-like expression and a highly controlled, dissonant chromaticism. Its textures seem
to evoke orchestral effects, as at the outset where the initially unharmonized melody
is supported by sustained, accented chords of a diminished seventh resolving to the
tonic, or moments later, when forte-piano alternations intensify the pattern of descending semitones.

There is something *Tristanesque avant la lettre* about the opening vertical sonority
of the Adagio; and, in fact, three of its four notes (E-sharp, B, G-sharp) are enharmonically identical to the so-called Tristan chord, even in their register (example 4.11).
As in *Tristan und Isolde,* the dissonance of this initial sonority generates a crucial semitone shift, which descends here rather than rising, as in Wagner's opera.[36] The composer
of *Tristan* greatly admired Mozart, particularly his works in the minor, and regarded
him as "der große Chromatiker"—a quality that undoubtedly inspired Wagner.

The movement unfolds in sonata form, with the second subject in D major characterized by hand crossings involving contrasts in dynamics and register, as the two-
note appoggiatura figures drawn from the first subject are inverted, resolving upward.
Another subject in D major, of serene character, leads to the close of the exposition
with a recall of the opening motive. Especially remarkable is the transition between the
end of the development section and the beginning of the recapitulation. Here Mozart
employs rising sequences of the opening two-measure unit of the main theme, which
carry the music from G minor to A minor and then to the tonic B minor. There is no
dominant preparation; the reprise sounds initially like a passing event evolving from
the modulations of the development. In the recapitulation, the theme of serene char-

---

36. Another feature that reinforces the parallel is the presence in both works of a melodic rising sixth
preceding the first vertical sonority.

acter remains in the sphere of the minor, but in the brief coda the music turns at the last moment to B major, closing pianissimo in the low register, with astonishing effect.

An admiration for J. S. Bach remained with Mozart until his final years and is reflected in one of his last independent piano pieces, the masterly contrapuntal Gigue, K. 574, in three voices, composed at Leipzig on 16 May 1789. The piece was written into the family album of the court organist Carl Immanuel Engel, evidently as a tribute to the Leipzig master, but it remains stylistically quite independent of Bach and, indeed, unlike anything else Mozart ever wrote. Particularly distinctive are the twisting angularity of the melodic lines, whose registral disparities enrich the polyphony, the bold dissonances, and the unusual pedal effects heard against shifting harmonies.

The Minuet in D Major, K. 355 (594a), is also clearly a product of Mozart's later years—how different it is from the childhood minuets in its chromatic textures and in the richness of its contrasts! The trio was added by Maximilian Stadler for the first publication of this movement in 1801. Alfred Einstein speculated that the minuet might originally have formed the third movement of Mozart's Piano Sonata in this key, K. 576, from 1789,[37] and Glock has pointed out a motivic similarity between the beginning of the minuet and the principal motive of the sonata finale, involving an inversion of the opening chromatic inflection.[38] The disappearance of the autograph score of Mozart's K. 576 makes it difficult to test this hypothesis. Perhaps because a four-movement format for a sonata was then so unusual, this fine movement was removed and made a musical orphan. If so, Mozart came very close to anticipating one of Beethoven's innovations of the following decade—the use of the four-movement scheme then associated with symphonies and quartets in the genre of the piano sonata.

37. Einstein, *Mozart, His Character, His Work,* 140.
38. Glock, program notes to the recordings *Mozart: The Complete Music for Piano Solo,* by Walter Gieseking, vol. 1 (Seraphim ID-6047).

CHAPTER 5

Four-Hand and Two-Piano Pieces

The Early Duet Sonatas

The first pieces Mozart composed for two players at one piano date from his child-hood and youth and were written for his own performance, together with his sister Marianne (Nannerl). The early duet sonatas assume special interest since no solo sonatas from this period exist.[1] Not all his early duets may have survived, but of those extant, the Sonata in C Major, K. 19d, would be the earliest, since it allegedly stems from May 1765, when Mozart was visiting London at the age of nine. This sonata was first published as Mozart's work in a Paris edition in the later 1780s, and it has been republished as such many times, including in the Henle edition and in a volume of the Neue Mozart Ausgabe in 1955. Writing in 1951, Hanns Dennerlein claimed that its authenticity was generally accepted.[2] However, more recently Mozart's authorship of this sonata has been questioned. In 1993, the piece was relegated to an NMA volume among *29 Werke zweifelhafter Echtheit* (Twenty-nine works of questionable authenticity). The editors of this volume of the edition, Wolfgang Plath and Wolfgang Rehm, stated that "the true author of the work is still to be investigated."[3] In a subsequent study of "Mozart and the Sonata K. 19d" from 1998, Cliff Eisen found no evidence to support Mozart's authorship, concluding that "so far as the sources, letters, and documentary evidence are concerned . . . Mozart's first *sonata* for keyboard four hands is K. 381."[4]

In view of the situation, we shall regard K. 19d as a piece that probably does not stem from Mozart, despite its longstanding association with his oeuvre. The piece still

1. Four early solo sonatas, in G, B-flat, C, and F, K. Anh. 99 (33d), 200 (33e), 201 (33f), and 202 (33g), respectively, have been lost. See the Neue Mozart Ausgabe, Serie IX, Supplement 25, vol. 1, forward, x–xi.
2. *Der Unbekannte Mozart, Die Welt seiner Klavierwerke,* 14.
3. Neue Mozart Ausgabe, Serie X, Supplement 29, vol. 2, forward, xvii.
4. Eisen, "Mozart and the Sonata K. 19d," in *Haydn, Mozart, and Beethoven: Studies in the Music of the Classical Period,* ed. Sieghard Brandenburg (Oxford: Clarendon, 1998), 91–99, quotation from 97.

merits consideration here as an early example of the piano-duet idiom. The adver-
tisements for appearances of the Mozart children from 1765 make clear that duet performances were on offer; hence, an announcement in the *Public Advertiser* from 13
May 1765, "For the Benefit of Miss MOZART of Thirteen, and Master MOZART
of Eight Years of Age, Prodigies of Nature," includes reference to performances "on
the Harpsichord by the little Composer and his Sister, each single and both together,"
and another announcement in the *Public Advertiser* from 9 July of that year declares,
"The Two Children will play also together with four Hands upon the same Harpsichord, and put upon it a Handkerchief, without seeing the Keys."[5]

The piano-duet idiom offers some possibilities that solo works do not. One of
these is the use of chordal simultaneities in all registers, as occurs at the outset of K.
19d; another consists in the enhanced opportunities for dialogical gestures and exchanges between the primo and secondo parts. Despite the undeniable stylistic limitations in K. 19d, the exploitation of these possibilities is noteworthy. For instance, the
beginning of this C-Major Sonata effectively pits two strongly contrasting gestures
against one another. Three massive tonic chords, which can be played forte, are set
against a more intimate response from the primo player alone, which can be performed piano (example 5.1).[6] This expressive four-bar response to the opening salvos
introduces distinctive sound textures in the form of trilled long notes with left-
hand accompaniment, set on weak beats of the meter in mm. 3 and 4. Then, following a reiteration of the three big chords, the secondo player is given a chance to
respond with the expressive phrase in the middle register. All of this musical material has an introductory character, and it is not restated at the recapitulation. The
main theme in the tonic actually begins in the primo part at the upbeat to m. 13, and
the three staccato repeated notes at the head of this subject suggest a rhythmic
diminution of the three half-note chords from the outset. The subsequent unfolding
of this subject also restates elements from the earlier phrases. For instance, the half-
note F resolving to E from m. 6 reappears in m. 16. The second subject in the dominant key begins in m. 21, and it too emphasizes a dialogical aspect, as phrases in the
primo with a measured stepwise falling contour in eighth notes are answered by a
more rapid swoop with a similar contour in sixteenths, played one octave lower in the
secondo.

The initial salvo of chords is restated at the threshold to the development section,
where two statements of the chords appear in close succession, carrying the music
from the dominant key of G major through a diminished sonority to the new key of
A minor. The range of modulation in the development is wide, with particular emphasis on B-flat major, the key of the lowered leading-tone.

5. Deutsch, *Mozart: A Documentary Biography,* 44–45. Mozart was actually nine years old at the time
in question.
6. Dynamic indications are not contained in the score, and such contrasts were hardly available with
instruments from the 1760s. On the other hand, performances of this work on the piano should not fail to
take advantage of the obvious and effective opportunities for dynamic contrasts.

Ex. 5.1 Sonata in C major for piano duet, K. 19d, formerly attributed to Mozart. Beginning of first movement

The outset of the middle movement of K. 19d, a minuet with trio, features musical rhetoric reminiscent of the expressive phrases at the outset of the first movement. Beginning on the dominant note, G, the melody moves through G-sharp to A before descending by step through a fifth to D, supported by dominant harmony. This four-bar phrase is given completely to the primo player, but the secondo joins in the lively, contrasting continuation, a phrase of seven measures ending with a cadence in G major. If this piece were by Mozart, it would show that his love of asymmetrical phrase structures began early.

The Allegretto finale is a "Rondeau," with appearances of a highly characteristic, vivacious theme in 2/4 meter interspersed with episodes, first in F major, then in C minor.[7] The rondo theme itself relies heavily on sequences of a nimble triadic figure as well as quick runs up and down the C-major scale. Its repetitive effect is highly persistent—not to say irritating or even exasperating—yet a rewarding perspective is opened by the final episode, which does not change the key of C major, but instead alters the tempo, slowing the music to adagio. The appearance of the Adagio is arresting, since it follows an abrupt interruption of the frenetic rondo theme (example 5.2). In 3/4 meter, this episode seems somewhat reminiscent of the minuet, particularly since it recalls the G–G-sharp–A motive in the same note values as are used in the second movement; more remotely, it also shows affinity to the first movement in its general melodic emphasis on the fifth and sixth scale degrees. But most striking is the transition back to the 2/4 rondo theme, now sped up to allegro (this is also shown in example 5.2). Following the fermata on the dominant-seventh chord in m. 159, the treble line inches upward toward the dominant with a three-note sixteenth-note upbeat, preceding the final plunge into the Allegro. This much is clear: the final accelerated reprise of the main theme is part of a joke, encouraging us to understand the entire movement in a humorous vein.

---

7. This subject is similar to the rondo theme in the final movement of Mozart's "Gran Partita," K. 361 (370a).

Ex. 5.2 Sonata in C major for piano duet, K. 19d, formerly attributed to
Mozart. Interpolation of Adagio episode in last movement

Ex. 5.2

There is no doubt about Mozart's authorship of the two sonatas, K. 381 (123a), in
D, and K. 358 (186c), B-flat, which were written at Salzburg in 1772 and 1773–74, respectively, and published about a decade later at Vienna as op. 3, nos. 1 and 2. These
are delightful and entertaining works, ideally suited to domestic music-making. There
was a ready market for such compositions in the late eighteenth and nineteenth centuries, particularly for pieces of modest technical difficulty. These sonatas demon-
strate Mozart's thorough assimilation of the sociable *galant* style of the day, as well as
his skillful handling of the duet idiom.

Ex. 5.3 Sonata in D major for piano duet, K. 381 (123a), I, beginning

Like the aforementioned C-Major Sonata, the Sonata in D Major, K. 381, opens with a festive sonority not attainable by a single player: a full-voiced, "orchestral" D-major chord sounding across four octaves (example 5.3). The sixteenth-note flourish in the treble emerges out of this splendid sound, and that motive in turn is immediately reinforced in three octaves to serve as upbeat to the quadruple-octave rising staccato scale that occupies the second measure. Mozart then alternates the D-major tonic harmony with falling dominant-seventh arpeggios in the succeeding measures, before introducing motives doubled in thirds and sixths in the treble over a tonic pedal point in the second part. In its rhythmic drive and accumulation of energy, the opening of this sonata shows impressive vitality. K. 381 begins as a celebration of the D-major tonality itself, with motives and scales arising out of the grand festive chord on the opening downbeat.

The Andante in G major and 3/4 meter of K. 381 foreshadows the Andante in this same key and meter in Mozart's solo Sonata in C Major, K. 545, a work written sixteen years later. Particularly notable is the graceful treatment of linear relationships in the opening subject. Whereas the initial two-measure phrases begin on D and C, the half-close on the dominant in mm. 7–8 extends this linear descent through a fourth, D–A, while enriching the texture with thirds, which were already present in the horizontal voice-leading of the opening phrases. The symmetrical phrase ending the whole sixteen-bar period, on the other hand, carries this linear descent through the fifth to its resolution on G, while further enhancing the sonority through the use of the higher octave in the treble.

The Allegro molto finale opens with resounding full chords paired with triplet motives in the secondo part. In the unfolding of this succinct movement, the diversity of rhythmic patterns, including dotted rhythms and especially triplet eighths, is especially important. The motivic material itself is highly conventional, but the flair of the music lies in its effective contrasts and dialogical gestures. Most colorful is Mozart's use of the lilting chromatic third as a "Scotch snap"—a descending motive in an inverted dotted rhythm of a sixteenth and dotted eighth—that yields to the D-major steamroller driving to the final cadence.

The beginning of the Allegro of the Sonata in B-flat Major, K. 358, from 1773–74, shows Mozart's increasing subtlety in thematic construction, and his enhanced abil-

Ex. 5.4 Sonata in B flat major for piano duet, K. 358 (186c), I, beginning

ity to impact a gradually increasing tension to the music through harmonic means. To that end, Mozart foregoes a massive chordal opening, and presents the opening motive in unison octaves to both players (example 5.4). After the music unfolds across the tonic B-flat major triad, he accelerates the rhythmic motion to steady eighth notes and then reapproaches the initial B-flat from below, while emphasizing pitches belonging to the subdominant harmony, E-flat major. In the ensuing phrases, this stress on the subdominant persists, inviting in response an increasingly forceful articulation of the tonic triad of B-flat major. Each of the three phrases in mm. 4–10 spell out the falling fourth from subdominant to tonic, or E-flat to B-flat. The dialogical structure of these phrases involves a dynamically weighted end-gesture, as the tonic harmony is asserted forte with a flourish in mm. 6 and 8 and then articulated in sixteenth-note figuration with block chords beginning at m. 10. The relatively lean opening of this sonata thereby becomes increasingly animated, culminating in mm. 12–16 in fanfare-like flourishes penetrating the high register over a pedal point on the dominant.

Mozart's focus on the unison triadic figure also dominates the coda and thus frames the movement as a whole. These seven closing bars are saturated with the initial falling motive in half notes as well as with the answering stepwise rising figure leading to the tonic, which is heard three times, the last time in a four-octave unison. This curtailment of the opening gesture thus provides the witty close to the Allegro.

The remaining movements, a 3/4 Adagio in the subdominant key, E-flat major, and a Molto presto finale in 2/4, are more straightforward in their expression and design. One common feature is their use of linear descending patterns. The first four measures of the Adagio outline a stepwise melodic descent from the dominant note, B-flat, through an octave; at the end of the sixteen-measure period, a similar descent to this pitch marks a cadence in B-flat major. In the finale, a linear descent from the tonic note, B-flat, is more subtly imbedded in the thematic structure: mm. 3–5 trace a stepwise fall through the fourth, B-flat–F, and mm. 9–15 contain a continuation of the linear descent through the fourth E-flat–B-flat, with the last of these steps decorated with short trills. Attention to such relations can be essential to a coherent performance. On the other hand, some layers of the accompaniment, particularly in the

Adagio, require a controlled evenness to avoid their becoming unduly prominent, cluttering the texture.

Another important, though often elusive, question relevant to performance is the expressive or psychological meaning of such melodic or linear patterns. For instance, the main themes of the slow movements of both K. 381 and K. 358 involve patterns of stepwise descent from the dominant to the tonic in the major mode. Mozart was, of course, highly familiar with the archetypal nature of configurations of this kind, and although there are numerous possibilities of realizing such a pattern, some common tendencies remain. In this instance, an attempt at generalization was once made by Deryck Cooke: "If to fall in pitch expresses incoming emotion, to descend from the outlying dominant to the point of repose, the tonic, through the major third, will naturally convey a sense of experiencing joy passively, i.e., accepting or welcoming blessings, relief, consolation, reassurance, or fulfillment, together with a feeling of 'having come home.'"[8]

Two-Piano and Duet Works of the Vienna Period

Many years later, at the beginning of his residence at Vienna in 1781, Mozart composed his Sonata in D Major for Two Pianos, K. 448 (375a). This work was written for Mozart's own performance with his excellent piano student Josepha Auernhammer, who also played the Concerto for Two Pianos, K. 365, with her teacher. Auernhammer was evidently enamored of Mozart, though the feeling was not mutual. The composer wrote bluntly to his father that "she is as fat as a farm-wench, perspires so that you feel inclined to vomit, and goes about so scantily clad that really you can read as plain as print: '*Pray, do look here.*'"[9]

Einstein wrote appreciatively about the sonata that "the art with which the two parts are made completely equal, the play of the dialogue, the delicacy and refinement of the figuration, the feeling for sonority in the combination and exploitation of the registers of the two instruments—all these things exhibit such mastery that this apparently superficial and entertaining work is at the same time one of the most profound and most mature of Mozart's compositions."[10] Arthur Hutchings has rightly questioned the word "profound" in this description, finding a lack of depth,[11] but there is no doubt that within the confines of the *galant* style, K. 448 is an exceptionally polished work.

With the two-piano idiom, Mozart could exploit a stereophonic dimension lacking in duet works on a single instrument, and he takes full advantage of this possibility in K. 448. The fanfare-like opening of the Allegro con spirito utilizes the full sound of both pianos, but the continuation uses exchanges of figuration and echo

---

8. Cooke, *The Language of Music* (New York: Oxford University Press, 1959), 130.
9. *Letters,* L. 421 (22 August 1781).
10. Einstein, *Mozart, His Character, His Work,* 273.
11. Hutchings, "The Keyboard Music," in *The Mozart Companion,* ed. H. C. Robbins Landon and Donald Mitchell (London: Faber and Faber, 1956), 56.

Ex. 5.5 Sonata in D major for two pianos, K. 448 (375a), I, beginning

effects to further the dialogue between the two players (example 5.5).[12] In the second subject, marked "piano" and "dolce," the first piano adds cute winks while listening to the first, and both instruments then join in a joint statement whose cadence in A major triggers a return of the brilliant sixteenth-note figuration so characteristic of this opening movement.

Particularly impressive is how Mozart builds up the sonority in this continuation after the dolce second subject. The sixteenth-note figuration in each measure consists of measured trills, which unfold into rising scales (example 5.6). Mozart switches each appearance of this motive between the instruments, while the resulting chain of motives rises by step over a pedal point. During the crescendo in mm. 53–54, he doubles the figuration at the third, and, at the arrival at forte in m. 55, a third voice is added, so that the figuration is fully bodied-out, with brilliant first-inversion sonorities resounding over the dominant pedal point in octaves. The following measures add yet another dimension to the sound, as sustained chordal syncopations in the second piano are played against the on-beat chords in the first piano. In its sheer luxuriance of sound, this passage is outstanding even for Mozart.

In some respects, the second and third movements of K. 448 follow well-established patterns: the slow movement is a lyrical Andante in G major in 3/4 time, and the fi-

12. Einstein has suggested that the opening of Mozart's sonata was influenced by the beginning of Johann Christian Bach's Clavier Concerto, op. XIII, no. 2, published in 1777. This movement is also in D major and carries the identical expressive marking of "Allegro con spirito." (*Mozart, His Character, His Work,* 136).

Ex. 5.6 Sonata in D major for two pianos, K. 448, I, mm. 48–56

nale a Molto allegro in 2/4, just as in Mozart's earlier duet sonata in this key, K. 381. Yet as in the first movement, Mozart creates unique effects through use of dual pianos occupying the acoustical space. In mm. 13–20 of the Andante, the echoing of identical lyric phrases takes on an almost unreal, music-box character, freezing time before the transition to the dominant key. The finale, on the other hand, contains passages in which motives are tossed back and forth between the pianos, with seemingly careless abandon.

One of Mozart's most fascinating works for two pianists is his Fugue in C Minor for Two Pianos, K. 426, from December 1783. This work was written at the height of Mozart's period of enthusiastic assimilation of J. S. Bach's contrapuntal style, when he arranged various fugues of the Leipzig master for trio or quartet performances at the musical gatherings held at Baron van Swieten's house in Vienna. Mozart later arranged this fugue for strings as well, adding the introductory Adagio, K. 546. The traditional Baroque idiom that is developed in this fugue for two pianos lays great stress on dissonant chromatic semitones and appoggiaturas. The intensity of the fugal writing is startling, foreshadowing the fugal textures in some of Beethoven's later works, such as the first movement of the Piano Sonata in C Minor, op. III, which exploits a variant of the same idiom. Beethoven was so taken by this piece, in fact, that he copied out the entire fugue in score.

Mozart's works for piano duet from the Vienna period also include a fragmentary Allegro, K. 357 (497a), from about 1788, as well as a fragmentary Andante, K. 357 (500a), presumably from 1791.[13] These pieces have been regarded as the fragments of a Duet Sonata in G Major, which were completed by J. A. André.[14] Mozart's manuscripts contain 98 measures of the Allegro and 158 measures of the Andante, which is also in G major. The mature stylistic idiom of the Allegro is evident at once in the treatment of chromatic inflections in the opening unison theme, as well as in the subsequent motivic development and the brilliant pianistic textures. As in the unison theme beginning the C-Minor Concerto, K. 491, Mozart does not spell out the entire tonic triad at the outset; the opening staccato notes G and B are followed by a striking drop to D-sharp, and the same motivic contour with a dissonant D-sharp is preserved when Mozart transforms this idea as a legato, dolce statement in mm. 8–9. The completed torso of the movement displays an intensive treatment of this opening motive. The Andante, on the other hand, has a more naive character, with a main theme that glides up and down the scale. Oddly, the primo and secondo parts often alternate instead of playing together. The last section notated by Mozart, in C major, employs a rather simple melody with one unexpected detail, a shift to A-flat followed by a drop of a tritone to D. The musical content of these movements and the fact that the manuscripts employ paper from different periods implies that these pieces do not actually belong together as parts of the same incomplete composition.

Another fragment is the Larghetto and Allegro in E-flat Major for Two Pianos, K. *deest*, a work probably composed around 1781–83, which exists in completions by the Abbé Stadler and more recently by Paul Badura-Skoda.[15] Several other fragmentary projects survive in various manuscripts. For two pianos, there is a part of a fugue in G major, catalogued as K. 375d (Anh. 45), as well as a fragmentary Allegro in C Minor, catalogued as K. 426a (Anh. 44), which represents an incomplete prelude to the Fugue in this key for Two Pianos, K. 426. These two projects evidently date from late 1785 or 1786. As these manuscripts show, compositions for two pianists remained an abiding interest of Mozart's throughout his time at Vienna.

The first and most impressive of the two complete duet sonatas from Mozart's Vienna years is the work in F major, K. 497, composed during the summer of 1786 and published the following year as op. 12. The broad scale of the opening Allegro di

13. See Alan Tyson, "Proposed New Dates for Many Works and Fragments Written by Mozart from March 1781 to December 1791" in *Mozart Studies,* ed. Cliff Eisen (Oxford: Clarendon, 1991), 213–26, esp. 217, 220, 222.

14. This work appears in *W. A. Mozart: Werke für Klavier zu vier Händen,* ed. Ewald Zimmermann (Munich: Henle, 1976).

15. The manuscript of this work came to light in the 1960s. See Gerhard Croll, "Ein Überraschender Mozart-Fund," *Mozart-Jahrbuch 1962/63:* 108–10 (with a facsimile of the first page of the Larghetto), and Croll, "Zu Mozarts Larghetto und Allegro Es-Dur für 2 Klaviere," *Mozart-Jahrbuch 1964:* 28–37 (with two facsimile pages). In this source, the Allegro was completed by Maximilian Stadler.

Ex. 5.7 Sonata in F major for piano duet, K. 497, I, mm. 151–156

molto is forecast through Mozart's use of a slow introduction, a device rarely employed in sonatas and more characteristic of symphonies.[16] Like Haydn in the slow introduction to his Symphony no. 73 ("La Chasse") of 1781, and many later examples, Mozart seems subtly to prefigure the thematic material of the Allegro in the introduction, despite its difference in meter (3/4 as compared to 4/4 in the Allegro di molto). Thus the unison opening of five quarter notes foreshadows not only a prominent semitone figure from the end of the exposition, but also one of the principal rhythmic motives of the Allegro, a series of five even beats often prefaced by a grace note. At the climax of the powerful development section, after the music has come to the threshold of a cadence in D minor, Mozart interpolates a silence and then reasserts this motive fortissimo in all the pitch registers, cutting off the cadence and leading to a series of modulations through other keys (example 5.7). The coda, on the other hand, dwells playfully on this motive in its ornamented form, and the closing passage echoes some of the same motivic half-steps as had sounded at the outset of the slow introduction.

In its sustained, euphonious, yet characteristic textures, sometimes suggestive of a wind serenade, the charming Andante in B-flat major is somewhat reminiscent of the Andante cantabile in E-flat major of the solo Sonata in B-flat, K. 333, from 1783, and bears a closer affinity to the Larghetto of the Piano and Wind Quintet in E-flat Major, K. 452, from 1784. The sonata concludes with a vivacious rondo finale in 6/8 time. Especially memorable is the rondo theme itself, which begins with a soft call to attention on the dominant in the middle of a measure. The melody has an air of playful naïveté, enhanced by the ornamentation and detached articulation; but the structural underpinning is solidly devised, and the stepwise rising bass line incorporates imitations of the motives from the tune. The first episode of the rondo develops and expands the descending melodic contour from the principal theme in a legato, cantabile context. In the central episode, on the other hand, the music turns to D minor, with

16. Mozart's "Linz" Symphony in C Major, K. 425, of 1783, and "Prague" Symphony in D Major, K. 504, from the end of 1786, include slow introductions, as does his Quintet for Piano and Winds in E-flat Major, K. 452, from 1784.

forceful ascending scales juxtaposed with the legato, cantabile theme. Even after the return of the main subject, the darker coloring persists in a powerful imitative passage in the minor, in which these scales replace the soft call-note from the outset of the movement, casting a momentary doubt on the graceful composure of the whole.

The Variations in G Major, K. 501, also from 1786, are one of the most outstanding Mozartian works for the duet medium. The theme itself is surely Mozart's own, unlike most of the subjects of his solo variation sets, which are typically borrowed from songs or arias by other composers. This beautiful Andante theme is characterized by many subtle touches, such as the expressive tension between F-natural and F-sharp introduced in the first half and the sensitive contrapuntal imitations of the opening motive of the theme in the second half. The first three variations are based on progressive subdivisions in rhythm, as reflected in the accompaniment in running triplet sixteenths, suggesting a bassoon part in Variation 2, and the even more rapid pianistic figures in thirty-second notes in Variation 3. In the course of the variations, each hand of each pianist is given enough to do, though the music does not draw attention to such matters of technique. The comic spirit of the third variation belongs to the world of Papageno in *The Magic Flute* and to the finale of Mozart's Piano Concerto in G, K. 453.

At the heart of the set is the poignant fourth variation in the minor, which alters the melodic structure of the theme to stress the lowered sixth degree, darkening its sonority. The inward passion and despair of the variation is conveyed through its chromaticism and underscored by syncopations and the contrasts of register and dynamics. After this somber interlude, the jubilant, march-like fifth variation in the major is all the more effective. Its brilliant impact is enhanced by the written-out repetitions, with the second presentation of each variation half rendered in swift thirty-second notes in the treble. The powerful momentum generated here demands direct continuation into the coda, which begins with a shift into the minor and a brief excursion onto the harmony of the flat sixth, E flat, as a triadic fanfare is asserted in forte across all the pitch registers in mm. 128–30 (example 5.8). This emphatic E-flat triad is reinterpreted as a German augmented-sixth chord, resolving to the dominant of G major in m. 132. We now hear a final reprise of the theme beginning in m. 133, with many delightful changes in detail. A deceptive cadence at the rise of the bass to E in m. 140 leads to a renewed emphasis on the telltale F-natural, and the main theme is stated by the tenor voice in the subdominant, C major, at m. 145 and echoed by the soprano in the subdominant at m. 149. A motivic reduction to essentials then guides the music lightly to the gently suppressed gaiety of the final cadence, with its exquisitely delicate allusion to the texture of the second variation.

The Sonata in C Major, K. 521, dates from the spring of 1787, as we know from Mozart's letter of 29 May to the Baron Gottfried von Jacquin, asking him to give the piece to his sister with instructions to practice it at once, "for it is rather difficult." The opening Allegro contains much brilliant passagework and many felicitous exchanges between the players, but it also shows a particularly close network of motivic relationships. The thrust of the arresting unison fanfare at the beginning is to the sixth

Ex. 5.8 Variations in G major for piano duet, K. 501, coda, mm. 127–155

continued

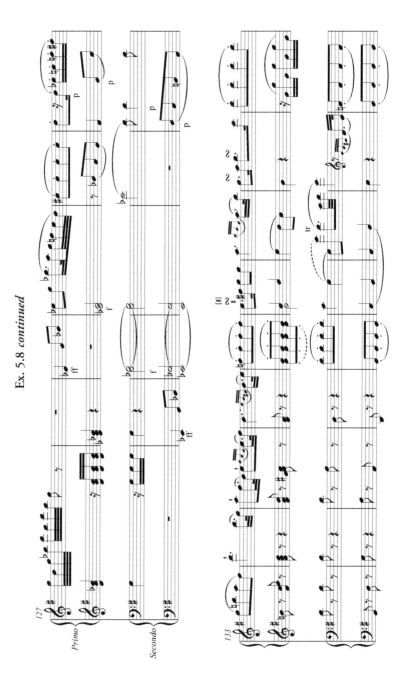

Ex. 5.8 continued

Ex. 5.9a Sonata in C major for piano duet, K. 521, I, beginning

Ex. 5.9b Sonata in C major for piano duet, K. 521, I, mm. 38–42

Ex. 5.9c Sonata in C major for piano duet, K. 521, III, beginning

degree of the scale, A, which is reached on the second beat of m. 2 (example 5.9a). This scale-step becomes a frequent point of emphasis in the outer movements of the sonata. In the dialogical phrases between the secondo and primo parts that immediately follow this opening unison theme, for example, the secondo emphasizes A with the support of subdominant harmony (m. 6), but this gesture is "corrected" by brilliant cadential passagework in the primo part, based on a progression of dominant seventh to tonic (mm. 8–9).

Ex. 5.9d Sonata in C major for piano duet, K. 521, III, coda, mm. 231–239

This same rhythmic motive driving to the sixth scale degree, transposed to the dominant, becomes the emphatic melodic peak of the second subject (m. 40) (example 5.9b). The following virtuosic subject in sixteenth notes makes a similar stress on the sixth degree, and yet another variant of the same idea recurs in the codetta of the exposition. Despite their obvious contrasts, the main themes of this movement assume thereby a kind of family resemblance, lending an audible unity to the whole.

The serene and lyrical outer sections of the following Andante enclose a turbulent, impassioned central episode in D minor, which reminds us at least distantly of the D-Minor Concerto, K. 466, composed the year before. Like the Romanze of K. 466, and several slow movements from the piano sonatas, as we have seen, this slow movement exhibits the adagio/andante archetype, whereby relentless destabilizing forces are pitted against the contemplative, even ecstatic expressive sphere in F major that begins and ends the movement. The frequency of this aesthetic strategy in Mozart's works invites interpretation and seems to point toward a dualistic perception of reality. In this case, one detail invites further reflection. Mozart's melody at the start of the Adagio rises from the dominant note, C, to the tonic and mediant, F and A. In this regard, it seems meaningful that the upbeat into the anguished middle section reproduces exactly this pattern transposed into D minor—a rise from A to D and F leading to an embellished high A placed on the first downbeat of the contrasting music. The stormy middle section thus begins as a transformation of the melodic gesture heard at the outset of the Andante.

The closing Allegretto is a rondo characterized by wit, high spirits, and a brilliant pianistic interplay in the episodes between appearances of the stately main theme. The movement is also visited by irony in its closing stages, at the transition from the reprise of the first episode to the last return of the rondo theme in its original form, where the music seems momentarily to lose its bearings, and at the later appearance of a phrase from the theme heard in the minor in the bass. This complexity has much to do with the sensitive role of the sixth degree of the scale—A—the same relation as was highlighted throughout the first movement. The Allegretto theme itself emphasizes this scale degree prominently in mm. 6–7 (example 5.9c). Consequently, the stress on the sixth degree remains an unresolved element, and Mozart returns with a vengeance to this phrase of the theme in his coda (example 5.9d). The secondo player poses the question in mm. 231–32 and brings matters to a crisis point in mm. 234–35, restating the motive with A-flat replacing A-natural, thereby triggering the momentary shift into the minor mode that is reinforced by the figuration of the primo player (mm. 235–36). Fortunately, the solution to the dilemma is given in mm. 236–39 to the secondo player: the problematical A-flat is enharmonically reinterpreted as G-sharp resolving to A, and the way is thus cleared for the return to C Major. The closing music then celebrates this restoration of order.

Two Works in F Minor from 1790–91

Our survey of Mozart's four-hand keyboard music would be incomplete were we not to consider two unusual works in F minor that are known in piano-duet arrangements: the pieces for clockwork organ, K. 594, from 1790, and K. 608, from 1791. The musical texts of these compositions are based on copies of the autograph manuscripts dating from the early nineteenth century, the autographs themselves having disappeared. Mozart's keen interest in mechanical instruments in this period is reflected as well in *The Magic Flute,* in Papageno's mysterious bells, an instrument that produces sounds with or without a performer.[17]

The origin of the mechanical pieces K. 594 and K. 608 is bound up with the strange and colorful activities of the Count Joseph Deym von Stržíté∕̌ (1750–1804), a Viennese personality who was well known to Mozart (and later Beethoven) and for whom Mozart wrote an Andante, also "for a little clockwork organ," K. 616. An aristocrat by birth, the count was known more commonly as "Hofstatuarius Müller," having lost his aristocratic title for a period on account of a dueling incident. He was an art collector, music enthusiast, and founder of a private museum—his *Kunstkabinett,* a gallery that was packed with plaster casts of statues from antiquity, colored wax figures of famous persons, and other attractions involving various mechanical music instruments: an automatic piano, a musical pyramid, a mechanical canary, flute-

---

17. Carolyn Abbate has probed the mysterious aspects of Pagageno's bells or Glockenspiel—an instrument described in the original libretto as "eine Maschine wie ein hölzernes Gelächter" (a machine like wooden laughter)—in her book *In Search of Opera* (Princeton: Princeton University Press, 2001), 78–85.

playing Spanish youths, and even the "Schlafgemach der Grazien" (Bedroom of the Graces). Müller-Deym's *Kunstkabinett* became a popular visitor's destination in Vienna, and he was eager to add to his collection. Soon after Mozart's death, the composer's death-mask joined that of Emperor Joseph II in Müller-Deym's gallery. A special feature of the wax-museum display was the multimedia dimension: the wax figures were enhanced by the presence of atmospheric lighting as well as by the disembodied effect of music heard on various mechanical contrivances. According to a contemporary description, a main part of the "Schlafgemach der Grazien" involved a sleeping figure lying on a bed, "softly lit by alabaster lamps," and "the most delightful music, specifically composed for the occasion," which sounded "from behind the figure."[18] Müller-Deym was surely proud to have engaged composers of the stature of Mozart and Beethoven to contribute music to his endeavors.

In 1799, the aging count married Beethoven's young piano student Countess Josephine Brunswick, who was thirty years his junior. Their union was driven by a double misunderstanding—Müller-Deym's hope for a substantial dowry and similar expectations of financial security on the part of Josephine's mother, the widowed mother Brunswick. Both hopes were unrealistic: following the hastily arranged marriage, Josephine dissuaded her mother from pressing for her separation from the count, who was seriously debt-ridden. At about this time, Beethoven contributed his pieces for Müller-Deym's musical clock.[19] Soon after the count's death in 1804, Beethoven fell strongly in love with Josephine; but as his feelings grew more amorous hers cooled, and she eventually married another aristocrat, the Baron Christoph Stackelberg.

To judge from their musical contributions, Mozart was more inspired than Beethoven in responding to Müller-Deym's commission. Nevertheless, he seems to have found the work somewhat distasteful at times. A letter to Constanze of 3 October 1790 may relate to the last of these pieces, K. 616:

> I compose a bit of it every day but I have to break off now and then as I get bored. If it were for a large instrument, the work would sound like an organ piece, then I might get some fun out of it. But as it is the work consists solely of little pipes, which sound too childish for my taste.

Both of the F-minor works under consideration here seem to have been associated with a particular project of Müller-Deym: his addition of a wax figure in memory of the recently deceased Field Marshall Gideon Ernst Freiherr Baron von Laudon (1717–90). In the *Wiener Zeitung*, the opening of the mausoleum display on 26 March 1791 was advertised as:

> splendidly illuminated until ten o'clock at night . . . the sight of it will not fail to surprise everyone who visits this mausoleum and thereby renews the memory of

18. A detailed account of Müller's *Kunstkabinett* is offered in Theodor Frimmel, *Beethoven-Handbuch* (Leipzig: Breitkopf and Härtel, 1926), 434–35.

19. See the entry for "Fünf Stücke für die Flötenuhr," WoO 33, in Georg Kinsky and Hans Halm, *Das Werk Beethovens. Thematisch-Bibliographisches Verzeichnis seiner sämtlichen vollendeten Kompositionen* (Munich: Henle, 1955), 474–75.

Ex. 5.10 Piano Duet in F minor, K. 608, beginning

continued

113

Ex. 5.10 continued

this great and meritorious man. . . . The seats are arranged in the best possible way and each person pays 1 fl. for a first place and 30 kr. for a second; upon the stroke of each hour funeral music will be heard, and will be different every week. This week the composition is by Herr Kapellmeister Mozart.[20]

Hutchings describes the transcriptions of K. 594 and K. 608 as "the most powerful, sonorous, and original piano duets Mozart ever invented."[21] Beethoven, too, shared a high opinion of these works, to judge from the copies of these pieces found among his effects.[22] There is indeed something peculiarly moving and impressive about these pieces. They possess a gravity that seems incongruous with Müller-Deym's glorified waxworks display and with the limited means of sonic production at his *Kunstkabinett*. Still, the idea of universalizing the "memory of a great and meritorious man" seems a worthy object, one that strongly foreshadows the Marcia funebre of Beethoven's "Eroica" Symphony, written more than a decade later. Like Beethoven's "Eroica," which bears only a superficial relation to any historical individual such as Napoleon Bonaparte but displays a much deeper connection to the mythic figure of Prometheus,[23] these Mozartian works clearly transcend their original context and any narrow tie to the departed Field Marshall Laudon.

Especially in K. 608, there is a grandeur and formidable objectivity that is reminiscent of Bach's *Art of Fugue*. This quality is felt at once in the first dozen measures, in the Baroque-style flourishes using dotted rhythms, the weighty chords stressing diminished-sevenths, and the stately pedal point on the dominant of F minor reached in m. 9. All of this is preparatory to the fugue that follows (example 5.10). The melodic trajectory of the fugue subject is anticipated with uncanny precision in its opening half notes, which fall a fifth and then rise by step. In the next three measures of steady eighth-note motion, this striving, ascending line twice reaches from A-flat to B-flat; the prominent motive here of the stepwise falling third has clearly been prepared from the beginning of the introductory section, where it appears in the dotted rhythm. Only at m. 18 does the chromatic continuation of the long fugal melody retrieve the initial pitch of C. At this juncture, the tonal answer of the fugue in the lower voice takes over to sustain the rising linear pattern, merging indivisibly into a larger structure. Einstein perceptively regarded "the function of the polyphony [as] a grandiose objectivity of expression, a monumental form of mourning that seeks to avoid the slightest trace of sentimentality."[24]

20. Cited in Patrick Gale, "Mechanical Organ and Armonica" in *The Mozart Compendium,* ed. H. C. Robbins Landon (London: Thames and Hudson, 1990), 309.

21. Hutchings, "The Keyboard Music," 57. It is not clear, however, that Mozart made the arrangements for piano duet.

22. Kinsky and Halm, *Das Werk Beethovens,* 474.

23. For a detailed discussion of the "Eroica" from this perspective, see my study *Beethoven* (Oxford: Clarendon, 1995), 86–95.

24. Einstein, *Mozart, His Character, His Work,* 270.

CHAPTER 6

Mozart's Creative Process

THE "DÜRNITZ" SONATA AND CONCERTO IN C MAJOR, K. 503

The popular image of Mozart's music as having sprung into existence fully formed as the miraculous product of genius, as is conveyed in Peter Shaffer's play *Amadeus* and in Miloš Forman's film of the same title, is seriously misleading. While Mozart did not make nearly as many sketches and drafts for his works-in-progress as did Beethoven, he nevertheless invested much labor in the compositional process, and he was by no means always satisfied with his initial attempts to work out compositions. Mozart not only composed in his head, but he tried out ideas at the keyboard and made written sketches and drafts, some of which have survived.[1]

Some scholars have long recognized that the notion of Mozart's having composed his important works rapidly and without much effort is inaccurate. The debate reaches back to early published writings on Mozart. In the first monograph devoted to Mozart, the book *W.A. Mozart's Leben* first published in 1798, Franz Niemetschek wrote concerning Mozart's creativity of the "incomprehensible ease, with which he composed most of his works."[2] On the other hand, Georg Nikolaus Nissen, in his *Biographie W. A. Mozarts* of 1828, claimed that "one doesn't believe the gossip at all, according to which he [Mozart] tossed off his significant works swiftly and hurriedly. He carried the main ideas with him for a long time, wrote these down briefly, worked out the principal matters fully in his head: only then did he write out the whole—and even then, not as quickly as one has imagined: he carefully improved his work and was extremely strict with himself regarding those compositions that he himself valued."[3]

1. A comprehensive study of Mozart's sketches is offered in Ulrich Konrad, *Mozarts Schaffensweise* (Göttingen: Vandenhoeck und Ruprecht, 1992). This book is supplemented by Konrad's article "Neuentdecktes und wiedergefundenes Werkstattmaterial Wolfgang Amadeus Mozarts. Erster Nachtrag zum Katalog der Skizzen und Entwürfe," *Mozart-Jahrbuch 1995:* 1–28.

2. Franz Niemetschek, *W. A. Mozart's Leben* (1798; facsimile reprint, including revisions and additions of the second edition from 1808, ed. Ernst Rychnovsky, Prague: T. Taussig, 1905), 45.

3. *Biographie W. A. Mozarts* (Leipzig: Breitkopf und Härtel, 1828), 649. The original quotation is as follows: "Man glaube überhaupt dem Geschwätz nicht, als habe er seine bedeutenden Werke nur flüchtig und

The surviving manuscript sources offer confirmation of Nissen's statement. Mozart often made revealing changes after having devised an initial version of a work. Some examples of this practice are mentioned in other chapters of this book. As we have seen, the rediscovery of the autograph manuscript of the Sonata in C Minor, K. 457, shows that the original conclusion of the finale was extended in extraordinary fashion. That compositional change is richly suggestive for the relationship of the sonata with the Fantasy, K. 475, with which it was published. Another instance of compositional deliberations carrying implications for the relationship between movements of a piece is offered by the surviving sketches for Mozart's Piano Concerto in A Major, K. 488, to be discussed in chapter 7.

The present chapter concerns two further instances in which Mozart returned to a work in progress to make substantial revisions. The Sonata in D Major, K. 284, is the last of the set of six sonatas completed by early 1775 at Munich. The reworking of its first movement offers insights into Mozart's evolving stylistic language at a pivotal point in his career. Our second example dates from more than a decade later, in 1786, when Mozart reshaped the piano entrance in the first movement of one of his most imposing works for piano, the Concerto in C Major, K. 503.

The Sonata in D Major, K. 284/205b ("Dürnitz"), First Movement

Much of the first movement of Sonata in D Major, K. 284, composed for Freiherr Thaddäus von Dürnitz at Munich, survives in an original version that was later thoroughly reshaped by Mozart. This canceled first version is preserved as part of the autograph score that contains the final version of K. 284 as well as the other five sonatas of the set, dating from 1774–75; this manuscript was formerly part of the collection at the Staatsbibliothek preussischer Kulturbesitz in Berlin, and it is currently held in Kraków at the Biblioteka Jagiellońska. The rejected draft for K. 284 contains no less than seventy-one measures, and it is fully realized, with dynamics and articulation markings. The draft is shown in example 6.1, together with the final version of the passage. When Mozart broke off work on his draft, he was well into the development section. In the revision, the development section was completely reconceived, and extended passages in the first and last sections of the exposition were rewritten as well.

Originally, Mozart employed the opening unison fanfare twice, with an ascent in register and filling-out of harmony when the gesture is repeated in m. 6. Against an accompaniment in staccato eighth notes, the right hand is given phrases highlighting

---

schnell hingeworfen. Er trug sich sehr lange mit den Hauptideen herum, zeichnete sie sich oft kurz auf, arbeitete im Kopfe die Hauptsachen ganz fertig: dann erst schrieb er das Ganze schnell nieder—und auch nicht so schnell, als man sich einbildet: er besserte sorgfältig nach, nur war er in solchen Compositionen, auf die er selbst Werth legte, äußerst streng gegen sich."

Ex. 6.1 Draft Version and Final Version of the Sonata in D major, K. 284 (205b), I

Fragment - First subject group

two-note sigh-figures. These single-voice lines marked "piano" contrast with the more robust texture of the forte passages, which suggest the texture of orchestral tutti passages.

In this draft version, short motives tend to be strung together in typical style for the time, and a literal repetition of phrases is more conspicuous, whereas in the revised passage Mozart offers a progression in which each change in the texture seems motivated by what happens before it. However, scholars have not agreed about the relative merits of the two versions. In a study comparing the canceled draft and the final

Final form - First subject group

version, László Somfai describes the fragment as "already a masterpiece, probably the best among the six sonatas of the set." He finds a "high level of organic elaboration in the discarded fragment" and regards the early version in this respect as surpassing the finished work.[4]

4. László Somfai, "Mozart's First Thoughts: The Two Versions of the Sonata in D Major, K.284," in *Early Music* 19 (1991): 601–13; quotations from 602, 605. Somfai provides a transcription of the draft, which I have reproduced with emendations in example 7.1. For instance, the bass note in the opening sonority of the draft is D, not C sharp, as is printed in his example 3 (606). Mozart's draft also appeared in the Neue Mozart Ausgabe, Serie IX, Werkgruppe 25, Band 1 (Bärenreiter, 1986).

Fragment - Second subject group

Let us examine the fragment in detail. It begins with a twofold statement of a six-measure unit,[5] which itself consists of two parts: a unison fanfare leading to a pedal point on the dominant, played forte, paired with a rhetorical continuation employing two-note sigh-figures, performed piano. In his article, Somfai describes the second statement of this dialogical phrase as a "variation" of the first,[6] but that term seems

5. In this instance, the phrases overlap, and a pattern of gestures in sixteenth-notes followed by expressive motives featuring sigh-figures appears not only in the opening twofold statement, but also in the continuation, with the sixteenth-note motion combined with the sigh-motives beginning in m. 15.

6. Somfai, "Mozart's first thoughts," Ex. 3 on p. 606.

Ex. 6.1 *continued*

4   Final Form - Second subject group

Fragment - Development section

end of the fragment

Ex. 6.1 *continued*

questionable, since apart from new voicing of the initial unison D as a full-voiced chord in m. 6 and a trill on the leading-tone in m. 5 there are no other changes; the second phrase is otherwise a literal repetition of the first. The tonic cadence of the two six-bar units overlaps with the ensuing phrase, so that the full-voiced D-major chord in m. 6 serves both as the end of the first phrase and as the beginning of the second.

Melodic continuity acts here as a primary agent of coherence. Hence the opening fanfare figure moves from the tonic note, D, to the dominant, A, and that pitch serves in turn as a repeated pedal point in the following three bars and also in a higher register as the initial pitch of the expressive four-note motive in mm. 2–3. A free inversion of that motive stresses the sigh-figure on A–G in m. 4. Mozart then doubles up the two-note phrases in m. 5, as the music moves toward the tonic cadence at the downbeat of m. 6. A stepwise descent through F-sharp–E and then D–C-sharp is outlined in the first and third of the two-note sigh-figures in m. 5. Hence the descending line as contained in the two rapid motivic figures of a falling fourth in the opening fanfare motto is outlined in larger note values in the melody as the music moves to the first cadence.

Once the cadence is reached in m. 11, the music of the first version unfolds in steady sixteenth-note figuration outlining turn figures, combined with octaves in the left hand. Beginning in m. 15, this figuration migrates to the left hand, as melodic inflections featuring the two-note sigh-figure unfold in the treble. This music already assumes a transitional function, and the ensuing mm. 20–24 present a pedal point on the dominant, A, preparing the beginning of the second subject group in A major. These five bars were taken over virtually unchanged into the final version of the sonata.

Let us now examine Mozart's revisions to this first section of the exposition. The change to the initial tonic chord is already arresting and significant. In place of a unison D in three octaves Mozart now employs a full voicing in the right hand, with added emphasis supplied through an arpeggiation of the chord.[7] At the same time, this initial sonority is curtailed to half its original length, with quarter rests placed on the second beat. Set off by silence, the opening sonority makes a more distinct impression, without thereby losing its connection to the gestures that follow.

Another striking change is that the gesture in the second bar now moves to A–F-sharp–B, creating a dissonance that needs to be resolved, with the second two-bar phrase balancing and resolving the first. When the music reaches the dominant m. 4, the rhythmic texture in eighth notes—representing a diminution of the quarter notes of the second measure—is continued in the bass motion, while Mozart continues with the following phrases beginning on the D in the octave above middle C. In the second version he has anticipated this progression already in the arpeggiation of the opening chord, which lays out the whole tonal space of the opening section.

There is now a gradually increasing rhythmic tension that integrates all of the thematic segments in the first subject group and transition, up to m. 21. After the phrases over the dominant pedal point in mm. 4–6, two transitional bars in running sixteenths resolve to the tonic in m. 9. This sixteenth-note figuration employs turn figures similar to those contained in the first version of the movement beginning in mm. 11. There, as we have seen, its function was already transitional. Here, by contrast, these two bars of sixteenths have been integrated into the opening theme, which is far broader than before. The original version of the movement displays a relatively loose, block-like construction, with a double statement of the main subject in mm. 1–6 and 6–11 followed by a transitional continuation in sixteenth notes. By contrast, the final version

---

7. One can also regard the beginning of the revised version as corresponding to m. 6 of the draft, which already contains the full tonic harmony. Seen from this perspective, Mozart's first critical decision was to discard the first five measures of the draft version.

impressively enlarges the opening theme, which reaches the transition only with the resolution of the augmented-sixth chord to the dominant octave A in m. 17.

The new idea Mozart introduced in mm. 9–12 is connected to the opening bars in tangible ways. Particularly important is the rhythmic correspondence. A half note (or quarter note and quarter rest) followed by five quarter-note impulses and another rest is common to both thematic segments, notwithstanding the sixteenth-motion in the second half of m. 1 (since each of these motivic groups is identical and is articulated within the space of one quarter-beat). Bars 9–10 can thus be regarded as a rhythmic variation of bars 1–2, and Mozart carries over a prominent feature of his original mm. 2–5 into the new idea, namely the steady movement in eighth notes. The newly articulated opening of the sonata, with rests marking off the motivic segments, allows Mozart to postpone the continuous rhythmic motion in eighths until mm. 9–12, when it seems motivated by the preceding acceleration to sixteenth notes in mm. 7–8.

The new subject introduced here has two voices heard above this steady eighth-note pulsation in the bass. In turn, the two-measure unit in mm. 9–10 is intensified as a rising sequence in bars 11–12. In the ensuing passage, orchestral-style tremolo figures in sixteenth notes are combined with a continuation of eighth-note motion in the bass, so that the composite texture is the most animated yet. However, starting at the arrival at the dominant pedal point in bar 17, the rapid sixteenths pass into the left hand while the right hand plays a pattern in eighth notes accelerating to sixteenths. Unlike most of the preceding passages, this music was retained from the original version. This idea represents a variant of the opening motive from m. 1, with the stepwise figure played first in rhythmic augmentation (in eighth notes) and then in sixteenth notes. Mozart thus recaptures the opening fanfare gesture just as the transition comes to an end.

Charles Rosen has singled out the first movement of Mozart's D-Minor Concerto, K. 466, from 1785, as manifesting "an important advance in purely musical skill—the art of sustaining an increase in rhythmic motion, that is, the creation of excitement," and he isolates no less than 13 steps in the gradual process in the first important climax for soloist and orchestra.[8] Such an advance in creating musical excitement through gradual changes in rhythmic motion is already unmistakably present, in somewhat simpler form, in the revised first movement of K. 284, a work composed a full decade before K. 466. In fact, the creation of such a dramatic progression through a series of carefully graduated steps was presumably a major factor behind Mozart's decision to rewrite his draft. Another motivation was the effort to recast this sonata on a more imposing level by enhancing its textures and its formal breadth.

Although much of the second subject area was left intact by Mozart, his departures from the draft in the last section of the exposition are revealing. Eight measures from this section were removed and replaced by ten new measures.[9] In turn, this revision

8. Charles Rosen, *The Classical Style: Haydn, Mozart, Beethoven* (1971; reprint, expanded ed., New York: Norton, 1997), 228–33; quotation from 228.
9. The measures replaced include the last seven of the draft as well as m. 43, whereas mm. 44–45 are retained in their original form.

was surely bound up with Mozart's dissatisfaction with the ensuing development section of the draft version—for, of the original development, virtually nothing remains in the finished work.

In the draft version, Mozart appends a two-measure cadential phrase in piano to the end of the exposition, immediately following a pair of robust cadences in forte, which sport trills in the right hand and rattling sixteenth-note figuration in the left hand. He then uses the soft two-measure cadential phrase as the motivic basis for much of the development. The motive appears eight times in the first twelve measures, and even the repeated-note figure of mm. 65–57 is derived from the three repeated pitches of the cadential motive, heard in rhythmic diminution.

Curiously, Mozart followed up on this basic compositional idea in the opening Allegro con spirito of his Sonata in D Major, K. 311, from 1777. The end of the exposition in that work incorporates a piano phrase featuring two-note sigh-figures in parallel sixths, a motive that dominates the first sixteen bars of the ensuing development. Thus Mozart's basic idea in the draft for K. 284 was not completely discarded, but found a home in his next piano sonata in this key.

To be sure, the contrast between a powerful, tutti-style scoring and a more intimate, expressive expression is retained and even heightened in the final version of K. 284. The first inserted material near the end of Mozart's exposition features a rhythmic motive employing a dotted eighth and two thirty-second notes (mm. 40, 43), an idea that is expanded into a whole measure of repetitions of this figure in octaves (m. 44) and which reappears in varied form in the penultimate bar of the exposition (m. 50). This thematic material is juxtaposed with arpeggiated chords (mm. 45, 51), foreshadowing the initial chord of the exposition (to be played as this section is repeated), whereas the cadence in A major (mm. 48–49) is now fortified by a trill sustained through one full measure. The more intimate expression in piano is nested into mm. 46–47, two bars that sound almost parenthetical in this context, since m. 48 could have followed directly from m. 45.

Why did Mozart completely recast the development of his evolving sonata? Part of the answer may lie in a desire to sustain momentum and rhythmic energy, since the final version of the development unfolds in unbroken sixteenth-note motion until the recapitulation. Another factor is surely motivic. The driving motive that appears in parallel sixths (or thirds) in mm. 52, 54, 56, and 58 deserves special attention in this regard. What is its connection to the exposition? This seven-note figure—with its stepwise move up a fourth and back—is audibly linked to passages in the first theme that Mozart added when he revised the movement.[10] This precise contour is embedded in the sixteenth-note figuration in mm. 7–8, following the first note of each eight-note group. Furthermore, this general motivic shape featuring a stepwise rise through a

10. Such figures have, of course, a conventional aspect, and similar motivic configurations can be found in other works, such as in the transition to the second group in the opening Allegro of the preceding Sonata in G Major, K. 283. Nevertheless, the specific network of motivic relations within a movement or work often assumes much significance in Mozart's music.

fourth is also reflected in the important two-measure phrases that Mozart placed at the heart of his rewritten opening section, mm. 9–12, while the intervallic shape suggests an inversion of the stepwise staccato figures in mm. 17–20. Yet another related passage is mm. 33–34 in the second subject group, with its stepwise melodic descent through a diminished fourth heard over an accompaniment in sixteenth notes. These motivic affinities are far-reaching, and go beyond the network of motivic correspondences in the first version.

László Somfai's claim about the two versions of this movement, that "from a modern analytical point of view, the organization of motives, the rhythm and textures—in general, the phenomenon of 'organic' elaboration—probably reached a higher level in the fragment than in the final form,"[11] seems hardly tenable. In its motivic subtlety, as well as its forceful rhythmic drive and brilliant textures, the second version of this opening movement of K. 284 represents an important advance. Closer to the mark is Einstein's observation that "Mozart himself must have had a personal or musical experience that suddenly lifted him to a new and higher level."[12]

The Concerto in C Major, K. 503, First Movement

If the compositional problem in K. 284 related especially to issues of continuity and musical development, the reasons for the revision of K. 503 were specifically associated with the relation of the piano soloist to the orchestral tutti. The evidence of Mozart's compositional process in this case is preserved in the autograph score of the concerto held at the Staatsbibliothek Preussischer Kulturbesitz in Berlin. In an article on this source published in 1953, Walter Gerstenberg isolated and transcribed 127 measures from the beginning of the concerto, describing these as a *particella*, or original outline draft, of the movement that was later revised when Mozart completed the piece.[13] Gerstenberg's work offers a valuable platform for further study of the genesis of K. 503.

More recently, the studies of Alan Tyson have broadened our knowledge of Mozart's working methods in ways that enrich the interpretation of this source. Tyson's main contribution has consisted in a close study of the papers used by Mozart for composing his music. Since Mozart used a considerable number of different paper types, and he needed to acquire new paper at regular intervals, his use of these papers reflects the chronology of his compositional activity. Furthermore, the investigation of Mozart's original papers has cast new light on a striking aspect of the Mozart sources: the survival of a substantial number of unfinished scores or fragments in various formats. Tyson observes about these sources that "in 1799 Constanze Mozart arranged for a careful catalogue of them to be compiled by the Abbé Maximilian Stadler, and after

---

11. Somfai, "Mozart's First Thoughts," 603.
12. Einstein, *Mozart, His Character, His Work,* 242.
13. Gerstenberg, "Zum Autograph des Klavierkonzertes KV. 503 (C-Dur). Anmerkung zu Mozarts Schaffensweise," *Mozart-Jahrbuch 1953:* 38–46.

she had disposed of all the available scores of her late husband's completed works to the publisher Johann Anton André in January 1800, the fate of the fragments, which had not been included in the sale, began to exercise her."[14] Despite the efforts of Constanze Mozart, publishers like Breitkopf and Härtel showed no interest in the fragments, which have long remained obscure. Only in 2002 was a full catalogue of these sources with facsimiles published as a volume of the Neue Mozart Ausgabe, edited by Ulrich Konrad.[15]

Tyson's investigation of these fragments and of Mozart's use of music paper led to an important conclusion: that some of his finished works began as fragments that were only completed after a considerable length of time had elapsed. It appears that Mozart's reputation for composing works swiftly was connected in part to his practice of setting aside torsos of incomplete works that could be taken up and finished when an occasion arose, such as a performance opportunity. Such was evidently the case with the first movement of K. 503. Mozart entered this work into his *Verzeichnüss* (thematic catalogue) with the date of 4 December 1786, and he premiered the work on the very next day, 5 December 1786. However, the three double-leaves at the beginning of the autograph score of K. 503 differ from the remainder of the score in that they consist of a rare paper type, one that turns up in six other examples. These include parts of the scores of the String Quartet in A Major, K. 464, an aria from *Davidde penitente*, K. 469, and three concertos, the works in F major, K. 459, D minor, K. 466, and C major, K. 467, as well as the whole of a string quartet fragment in A major, K. 464a. All of these works date from between December 1784 and March 1785, a period nearly two years earlier than Mozart's completion and performance of K. 503 in December 1786.

All of this indicates that the *particella* for K. 503 discussed by Gerstenberg almost certainly dates from the period, around late 1784 and early 1785, when Mozart was intensely occupied with piano concertos and brought to fruition three such works, K. 459, K. 466, and K. 467. The fact the one of these pieces—K. 467—was in C major, may perhaps have discouraged him from completing another concerto in the same key at that time. In any case, although Mozart composed three further piano concertos during the following 1785–86 season—K. 482, K. 488, and K. 491—it was not until the end of 1786 that he returned to his draft for what became K. 503, which was to become the very last of the great series of twelve Viennese piano concertos that began with K. 449, in E-flat major, in 1784.

Mozart's draft is reproduced in example 6.2a, and the final version of the opening solo passage is shown in example 6.2b. The transcription of the draft basically follows Gerstenberg's version, though empty staves have been deleted and emendations have been made to restore Mozart's strokes as articulation marks. The reconstruction of the draft is made possible through distinct differences in the color of the ink. When

14. Tyson, *Mozart: Studies of the Autograph Scores*, 125.
15. Ulrich Konrad, ed., Neue Mozart Ausgabe, Serie X, Supplement 30/4: *Fragmente*, (Kassel: Bärenreiter, 2002).

Mozart returned to his draft, he filled out the many empty systems in the pages of the draft, rewrote parts of the solo piano passage on folio 5r, and then canceled all of folio 5v. Consequently, he inserted a new leaf, folio 6, into his score. The original folio 6 thus became folio 7, but it corresponds in its paper type to the opening pages of the draft and represents the missing leaf that was paired originally with folio 5.

What did Mozart alter in his draft, and why? The change involved a thorough reshaping of the opening solo piano passage with orchestral accompaniment, which was expanded from fifteen to twenty-one measures. The first bars of the solo, in which the piano responds to soft inflections in the strings, were left unchanged. However, beginning in mm. 96–97, Mozart's refashioning of the piano part involved a fundamental rethinking of the original version. In order to appreciate the revision, it is indispensable to reflect on the challenging context of this solo passage following an imposing and weighty orchestral ritornello.

This Allegro maestoso opens with a pair of weighty orchestral phrases in forte rooted on the tonic and dominant, spread across broad registers of pitch and grounded by the taps and rolls of the timpani. In all the Mozart piano concertos, there is no other opening that so much depends on the effect of sheer massive sonority; indeed, the first four measures of each of these eight-bar phrases involve no harmonic shift whatsoever. Such an opening cannot be effectively transferred to the solo piano by itself, which would sound hopelessly weak by comparison. Presumably for this reason, Mozart decided to introduce the solo indirectly, in response to a series of cadential phrases in the strings, played piano. As the piano continues, Mozart gives to the soloist a version of another piano phrase—the inflection heard twice in the strings in mm. 70–72 of the orchestral introduction.

Thus, in K. 503, Mozart faced a special challenge with the opening piano passage, inasmuch as his "standard operating procedure" in lyrical movements—to borrow David Rosen's phrase—would not apply. It would not do to have the piano initially mimic the opening theme of the orchestral introduction, as occurs in other later concertos such as K. 488, K. 537, or K. 595. Nor was it viable to devise the piano entrance as an expressive recitative-in-tempo passage, as in the two concertos in minor, K. 466 and K. 491, in which the agitated tension of the orchestral ritornello is reshaped into the more personal utterance of the soloist.

The problem in Mozart's initial attempt at the opening piano passage is twofold: it lacks sufficient stature to enable the soloist to assert himself or herself against the orchestra, and it fails to build a convincing transition in sonority and character to the massive reassertion of the opening theme in the tutti that occurs in m. 106 of the draft, corresponding to m. 112 of the finished work. It is revealing that in his draft, just as in the completed version, Mozart avoids including the solo with the first six measures of this emphatic restatement of the main theme. However, the lighter orchestration of the last two measures of this eight-bar unit offered that opportunity, and here the solo reenters with sixteenth-note figuration in the high register, a texture of sound heard above the bassoons and oboes and the sustained dominant-seventh chord in the strings.

Ex. 6.2a Draft Version of the Concerto in C major, K. 503, I

That distinctive texture of sound—with the rapid piano figuration heard in the high register over the woodwinds—became a key element in Mozart's expansion of the piano entrance once he returned to the work in 1786. But just as important is the higher degree of articulation given to the phrasing of the passage. In the draft version, the last eight measures of the piano solo unfold continuously, with no articulating pauses in the right hand of the piano. The rewritten version contains several such breaks. An emerging quality of insistence invests the threefold phrases emphasizing the falling dyad F–B in mm. 96–98, and the psychological impression emerges that the soloist

will not remain content with understated rhetoric. The richer sonority of parallel 6/3 chords and syncopation in mm. 99–100 show an increasing resourcefulness, and the following two-bar phrase, in mm. 101–102, returns to the telltale F with a new twist. In place of the predictable V–I cadences in those rather unimaginative orchestral gestures in mm. 91 and 93, the soloist now harmonizes the F as part of a diminished-seventh chord leading through a deceptive harmonic shift to the sixth degree. Skillful individual innovation thus competes with the massive yet limited resources of the crowd. In the ensuing two-bar phrase, in mm. 103–104, virtuosity begins to play a role for the first time. This phrase is a variation on mm. 99–100, a variation in which brilliant sixteenth-note scales and broken octaves sweep through registers yet untouched by the piano. Following the same pattern is m. 105, which offers an elaboration of the content of m. 101, accompanied softly by the strings.

The turning point in the entire piano passage comes at m. 106, with the entrance of the horns to articulate the G pedal point in the tonic 6/4 chord as the soloist moves into the high register. The flute, oboes, and bassoons join their sonorities with the piano, with the upper oboe line corresponding closely to that of the piano, though

played one octave lower. These orchestral instruments are missing altogether from the early version of the passage in Mozart's *particella,* which is altogether more placid and less eventful than the final version. In the last three measures of the finished work, the piano's descending figuration is reversed through a rising chromatic scale, followed by restatement of the I 6/4–V7 in a halting rhythm that seems to foreshadow the orchestral chords to come. To a much greater extent than the first version, Mozart's expanded passage for the solo piano conveys a sense of growing strength and confidence. The solo passage here seems to *lead into* or even help *bring about* the powerful main theme in the tutti, rather than merely precede it.

The autograph score of K. 503 thus offers a wealth of insight into the ways in which a single solo piano passage can accomplish a crucial psychological transition while interacting with instrumental groups from the orchestra. But the value of this autograph

score for study of the creative process is not confined to this one example. Layers of successive compositional work can be identified throughout the score. As Gerstenberg observes, many passages, especially for the pianist's left hand, are in a distinct yellowish ink and were clearly filled in later.[16]

It is not surprising that the last part of the musical text to be completed was the piano solo part—particularly those aspects of the texture that would be realized through patterns of figuration. Indeed, in the autograph score of one of the subsequent concertos, the "Coronation" Concerto, K. 537, Mozart notated little for the left hand in extended passages of the outer movements and in the entire slow movement, even

16. "Zum Autograph des Klavierkonzertes KV. 503," p. 39; see esp. note 4.

though he performed this piece more than once. Other concertos as well, such as K. 482 and K. 491, contain passages in which Mozart has outlined just a few sustained pitches without realizing the full texture; such passages tend to appear before major cadences, when a sudden interruption of the rhythmic momentum would be especially inappropriate and disconcerting.[17] One reason for the use of such shorthand

17. For perspectives on Mozart's fragmentary notation and the role of improvisation in the concertos, see, among other studies, Robert Levin's essays "Improvisation and Musical Structure in Mozart's Piano Concertos," in *L'interpretation de la Musique Classique de Haydn à Schubert. Colloque international, Evry, 13–15 octobre 1977* (Paris: Minkoff, 1980), 45–50, and "Improvised Embellishments in Mozart's Keyboard Music," *Early Music* 20 (1992): 221–233, esp. 226–232; and Friedrich Neumann, *Ornamentation and Improvisation in Mozart* (Princeton: Princeton University Press, 1986), esp. 240–56.

Ex. 6.2a *continued*

Ex. 6.2b Final Version of the Piano Entrance in the Concerto in C major, K. 503, I

may have been a reluctance on Mozart's part to fix the text in a single configuration. In specific performances, he could choose among different possibilities of textural realization.

Hence it remains uncertain whether the yellowish ink layer of writing in the score of K. 503 preceded or followed Mozart's first performance of that work on 5 December 1786. In various details, his initial performance of the concerto surely did not coincide with the printed text we know. Some of his late revisions also affect structural features, as with his decision to delete a measure in the slow movement preceding bar 100, which prolonged the diminished-seventh harmony while connecting the piano arpeggios in the high register in m. 99 with the low register at the beginning of the following measure.

With K. 503, as with several of the other great piano concertos from the Vienna years, the greatest gap between aesthetic realization and the preserved text remains the problem of the missing cadenzas. This situation reflects ironically on overly literalist attitudes toward Mozart's musical texts. These texts are not only incomplete, but could scarcely ever have existed in one definitive version. It is more appropriate to inquire into the meaning, rather than merely the letter, of Mozart's musical legacy, recognizing the continuing challenge these works pose for active, imaginative interpretation.

CHAPTER 7

The Piano Concertos

Mozart's piano concertos represent one of the richest legacies in a single genre by any artist and overshadow, in their importance and quantity, the contributions of subsequent composers to this form. Whereas Beethoven left four supreme examples in the concerto genre (the last three piano concertos as well as the Violin Concerto), Mozart produced more than a dozen piano concertos of the very highest caliber. The piano concerto served Mozart as the piano sonata served Beethoven, as a primary vehicle for this own keyboard virtuosity and evolving compositional powers. From the Concerto in E-flat, K. 271, from 1777, to the final Concerto in B-flat, K. 595, from 1791, the concerto was one of Mozart's most progressive genres, in which innovations in form, orchestration, and texture make an early but decisive appearance, sometimes foreshadowing his symphonic and operatic styles.

Widespread recognition of the importance of Mozart's concertos occurred by the 1790s. Writing in 1796, August Eberhard Müller observed about Mozart that

> this excellent man, whom Germany first began to honor sufficiently after his death, combined in his concertos much harmonic richness and novelty with charming and often ingratiating melody, a very rich and often audacious fantasy, altogether an uncommon variety, [with the] pomp and splendor of a fully realized accompaniment and a soothing sensitivity and grace in the woodwind instruments. [He] gave the virtuoso in his solo passages enough opportunity for brilliant display—but never demanded the impossible from them, and wrote on that account as excellently and very practically for performance as did otherwise perhaps only the great Philipp Emanuel Bach.[1]

1. Müller, *Anweisung zum genauen Vorträge der Mozartschen Clavier Concerte hauptsächlich in Absicht richtiger Applicatur* (Leipzig: Schmiedt and Rau, 1796), 1. A comparison of first movements of concertos by C. P. E. Bach and Mozart is found in Jane R. Stevens, "The Importance of C. P. E. Bach for Mozart's Piano Concertos," in Neal Zaslaw, ed., *Mozart's Piano Concertos: Text, Context, Interpretation* (Ann Arbor: University of Michigan Press, 1996), 211–36.

The structural framework of Mozart's concertos entails a three-movement plan, with a central slow movement followed by a finale most often in rondo form or, less frequently, by a sonata design or set of variations. The longest and most complex of the three movements is generally the first. Comparison can be drawn with sonata-allegro procedure, but Mozart's concerto forms resist easy categorization and, unlike a symphony or sonata, rely fundamentally on the dramatic interplay between orchestra and soloist. Some of the themes in the opening orchestral ritornello of a first movement may not appear in the ensuing solo exposition, but return only in the development or recapitulation. Other themes may be heard only from the orchestra or soloist, but are not interchanged between them. A basic principle of the Mozart concertos is that the recapitulation restates and resolves materials from both the opening orchestral ritornello and the ensuing solo exposition in the tonic key, while often changing the original order of presentation of the themes. Both the solo exposition and the recapitulation are normally ended by a display of rapid, showy passagework from the soloist leading to a cadential trill. Following the tonic cadence by the soloist in the recapitulation, a short orchestral tutti passage then leads to an extended improvisatory passage, or cadenza, before the orchestra returns to close the movement.

In creating his first concertos in 1767, Mozart supplied orchestral accompaniments to keyboard sonatas by other composers, including Eckard, Honauer, Raupach, and Schobert—German-speaking musicians whom the Mozarts had met in Paris—as well as C. P. E. Bach (K. 37, K. 39, K. 40, K. 41). The sources for these three-movement arrangements are as follows: K. 37—Raupach, an anonymous source, Honauer; K. 39—Raupach, Schobert, Raupach; K. 40—Honauer, Eckard, Bach; K. 41—Honauer, Raupach, Honauer. The piano part of these pasticcio concertos reproduces the original works, while shaping a broadly balanced form. In the first movements, for example, Mozart's contribution consisted in the addition of four orchestral ritornelli: one preceding the solo entrance, one reinforcing the arrival in the dominant key, one after the recapitulation in the tonic, and finally another tonic ritornello to close the movement. Several years later, by 1772, Mozart made concerto transcriptions of three sonatas from the op. 5 set by Johann Christian Bach that had first been published in 1766. These three transcriptions are grouped under the single catalogue number K. 107.

The first original keyboard concerto by Mozart is K. 175, in D major, written at Salzburg in December 1773, when he was eighteen. The originally intended solo instrument in this work may have been harpsichord or organ. The orchestration, including trumpets and drums in addition to strings, oboes, and horns, is the largest in any of the six Salzburg keyboard concertos. The D-Major Concerto was well received by audiences, and Mozart revived it years later for performances as piano soloist at Mannheim in 1778 and again after his move to Vienna, when he wrote a new finale for it, the rondo-variations K. 382, which are lighter in character than the original finale and may have better appealed to popular taste. The rhythmic vitality of the opening Allegro, the dream-like mood of the Andante, and the polyphonic ingenuity of the original sonata-form finale of K. 175 stand out among the early concertos. C. M. Girdlestone provocatively described this work as "a final personal outburst before the slumber of the years of *galant* music,"[2] when Mozart revealed comparatively little of his personal genius but much skill in assimilating the fashionable musical styles of the eighteenth century. Girdlestone's characterization has some validity, but it is too sweeping, in view of works like the solo sonatas, K. 279–284 from 1775–76.

Mozart at Salzburg: The "Jenamy" Concerto in E-flat Major, K. 271

Less distinctive than K. 175 and more reflective of the taste of the age are Mozart's Concertos in B-flat, K. 238, in F, K. 242, and in C, K. 246, all of which were written in the space of three months in early 1776. K. 238 is notable for its delicate scoring, with flutes substituted for oboes in the slow movement, and especially for its handling of the solo-tutti relationship, which is more resourcefully integrated than in K. 175. This raises the matter of Mozart's formative models for his concerto designs during the 1770s. As Martha Feldman has shown, the first movement of K. 238 shows a strong formal correspondence to Giunia's bravura aria "Ah, se il crudel periglio," in Mozart's *opera seria Lucio Silla,* K. 135, from 1772. Feldman argues convincingly that Mozart "adapted to the concerto what he learned from arias . . . exploit[ing] the process of tutti-solo exchange toward a purposeful, directed discourse, rather than letting this exchange create the more diffuse patterns to which concertos sometimes fell prey."[3] K. 238 is an important outcome of this cross-genre fertilization, even if it otherwise seems less impressive than many of the concertos that followed it.

Whereas this Concerto in B-flat Major was written for Mozart's own use, the F-Major Concerto K. 242 was composed for the Countess Maria Antonia Lodron and her two daughters, originally in a setting for three pianos, while the C major Concerto K. 246 was composed for the modest keyboard abilities of Countess Antonia Lützow, a niece of the archbishop and wife of the commandant of the Salzburg fortress. During the 1777–78 journey to Mannheim and Paris, Mozart used K. 246 mainly for his pupils rather than himself; it remains an excellent introduction to the Mozart concertos for the inexperienced player. Both of these commissioned concertos for aristocratic dilettantes residing at Salzburg display Mozart's skill in tailoring his music to the needs of the occasion. The Lodron daughters, Aloysia and Josepha, were 15 and 11 years old, respectively; Josepha was offered a part of little difficulty, which nevertheless has moments of soloistic presence. The role of the orchestra is reduced; the exchanges between the two main players can become somewhat monotonous. Mozart arranged this concerto without the third keyboard, and played the two-piano version with his sister Nannerl by 1780.

2. Girdlestone, *Mozart's Piano Concertos* (London: Cassell, 1948), 78.
3. Feldman, "Staging the Virtuoso: Ritornello Procedure in Mozart, from Aria to Concerto," in *Mozart's Piano Concertos: Text, Context, Interpretation,* ed. Neal Zaslaw, 175–76. Feldman's detailed comparison of the first movement of K. 238 to the aria is found in pp. 166, 168–170.

More important artistically is another double concerto, the work in E-flat, K. 365 (316a), for two pianos and orchestra, a piece from 1779–80, which was presumably written for Mozart himself with his sister, to judge from the well-balanced virtuosity of the solo writing. Like other works by Mozart in this key, the concerto opens with an unharmonized and broadly majestic subject spelling out the triad of E-flat major. At the entrance of the soloists, Mozart at once exploits the opportunity afforded by a pair of pianists by embellishing the initial prolonged note through trills across four octaves, while the triadic continuation is elaborated through neighbor-note figuration in sixteenth notes. This figurative variation of the initial motive in K. 365 resembles the textures of the first variations of Mozart's variation sets, as in the "Ah, vous dirai-je Maman" set from 1781. The opening Allegro of K. 365 shows a special richness of thematic invention, and it is stylistically more brilliant and less predictable than K. 242; at the recapitulation, for instance, the soloists bring a surprising shift into the minor mode. This double concerto is an attractive and imaginative work, but it does not transcend the sphere of delightful entertainment and colorful juxtaposition—this is not yet the great Mozart.

Most important of all the concertos from Mozart's Salzburg period is the earlier work in the same key of E-flat major for one soloist, K. 271, which was completed in January 1777. Curiously, this piece has long been widely known as the "Jeunehomme" Concerto. The designation "jeune homme," or "young man," for K. 271 appears in the collaborative study of Mozart by Wyzewa and Saint-Foix, although the authors note that Mozart and his father actually referred to the woman pianist who commissioned the work as "Jénomé."[4]

In 2003, Michael Lorenz discovered that the mystery woman was actually Louise Victoire Jenamy (1749–1812), the eldest child of Jean Georges Noverre (1727–1810), a famous French dancer and ballet master, who was one of Mozart's best friends.[5] When her father was hired by the Viennese court, Victoire Noverre came to Vienna in the summer of 1767; in September of that year she married the wealthy merchant Joseph Jenamy (1747–1819). Victoire Jenamy was an outstanding pianist; after her performance at a ball for the benefit of her father on 17 February 1773, a critic for the *Realzeitung* wrote that "His [Noverre's] daughter played a concerto on the *Clavier* with much artistry and ease." It was she who commissioned Mozart's K. 271 at Vienna in 1776. In late 1776 or early 1777 she passed through Salzburg on her way from Vienna to her father in Paris, so her visit to Salzburg coincided with the completion of Mozart's concerto.

Alfred Einstein regarded this concerto as "one of Mozart's monumental works . . . Mozart's 'Eroica,'" while for Charles Rosen it is his "first large-scale masterpiece in

4. Wyzewa and Saint-Foix, *Wolfgang Amadé Mozart*, 2:362. Actually, Mozart usually used the correct form "Jenamy" and his father "Genomai."
5. See Lorenz, "The Jenamy Concerto," *Newsletter of the Mozart Society of America* 9 (2005), 1–3; and "'Mademoiselle Jeunehomme' Zur Lösung eines Mozart-Rätzels" in *Mozart Experiment Aufklärung* (Essays for the Mozart Exhibition 2006) (Vienna: Da Ponte Institut, 2006), 423–29. The following comments concerning Jenamy are based on Lorenz's work.

any form" and for Alfred Brendel, a "wonder of the world."[6] The astonishing innovations of the piece deepen the dramatic relationship between tutti and solo and sometimes suggest an affinity to the world of Mozart's operas. In a brilliant stroke, Mozart introduces the soloist already at the beginning of the opening ritornello, in two-fold response to the opening triadic fanfares of the orchestra. It is a device he never repeated, though it left its mark on the later concertos of Beethoven and the Romantic concertos of other composers, where the piano frequently appears at the outset. Mozart characteristically reinterprets this surprising gesture at the beginning of the recapitulation, where the roles of soloist and tutti are reversed, with the orchestra answering the piano. Another significant feature of this concerto is the manner in which forceful rhythmic gestures are effectively juxtaposed with a more poignant and personal voice. Such a contrast is heard already near the end of the ritornello, where a climactic chord supporting the high melodic pitch D-flat is followed by recitative-like phrases in the strings. These expressive phrases are later transferred to the piano solo, which seems thereby to respond affectively to the orchestral discourse. The stress on the pitch D-flat, on the other hand, is not merely a local feature but returns prominently in the development, introducing tensions that even spill over into the beginning of the recapitulation. The climactic chord supporting D-flat and the recitative-like phrases, then, are not merely abstract thematic ideas, but contribute to a larger dramatic conception governing the form as a whole.

These features of K. 271 are linked in far-reaching ways with his other concertos and show how resourcefully Mozart developed basic dialogical strategies that are present in other musical genres as well.[7] In some of his first concertos, an initial forte motive paired with a piano answer is reinterpreted at the recapitulation as an orchestral statement and response by the soloist. For that reason, A. Peter Brown suggested that in K. 271 Mozart transfers the "recapitulatory dual statement with its orchestral/solo contrast to the beginning of the movement."[8] Some of the later concertos cultivate dialogical relationships in comparable ways. The F-Major Concerto, K. 413, for instance, opens with a four-measure phrase that begins forte in the tutti, followed by a more lyrical continuation for strings alone, establishing a pattern of phrases that is then allocated to the orchestra and soloist at the beginning of the solo exposition and at the recapitulation. An especially subtle example in this context is the first movement of the later concerto in this key, K. 459. The opening ritornello of this piece begins with an eight-measure piano phrase followed by an eight-measure forte statement. In the solo exposition, that configuration lends itself to a pair of phrases, both of which are played piano: an opening soloistic statement of the theme followed by the second phrase in the oboes and bassoons, accompanied by the piano. As David

6. Einstein, *Mozart, His Character, His Work*, 294; Rosen, *The Classical Style*, 198; Brendel, *Music Sounded Out*, 11.

7. See chapter 2 for a detailed examination of dialogical gestures in the first movement of his Sonata in G Major, K. 283.

8. Brown, "On the Opening Phrase of Mozart's K. 271: A Singular, Yet Logical, Event," *Mozart-Jahrbuch 1980/83: 317.*

Rosen observed, an unusual trait of K. 459 is that the recapitulation is initiated not by the orchestra, but by the soloist. This is one of only two concertos by Mozart with such a "solo recapitulation," the other being K. 271.[9]

Why does Mozart depart in these two concertos from his usual procedure of assigning the beginning of the recapitulation to the orchestra? In both works, the very strong focus on the initial motive may play a role. In K. 271, the opening unison triadic figure is asserted twice in forte, and many of the ensuing motives—including the soloist's immediate reply—bear a family resemblance to it. In K. 459, the rhythmic motive of repeated notes ♪♪♩♩ is even more prevalent, since it is found in three of the first five measures as well as in very many subsequent passages. However, sheer logic would seem to favor the path not taken. After all, in K. 271, the opening unison forte motive seems clearly orchestral—the voice of the mass—whereas the harmonized reply seems to befit the more nuanced persona of the soloist. On the other hand, the opportunity of beginning the recapitulation in K. 459 with the main theme forte in the orchestra seems obvious, since both the ritornello and solo exposition had begun piano.

An understanding of such departures from Mozart's "standard operating procedure"[10] requires an appreciation of his wit. In K. 459, the saturation—not to say obsession—with the opening rhythmic figure reaches its climax at the very end of the development: the woodwinds and strings exchange the motive repeatedly, dividing the orchestra against itself through the persistent antiphonal treatment of the head motive. This competitive situation opens a space of opportunity to the soloist, who unexpectedly assumes leadership, initiating the recapitulation with a quiet, unassuming statement of the main theme. Rosen slyly observed that "the rhetorical ploy might be expressed by the old proverb that provides the title of Sarti's best-known opera: "Fra I due litiganti il terzo gode" (When two quarrel, the third profits).[11]

At the recapitulation of the Allegro in K. 271, Mozart mischievously overturns established patterns. The pattern of tutti-solo exchange had become familiar not only from the opening of the movement, but from the beginning of the solo exposition as well as the outset of the development section. The development opens with a twofold orchestral statement of the fanfare in forte, in the dominant key, B-flat major. Nevertheless, the pianist's emphasis on variants of the fanfare motive in the ensuing passages prepares the pivotal reversal at the recapitulation: now the pianist seizes the first word, hammering out the head motive in three octaves, thereby taking control away from the orchestra (example 7.1).

What clinches the effect is the gentle answering phrase, which is now given to the strings, at the dynamic level of piano. The soloist's continuing active role is confirmed in the following passage, beginning with the repetition of the fanfare motive. Al-

9. Rosen, "'Unexpectedness' and 'Inevitability' in Mozart's Piano Concertos," in Zaslaw, *Mozart's Piano Concertos,* 261–84.

10. A term employed by David Rosen and elaborated in his essay "The Composer's 'Standard Operating Procedure' as Evidence of Intention: The Case of a Formal Quirk in Mozart's K. 595," *Journal of Musicology* 5 (1987): 79–90.

11. Rosen, "'Unexpectedness' and 'Inevitability' in Mozart's Piano Concertos," 263.

Ex. 7.1 Concerto in E flat, K. 271, I, beginning of recapitulation, mm. 195–202

though this gesture returns to the orchestra, the solo reply is now enlivened through sixteenth-note figuration and through the harmonic emphasis on the crucial pitch D-flat in m. 202, which ushers in a developmental episode placed after the beginning of the recapitulation.

Einstein's allusion to K. 271 as Mozart's "Eroica" points to the role of the second movement, an Andantino in C minor, as a great tragic utterance in which, in his words, "the melody is so eloquent that at any moment it could break into genuine recitative"[12]—as indeed occurs in the piano near the conclusion of the exposition and recapitulation. The anguished expression of the main theme is lodged above all in its emphasis on the lowered sixth scale degree, A-flat, as is felt in the canonic phrases in the violins in mm. 1–3, the melodic peak of m. 6, and especially in m. 11, the climax, where the sustained A-flat is supported by a D-flat harmony. The superimposition of the piano's phrases over this theme heightens the poignancy.

Mozart's solo cadenza to this movement takes on a searching character, as if the pianist, temporarily relieved from the somber resignation of the tutti phrases, seeks a new outcome. In this context, the D-flat chord in m. 136 not only recalls the climax of the ritornello in m. 11, but also those analogous sonorities in the first movement that had prompted such recitative-like phrases, such as the diminished-chord supporting D-flat in mm. 45–46. Momentarily, the cadenza finds consolation on the harmony of A-flat major (mm. 140–41), before veering back to C minor in a passage that outlines each of the three possible diminished-seventh chords, each marked by a fermata (example 7.2).

When the orchestra re-enters, it is on that D-flat harmony supporting high A-flat corresponding to m. 11, but the mutes that had previously softened the anguish are now removed. Three bars of recitative remain in the piano, ending with the drooping semitone inflection A-flat–G, before the hard objectivity of the cadence is pronounced firmly, like an inevitable, fateful outcome.

The dazzling virtuosity and humorous high spirits of the Presto finale make room for a more serious, poetic expression, through Mozart's interpolation of an elegant minuet and variations into the heart of the rondo design. As Heartz has suggested, the use of A-flat major for this Menuetto cantabile assumes an important resolving function in the overall design of the entire work, since it "prepares us to accept A-flat, a source of painful anguish before, now as a place of elegant repose . . . discharg[ing] the accumulated pathos of the *Andantino*."[13] Furthermore, Mozart incorporates passages into the bustling, *perpetuum mobile* sections of the rondo framing the minuet that clearly recall the rising triadic motives and even the emphasis on D-flat from the opening movement (mm. 196–207, 324–341). The head motive of the main rondo theme, on the other hand, is a turn figure on the tonic note E-flat, which is woven into the continuous eighth notes of the piano version but given to the violins and oboes when the orchestra takes up this subject. The movement is one of Mozart's boldest and most exuberant finales—indeed, the entire concerto is a major landmark in the evolution of his mature style. No later concerto goes beyond K. 271 in achieving a satisfying interrelationship between the three movements of the design. In the closing moments, the piano extracts the frisky turn figure from its driving figuration, joining with the orchestra in a closing diminuendo to pianissimo that sets a trap, clearing the way for the two emphatic forte chords that cap this extraordinary work.

---

12. Einstein, *Mozart, His Character, His Work,* 294. The term Andantino indicates a tempo slower than Andante.

13. Heartz, *Haydn, Mozart, and the Viennese School,* 634.

Ex. 7.2 Concerto in E flat, K. 271, II, cadenza to end of movement.

The revelation that K. 271 was a commission from Victoire Jenamy raises intriguing questions about the compositional background of the concerto. Michael Lorenz suggested that the slow minuet in the finale may be seen as an allusion to Noverre the dancer.[14] Could the mournful slow movement be connected to the apparent failure of her marriage? In April 1778, Mozart met Jenamy again at her father's home in Paris; it has not yet been proven that she ever returned to Vienna. A Viennese source notes that she died childless on 5 September 1812, but the place of her death has not yet been identified.

In a letter to his father from Paris, dated 11 September 1778, Mozart writes that "I will give 3 concertos to the engraver, the ones for jenomy and litzau and the one in B-flat."[15] The works in question are K. 271, K. 246, and K. 238, his three concertos for one keyboard from 1776–77. The intended publisher was Sieber, who would soon issue Mozart's Sonatas for Violin and Piano, K. 301–306. Mozart adds that "if I can, I shall do the same with my six difficult sonatas," which we know to be K. 279–284. His efforts to arrange these publications failed, and of his twenty-three keyboard concertos, only seven were published in his lifetime.

The Social and Political Context

In approaching Mozart's piano concertos from the Vienna period, it is helpful to consider their social and political context. The reception history of Mozart's concertos raises some important issues that have received little attention. One such matter is his remodeling of his first original concerto, K. 175, after moving to Vienna in 1781. When Mozart presented this concerto at his academy in Vienna on 3 March 1782, it contained a newly composed finale, as we have seen. The performance aroused wild enthusiasm. Mozart wrote to his father of "*the last rondo* which I composed for my concerto in D major and which is making such a furor in Vienna" and asked Leopold to "guard it like a *jewel*—and not give it to a soul to play. . . . I composed it *especially* for myself."[16] In a later reference to the movement, from 29 March 1783, Mozart uses the unusual hybrid term "variazion Rondeau."

Commentators on the movement have been puzzled by Mozart's formal designation as well as his enthusiastic evaluation of the piece. Bernd Sponheuer, for instance, wrote that "there can be no doubt but that K. 382 is in the first instance a variation movement."[17] With a few exceptions, the critical reception of the replacement movement has been negative. For Girdlestone, the new finale was "a series of insipid variations which are a very poor substitute for the beautiful original *sonata*," whereas Flothuis found it "somewhat disappointing" in "its primitive alternation of the tonic and

14. Lorenz, "The Jenamy Concerto," 3.
15. *Letters,* L. 331.
16. *Letters,* L. 445 (23 March 1782).
17. Sponheuer, "Zum Problem des doppelten Finales in Mozarts 'erstem' Klavierkonzert KV 175," *Archiv für Musikwissenschaft* 42 (1985): 117: "kann kein Zweifel daran bestehen, daß es sich bei KV 382 in erster Linie um einen Variationensatz handelt. . . ."

dominant harmonies" and Kerman described the movement as "a shamelessly popular display piece."[18] A defender of the substitute finale, Elaine Sisman, expressed the quandary as follows:

> Was Mozart consciously, even cynically, pandering to the public? Did his self-praise represent a tactic to reinforce his success to his father? Had his aesthetic judgement insufficiently evolved? Or have our traditional modes of understanding and valuation not been fully adequate?[19]

While Sisman found novelty in the use of the sprightly theme as a rondo refrain within the series of variations, it is also evident that Mozart's K. 382 involves a combination of glittering textures with a highly repetitive, even rather simplistic treatment of the main tune. Whereas the original contrapuntal finale of the concerto can be seen as a springboard for movements as substantial as the finales of the Concerto in F Major, K. 459, or even the "Jupiter" Symphony, the replacement finale eschews such complexity and most of the variations remain close to the original theme. This opening subject unfolds as a predictable alternation between tonic and dominant harmonies; the accompaniment in sixteenth notes acts as filler material, and the rhythm and detached articulation of the bass mirrors the upper line. (example 7.3). The principal motive consists of three staccato eighth notes on the dominant that drop a third to a decorative trill. This motive initially occupies one measure each of tonic and dominant harmony, before it is compressed into half-bar units leading to the dominant in m. 4.

Resolution of the quandary comes from the recognition that Mozart was employing a vocal theme familiar to his audience. There was surely an inside joke that helps account for the sensational audience response. Another sign of this success is the sale of copies of the rondo as a separate work as advertised by Lorenz Lausch in the *Wiener Zeitung* in April 1785.[20] In a revealing study, Manfred Hermann Schmid showed that the theme used by Mozart in K. 382 was employed before Mozart, such as by the Dresden composer Joseph Schuster in 1780, and that a variant of the tune later became well known as the French song "Fleuve du Tage," as in published solo and duet settings of the text by Hélitas De Meun with music by Benoît Pollet from 1818 and in many subsequent versions.[21] De Meun and Pollet presumably arranged the song from earlier versions that were probably not of French origin. What is involved here is a song of departure, as the hero bids farewell to "the beloved land, where I first glimpsed the light of the world."[22] It appears that Mozart turned this song of departure into a

18. Girdlestone, *Mozart's Piano Concertos*, 81; Marius Flothuis, *Mozart's Piano Concertos* (Amsterdam: Rodopi, 2001), 10; Joseph Kerman, "Mozart's Piano Concertos and Their Audience," in *Write All These Down: Essays on Music* (Berkeley: University of California Press, 1994), 333.

19. Sisman, "Form, Character, and Genre in Mozart's Piano Concerto Variations," in Zaslaw, *Mozart's Piano Concertos*, 336.

20. John Irving, *Mozart's Piano Concertos* (Aldershot: Ashgate, 2003), 175.

21. Schmid, "Variation oder Rondo? Zu Mozarts Wiener Finale KV 382 des Klavierkonzerts KV 175," *Mozart Studien*, ed. Manfred Hermann Schmid (Tutzing: Schneider, 1992), 59–80.

22. Schmid speculates that the text employed by De Meun and Pollet, referring to the Spanish river Tajo, which was described as the gold-bearing "Tagus aurifer" already by Pliny and Ovid, might have car-

Ex. 7.3 Rondo in D Major, K. 382, mm. 1–5

farewell march, alluding pointedly to the end of his service to the archbishop of Salzburg. In a letter to his father, Mozart describes how after the performance of K. 382 on 11 March 1783, he walked off the stage and was called back by the continuing applause of the audience. Other dimensions of the situation may yet be clarified if further evidence comes to light.[23] But this context already helps clarify the very unusual treatment of the given theme in K. 382, including its parodistic features, such as the overemphatic tick-tick-tick rhythm assigned to many instruments, with the violas consigned to repetitions of a single note. The theme itself is treated like a rondo

---

ried an association to the "Salzburger Midas," an expression Mozart and his father often used in referring to the archbishop (Schmid, "Variation oder Rondo?" 66).

23. Sisman suggests that Mozart may have improvised extensively in performing K. 382, using the invariant ritornello "as a springboard to further flights of fancy" (Sisman, "Form, Character, and Genre," 336).

refrain or ritornello, which helps to explain Mozart's formal designation. Near the conclusion, the ritornello returns as a quickened 3/8 Allegro; and in the coda, the mock-festive scoring with trumpets and timpani is combined with the solo and ritornello. There is a special point to the apparent superficiality—or "malicious gaiety," in Olivier Messiaen's formulation[24]—of this unusual set of variations on a preexisting theme, suggesting that an awareness of Mozart's humor is essential to appreciation of the music.

If the surface glitter and wit of K. 382 reflects his shrewd concern to please his Viennese audiences in 1781, subsequent events confirmed the limited lifespan of the subscription concert series for which so many of Mozart's piano concertos were composed. At the time of his break with Salzburg, Mozart wrote to his father on 2 June 1781 that "Vienna is certainly the land of the clavier! And, even granted that they do get tired of me, they will not do so for a few years, certainly not before then. In the meantime I shall have gained both honor and money."[25] The zenith of his activity as a piano soloist in Vienna—and of his piano concerto production—was reached by 1785, but the following year already saw a virtual collapse of Mozart's soloistic activities.

Did Mozart's novelty wear off or can we identify other causes for this decline in his fortunes? A revealing document from these years is the list of 176 subscribers to his three private concerts held in the Trattnerhof on 17, 24, and 31 March 1784. The programs for these concerts included, among other works, the new piano Concertos in E-flat Major, B-flat Major, and D Major (K. 449–51), the first three of the remarkable succession of twelve concertos that would end with K. 503, in C major, in late 1786. The subscription list includes a large proportion of aristocratic subscribers. Comparison of Mozart's list with Johann Pezzl's *Skizze von Wien* (Sketch of Vienna) from 1786–90 confirms that nobility of the first rank—princes, counts, and barons—were well represented.[26] This social stratum suggests a possible reason for the rapid erosion of Mozart's base of support beginning in 1786—offense caused by the performances, beginning in May that year, of the first of his operatic collaborations with librettist Lorenzo da Ponte: *Le Nozze di Figaro*, based on Pierre-Augustin Caron de Beaumarchais's controversial banned play critiquing the aristocracy. A critic in the *Realzeitung* began his review of *Figaro* by stating that "nowadays what is not allowed to be spoken is sung," and he referred to the cabals that polarized opinion and contributed to the opera's limited success at Vienna in 1786. Volkmar Braunbehrens concludes that "the opera was obviously boycotted by the Viennese nobility and could only establish itself later under different political conditions."[27] After only nine performances it was swept from

24. Messiaen identifies a quality of *gaieté malicieuse* in his discussion of his movement in *Les 22 concertos pour piano de Mozart* (Archimbaud/Birr: Librairie Ségier, 1987), 31.

25. *Letters,* L. 408.

26. See H. C Robbins Landon, *Mozart and Vienna, Including Selections from Johann Pezzl's 'Sketch of Vienna' (1786–90)* (London: Thames and Hudson, 1991), 70–71.

27. Braunbehrens, *Mozart in Vienna, 1781–1791,* trans. Timothy Bell (New York: Grove Weidenfeld, 1989), 283; originally published Munich: Piper, 1986. The fact that the reformist emperor Joseph II supported the opera and that it was revived in 1789 in no way undermines the thesis that it caused offense to

the stage by the greater popularity of a much less substantial work—Martin y Soler's *Una cosa rara.*

It is hard to imagine that Mozart's artistic activities at Vienna remained untouched by social and political concerns during the years preceding the outbreak of the French Revolution. Regarding *Figaro,* Michael Levey commented that "Da Ponte claimed to the Emperor that he had omitted things in the original play which might offend decorum, but, despite what is usually supposed, he and Mozart not only kept in much of Beaumarchais's revolutionary cheek . . . but added some of their own. From a brief parting line of Figaro's when he leaves the Countess's boudoir in act 2, '*et puis dansez, Monsiegneur*' (and then dance, my Lord), they created Figaro's first aria in act 1, threatening as much as mocking his master: 'Se vuol ballare, Signor Contino, il chitarrino le suonerò' (If, my dear Count, you feel like dancing, it's I who'll call the tune)."[28] As Levey observed, Beaumarchais also promoted another social revolution that found a deep resonance in Mozart: reform of the role of women in society. Consequently, the "ultimate outwitting of the Count comes—not from Figaro but from the Countess and Susanna."[29] Georg Knepler wrote pointedly about the period beginning in 1789 that

> it is not among musicology's most glorious achievements that it should so stubbornly cling to the belief that the greatest composer of the age was one of the few who did not await the success of the Revolution with "feelings of passion," that so astute and sensitive an observer as Mozart, of all people, should feel nothing of this "sublime feeling" or "enthusiasm of the spirit," that the composer of *Figaro* and *Don Giovanni* should not have noticed that the nobility had been abolished in France, the same nobility that he had looked upon with derision and contempt from the day he was capable of critical thought.[30]

Such considerations lead to a further question: to what extent were Mozart's piano concertos shaped by the social context in which they were composed and performed? Kerman has proposed that "the solo part and the orchestral part in a concerto can be read as a composite metaphor for Mozart and his audience in *their* relationship" and that the "inner drama of concerto relationship can be viewed as the projection of an actual social dynamic."[31] According to this model, the exchange and mimicry that typifies much in the genre symbolizes social harmony, affirming the common ground between the individual and the collective. Can it be, then, that an increasing complexity or tension in the "inner drama of concerto relationship" in Mozart's Viennese

---

Mozart's aristocratic supporters. There is a strange parallel between Mozart's difficulties beginning in 1786 and the political and personal problems that beset the increasingly isolated emperor.

28. Levey, *The Life and Death of Mozart* (1971; reprint, London: Abacus, 1995), 192.

29. Levey, *The Life and Death of Mozart,* 192. See 188–96 for Levey's discussion of Mozart's collaboration with da Ponte.

30. Knepler, *Wolfgang Amadé Mozart,* trans. J. Bradford Robinson (Cambridge: Cambridge University Press, 1994), 295; originally published, Berlin: Henschel Verlag, 1991. The quotations within the excerpt cited are drawn from Hegel's writing about the French Revolution in his *Vorlesungen über die Philosophie der Weltgeschichte.*

31. Kerman, "Mozart's Piano Concertos and Their Audience," 323, 328.

concertos strained the expectations of his audiences and that, as Kerman suggests, this same phenomenon betrays Mozart's growing alienation from his public? The writer who has gone farthest in interpreting the solo/orchestral relationship as socially conditioned is Susan McClary. For her, the concerto involves "a soloist and a large, communal group, the orchestra . . . [enacting] as a spectacle the dramatic tensions between individual and society."[32] McClary's appeal to hear in Mozart "not one clear, unambiguous message . . . but rather a dynamic forcefield of characters and strategies"[33] is urgently important, but the assessment of dialogical relationship requires more refinement, with attention paid to the ways in which Mozart's most advanced concertos still cultivate collaborative exchange. An underdog role of the soloist as "Other, rather than collaborator" is taken for granted by McClary; but in the eighteenth century, the role of soloist surely corresponded less to an alienated individual than to a princely leader, who even if rule-abiding is invested with arbitrary power and influence. McClary's model of power relations between soloist and orchestral can thus be turned on its head. As Manfred Hermann Schmid has observed, Hans Georg Nägeli, writing in 1826, employed the metaphor of prince and people (*Fürst und Volk*) in assessing the relationship between soloist and tutti in Mozart's piano concertos.[34]

Already in 1793, Heinrich Christoph Koch had compared the concerto to Greek tragedy, whereby the modern orchestra assumed the role of the chorus. In Koch's view, the concerto shows "a passionate conversation of the soloist with the accompanying orchestra; he conveys his impressions, [and] the latter signals to him through short interspersed statements its approval, soon affirming his very expression; or it seeks in the Allegro to further arouse his sublime feelings; soon it laments, then consoles him in the Adagio."[35] Koch based this understanding of the concerto especially on compositions by C.P.E. Bach, unaware that Mozart had brought the genre to new heights, in which the soloist and orchestra interact in extensive and unprecedented ways. In that process, Mozart drew on the resources of the *opera buffa*, whereby the music embodies psychological qualities and changing dramatic events in its rhetoric and structure. A blending of sonata style with ritornello procedure is characteristic of Mozart's concertos, and he explored a broad range of compositional options at many points,

32. McClary, "A Musical Dialectic from the Enlightenment: Mozart's *Piano Concerto in G Major, K. 453*, Movement 2," *Cultural Critique* 5 (1986): 138.

33. McClary, "A Musical Dialectic," 147.

34. Hans Georg Nägeli, *Vorlesungen über Musik* (Stuttgart and Tübingen, 1826), 161, cited in Manfred Hermann Schmid, *Orchester und Solist in den Konzerten von W. A. Mozart* (Schneider: Tutzing, 1999), 18.

35. Koch, *Versuch einer Anleitung zur Composition*, iii (Leipzig, 1793; reprinted Hildesheim, 1969), 331 ("eine leidenschaftliche Unterhaltung des Concertspielers mit dem ihn begleitenden Orchester; diesem trägt er seine Empfindungen vor, dieses winkt ihm durch kurze eingestreute Sätze bald Beyfall zu, bald bejahet es gleichsam seinen Ausdruck; bald sucht es im Allegro seine erhabenen Empfindungen noch mehr anzufachen; bald bedauert, bald tröstet es ihn in dem Adagio"). In her translation of Koch's treatise, Nancy Kovaleff Baker renders "leidenschaftliche Unterhaltung" as "passionate dialogue" (Herinrich Christoph Koch, *Introductory Essay on Composition: The Mechanical Rules of Melody, Sections 3 and 4* (New Haven: Yale University Press, 1983), 209). See in this regard Simon P. Keefe, *Mozart's Piano Concertos: Dramatic Dialogue in the Age of Enlightenment* (Woodbridge: Boydell and Brewer, 2001), 9–10; and Manfred Hermann Schmid, *Orchester und Solist in den Konzerten von W. A. Mozart*, 16.

such as in the development and recapitulation of opening movements.[36] As we have seen with K. 271, the individual works can display numerous original features.

In evaluating this "thrilling . . . antithesis of the individual and the crowd," as Tovey put it,[37] we thus discover a wide range of situations, in which the collaborative model often retains validity, but is also put to the test. An enhanced role of the soloist as individual agent is already present in the B-flat Concerto, K. 450, from 1784, the first work that Girdlestone saw as achieving "with marvelous art [the] balance between personal and social ideals."[38] No less fascinating is the solo-orchestra interaction in the two concertos in the minor, K. 466 and K. 491, and especially in the first movement of the work in C minor, the penultimate concerto in the series completed by 1786.

The Viennese Concertos of 1782–84: K. 413 to K. 459

The first of Mozart's concertos composed at Vienna, the work in F, K. 413, from 1782, is less distinguished and innovative than K. 271. Girdlestone writes that "like K. 238, 242, and 246, it is a product of the *ancien régime,* one of the few works of Mozart's prime which can be so styled. Everything in it is measured and well ordered."[39] Despite its retrogressive cast, K. 413 shows some unusual features, such as the 3/4 meter of the opening Allegro and subtle thematic rearrangements within the returns of the minuet theme in the finale that enhance the interest of the rondo design. Like K. 413, the two companion works in A, K. 414, and in C, K. 415, have tended to be overshadowed by the greater concertos in these same keys that Mozart produced a few years later. (The first movement of K. 415, for example, with its *alla Marcia* idiom and canonic imitations in C major, foreshadows the style not only of Mozart's later concerto K. 503, but also that of the "Jupiter" Symphony.) The woodwind parts are not structurally essential in these concertos from 1782, and Mozart authorized performances of the pieces *a quattro,* by a pianist with only string-quartet accompaniment. The works are nevertheless attractive and highly crafted, especially the A-Major Concerto.

Particularly memorable is the Andante of K. 414, with its sublime, hymn-like main theme, which seems to quote J. C. Bach's 1763 overture for the revival of Baldassare Galuppi's "La calamità dei cuori" (The calamity of love) and may represent an homage to the older master, who had died shortly before, in January 1782. The continuation of the orchestral ritornello beginning in m. 9 unmistakably recalls the first two bars of the main theme of the first movement of K. 414, with its rise through the tonic triad followed by a stepwise descent. Various themes in this delightful concerto em-

36. Despite occasional controversies over the formal terminology appropriate to Mozart's concertos, terms such as "solo exposition" and "development" remain useful. For a discussion of the terminological issues in an historical context, see especially Schmid, *Orchester und Solist in den Konzerten von W. A. Mozart,* 20–30.

37. Donald Francis Tovey, *Essays in Musical Analysis,* vol. 3, *Concertos* (London: Oxford University Press, 1981), 6.

38. Girdlestone, *Mozart's Piano Concertos,* 197.

39. Girdlestone, *Mozart's Piano Concertos,* 130.

ploy such scalar descending figures. Already in the opening subject of the first movement, for instance, Mozart reshapes the scalar descent through an octave from E in m. 2 as a rhythmically augmented, syncopated descent from A in mm. 5–8, an idea that forms the gestural climax of the theme. The prominence in the development of this Allegro of the key of F-sharp minor foreshadows the later Concerto in this key, K. 488.

The C major Concerto, K. 415, also displays such motivic interconnections between its movements. The sweeping conjunct motion beginning on C in the opening march-like Allegro reappears transformed in the gliding lyrical contour of the Andante in F major, which Levin calls the "most operatic middle movement since that of K. 271."[40] Its melody is shaped around C, the dominant, and unfolds as a series of increasingly passionate descending gestures to this note from D, from F, and from A. This last fall of a sixth is expressed through sixteenth notes, whose momentum helps destabilize the C in m. 4, as the line shifts downward through A to G in m. 5. Then comes the melodic crux: a soaring upward leap through a tenth to the highest note, B-flat, a gesture then balanced by a long lyrical descent, leading to the end of the theme in m. 8. This Andante has been underestimated, in part because of its reliance on embellishment of this main subject,[41] but the theme is beautifully shaped, and the movement displays other subtle features, such as the chains of trills that appear before the reprise and in the coda.

A rejected sketch for this slow movement shows that Mozart contemplated using a very different theme in C minor, whose descending contour closely parallels the main subject of the jovial finale, in C major and 6/8 time. While discarding this idea for the slow movement, he introduced a pair of pathos-laden Adagio episodes into the Allegro finale, in mm. 49–64 and 216–231. A return of the 6/8 tune dispels the melancholy C-minor music, but the conclusion brings a *decrescendo* to *pianissimo* in the final moments. K. 415 was first performed at Mozart's academy on 23 March 1783, together with K. 175/382 and the "Haffner" Symphony, K. 385, in the presence of Emperor Joseph II. Although trumpet and drum parts are lacking in the first publication of the concerto by Artaria in 1785, Mozart could well have added these instruments for the première, especially since the other works on the program used them.[42]

The Rondo for Piano and Orchestra, K. 386, was formerly regarded as a discarded finale of the Concerto in A, K. 414, but Tyson's recent investigation of the autograph sources indicates that it may have been an independent work in one movement—a unique case among the Mozart piano concertos.[43] It shares the same tempo indica-

40. Levin, "Mozart's Keyboard Concertos," 362.
41. Girdlestone is scathingly dismissive of this Andante, writing of its "complete insignificance," its "repetition mania," and that "its commonplaceness is constant from end to end." (*Mozart's Piano Concertos*, 154).
42. John Irving, *Mozart's Piano Concertos*, 198.
43. See Tyson's chapter "The Rondo for Piano and Orchestra, K. 386," in *Mozart: Studies of the Autograph Scores*, esp. 275–89.

tion of Allegretto and the same 2/4 meter with the finale of K. 414, but differs in its scoring, featuring an elaborate cello part.

In a famous letter, Mozart described his trilogy of concertos from 1782 as "a happy medium between what is too easy and too difficult; they are very brilliant, pleasing to the ear, and natural, without being vapid. There are passages here and there from which the connoisseurs alone can derive satisfaction; but these passages are written in such a way that the less learned cannot fail to be pleased, though without knowing why."[44] Although his ambition to appeal to both connoisseurs and amateurs (*Kenner* and *Liebhaber*) might seem conventional enough, the conscious pursuit of such aesthetic balance provokes reflection. Mozart's "happy medium" seeks to avoid empty virtuosity as well as mere complexity; in his view, intricate passages "cannot fail to please" the "less learned." His regard for the overall impact of his music on relatively untutored listeners remained an enduring concern, to judge from many of his subsequent concertos, in which innovation and accessibility often prove so compatible.

The great period of Mozart's piano concertos dates from 1784–86, three of his most successful seasons as virtuoso performer before the Viennese public. In their sharply defined expressive characters, richness of invention, and formal innovation, the twelve works from these years represent an unsurpassed achievement and have become the basic canon and cornerstone of the concerto repertoire. Mozart started to compile a personal catalogue of his compositions with precisely this series, entering the Concerto in E-flat, K. 449, on 9 February 1784. Two more concertos soon followed: K. 450 in B-flat and K. 451 in D. Following the completion of Mozart's Quintet for Piano and Winds, K. 452, he composed yet another piano concerto, the work in G major, K. 453, finished on 12 April 1784. The beginning of Mozart's work catalogue, bearing the dates and incipits of these four concertos, is shown in the photo gallery.

The E-flat Concerto, K. 449, is written for a smaller orchestra than its companion works, with oboes and horns ad libitum, as in the concertos from 1782. As Tyson has pointed out, the score of the concerto indicates that Mozart began composition of the first movement already in 1782, writing out a *particella* as far as m. 170.[45] This is one of several instances in which Mozart began work on a concerto and then put the work aside for an extended period before completing it. Such evidence also exists for the A-Major Concerto, K. 488, and the C-Major Concerto, K. 503, as well as for the final Concerto in B-flat Major, K. 595.

Nevertheless, K. 449 is a highly original composition that marks an advance in Mozart's style, showing, in Einstein's words, a "thematic variety and unity and an ingenuity of form that reveal the joy of the creative spirit at the highest."[46] Like K. 413, its opening Allegro is not in the typical march time in duple meter but in a more unstable

44. *Letters*, L. 476 (28 December 1782).
45. Tyson, *Mozart: Studies of the Autograph Scores*, 153–55. The autograph score of K. 449 is held in the Biblioteka Jagiellońska, Kraków.
46. Einstein, *Mozart, His Character, His Work*, 301.

3/4 meter. The arresting initial phrase implies an ambiguity of key, emphatically spelling out the C-minor triad before a trill signals arrival at the dominant of E-flat major. This restless, unstable quality is characteristic of the whole movement. The second theme of the opening ritornello beginning at the upbeat to m. 17 exploits the initial harmonic ambiguity, bringing a surprising, impassioned shift to the key of C minor. Mozart employs this theme sparingly, reserving it for the tutti passage leading to the cadenza and for the beginning of the cadenza itself. The opening Allegro vivace of K. 449 is particularly rich in its dialogical relationships and its energetic interplay of motives.

The Andantino, by contrast, is a calm cantilena in which Mozart restates the exposition beginning in the remote key of the lowered leading-note, creating thereby an effect of development before the reprise in the tonic B-flat major. Most impressive of all is the contrapuntal finale, whose returns of the rondo theme are never literally repeated, but constantly and gracefully varied in a movement where technical sophistication is inextricably merged with the comic atmosphere reminiscent of *opera buffa*. In the coda, the duple meter yields to a lively 6/8, and up to the end, the soloist offers witty, impetuous responses to the gentle motives in the strings, bringing the work to a close on a pair of forte chords.

Mozart himself wrote to his father about the concertos K. 450 and 451, "I consider them both to be concertos which make one sweat; but the B-flat one beats the one in D for difficulty."[47] In the same letter, Mozart described K. 450 in B-flat as the first of three *grossen Concerten* (grand concertos), together with K. 451 and K. 453. Unlike K. 449, which was written for Babette Ployer, one of his pupils, Mozart wrote K. 450 for his own use. This B-flat Concerto is indeed unusually virtuosic in style—more so, perhaps, than any of the other concertos—and Mozart wrote out brilliant cadenzas for it. But another striking feature of this important work is the new independence of the woodwind parts, which is proclaimed at once in the chromatically rising figures in thirds heard in the oboes and bassoons and answered by the strings (example 7.4).

Mozart employs variants of the rising motive in the ensuing phrases: the initial upbeat of two eighth notes is changed to three eighths in m. 4. This has metrical consequences: the 4/4 gait at the outset shifts to *alla breve* as the winds take up their three-fold slurred version of the idea in mm. 4–6. At the same time, Mozart fragments the accompaniment motive of repeated B-flats in the horns and low strings from mm. 1–2, reshaping this rhythmic pattern as shorter, detached notes leading to whole notes in mm. 2–3. Then the rising melodic figure is again altered as it appears in octaves in the oboes and bassoons in m. 8. A pattern of foreshortening ensues, with the ascending figure in eighths answered by descending motives in eighths and sixteenths in the strings, generating increasing momentum and excitement. The sheer abundance of evolving relationships in such passages is not so well captured by Leopold Mozart's metaphor of the unfolding thread; this is more like a rich tapestry of integrated events.

The gradual integration of the dialogic exchanges between winds and strings leads to an assertion of the full orchestra forte in m. 14, with the emergence of a new theme.

47. *Letters,* L. 514 (26 May 1784); translation emended.

Ex. 7.4 Concerto in B flat, K. 450, I, mm. 1–10

The rhythmic structure of each of the various ascending figures at the outset of K. 450 involves upbeats leading to pronounced stress on strong beats of the duple meter. This enables Mozart to shape the later theme beginning at the upbeat of m. 26 as a contrasting idea: its melody, marked piano, unfolds as a series of syncopated falling thirds in the strings over a bass texture similar to the opening theme. This eight-measure theme is then repeated in the oboes and bassoons, as the strings play a new counterpoint in flowing eighth notes. Then, beginning at the entrance of the horns at m. 41, Mozart writes a crescendo over a passage featuring a rising stepwise progression; its last bars, expressed as quarter notes in the oboes and violins in mm. 44–45, can be heard as a diatonic variant of the rising chromatic motive from the outset of the piece.

The first movement of K. 450 offers a chain of ingeniously subtle variations of the basic motivic ideas, in an orchestration highlighting the winds, thereby allowing for enhanced dialogic possibilities between sections of the orchestra as well as between the tutti and soloist.

The pianist's enhanced role in K. 450 has two main aspects: a declamatory, rhetorical voice, on the one hand, and a driving figurative virtuosity, on the other. Mozart grants a dozen measures to the soloist as an extended anacrusis even before the opening theme in the oboes and bassoons is restated, not to mention the possibility of a further improvisatory "lead-in" at the fermata preceding this structural return (example 7.5).

The entire opening solo passage rests squarely on the tonic harmony, with the soloist declaiming on high B-flat and then filling out the tonal space reaching down two octaves to the B-flat below middle C. Here, too, a process of constant ongoing variation enlivens the discourse: the initial arpeggiated quarter note and quarter rest lead to a sustained half note, which is tied to the descending figuration of the next measure; then Mozart replaces the tonic pitch in the lower octave by an appoggiatura resolving to the tonic, C–B-flat, before repetition of the falling figuration carries the passagework into the middle register. The big gesture of downward swooping is now enlarged into a more emphatic, upward curve, bodied-out through steady sixteenth-note motion in the right hand and reinforced by the bass octaves in the left hand. Through many discrete stages, the passage gains in intensity; and Mozart reserves the richest figurative texture to the last measures, adding sixteenth notes in the left hand as the music penetrates to the highest register in the right hand.

Can the expressive meaning of Mozart's initial solo statement be further specified? The pianist's opening gesture is indeed intimately bound up with the orchestra's forte ritornello statements near the close of the tutti exposition, beginning in mm. 45 and again in mm. 49 (example 7.6). This motive, which features a repeated B-flat, a move to the upper third, D, and then a stepwise descent from the B-flat through A to the sixth degree, G, is clearly audible in the first two measures of the solo passage. At the same time, this melodic contour is not reproduced literally, but is significantly reshaped. The pianist plays these notes in the same high register in which they had sounded in the violins and oboes, but decorates the initial attack through the upward arpeggiation and sets off the second B-flat by a rhetorical delay, while sustaining that pitch as a tied half note rather than a dotted quarter. The increased textural density of the swooping sixteenths enlivens the continuation, transforming the rather conventional figure from the orchestra into brilliant individualized display.

In terms of gestural meaning, the pianist has listened intently to the orchestral discourse and responded in a manner that is collaborative yet challenging. This competitive asymmetry underscores the double-edged nature of Mozart's concertos. Regardless whether a fortepiano or modern piano is chosen, the soloist is often at risk of being overwhelmed by the collective mass of the orchestra, but the more nuanced, differentiated language of the soloist can counteract this disadvantage. In K. 450, Mozart

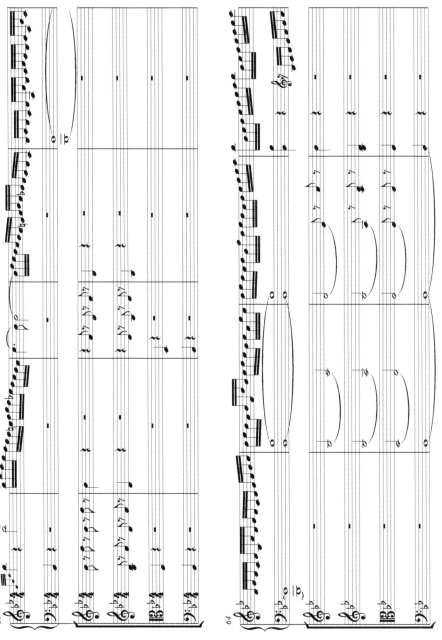

continued

Ex. 7.5 continued

Ex. 7.6 Concerto in B flat, K. 450, I, orchestral ritornello, mm. 48–51

often gives the piano a distinctive expressive voice independent from the orchestral discourse. Following the opening theme, and in response to a short but emphatic orchestral gesture, the soloist plays a sensitive rhetorical phrase legato in G minor; soon thereafter, the true second subject in F major, withheld from the opening orchestral ritornello, is first heard from the pianist. The development, on the other hand, is launched through the powerful reinterpretation by the soloist of a placid and banal cadential phrase in the orchestra—the kind of standard formulaic gesture found in countless works by many composers. The urgency of this reinterpretation is underscored by the sudden turn to F minor, the chromaticized figuration in running sixteenth notes, the contrapuntal shaping of the passage, and the unfolding of modulations leading to C minor and G minor.

If the generation of this large-scale momentum is largely a deed of the soloist, the recapitulation provides the setting for Mozart to revisit the subtleties from the outset of the work. When the strings first sound the thematic hallmark of the chromatic thirds below a sustained piano trill, this is not yet the recapitulation, since the passage rests on the dominant. Mozart mischievously gives the strings the opening motive and treats it in sequence so that the end of the rising chromatic line reaches D and E-flat, the very notes that will signal the return to B-flat major. Then the piano takes up the motive, composing it out in the lofty high register for a long breathtaking moment with sequences based on the dominant-seventh sonority. After deliciously overshooting his goal in these motivic elaborations, Mozart accomplishes a delicate landing in the tonic, a cadence marked by the original characteristic orchestration of oboes and bassoons, but with the piano now answering the winds. The recapitulation is a skillful blending of the solo exposition materials with those from the ritornello, and the movement ends playfully, with the motives that had earlier introduced the soloist.

The slow movement consists of variations on a solemn, hymn-like theme, marked "Andante." This is the first set of slow-movement variations in the piano concertos. The binary theme contains alternation between the orchestra and piano in turn, thus already harboring elements of variation. Mozart's revision of the melodic contour of the melody in his autograph score sheds light on its linear relations and climax structure.[48] The first eight measures of the original violin melody and the revised final version are shown in example 7.7a–b. The original version is less eventful; its fifth to seventh measures, based on upward transposition of the stepwise motive of a third, seem relatively mechanical. In his revision, Mozart employed a stepwise falling line in mm. 3–4, a motive that engages with the gesture in mm. 1–2 without simply reproducing it. The A-flat in m. 3 fills in the gapped pitch from m. 1 while recapturing its descending contour; the E-flat–D figure in m. 4 goes beyond the lowest note heard in m. 2. By so reshaping the motivic components, Mozart makes room at the beginning of m. 6 for a striking upward leap of an octave to C—a melodic goal that was already touched upon in m. 2. In the lower octave, C will also serve as the penultimate note of the linear descent through an octave from B-flat—a guiding idea in the shape of the whole theme. Mozart's revision is instructive, since it catches him in the process of achieving that tensional balance so characteristic of his style.[49] The melodic emphasis on the high C from mm. 2 and 6 of the theme is not forgotten in the ensuing variations, and it recurs prominently in the solo at the beginning of the coda.

The B-flat Concerto closes with a spacious sonata rondo in 6/8 time, a movement of joyous, even dazzling character, brimming with virtuosity. Mozart's wit is reflected, above all, in the lively and even mischievous exchanges of the main motive between the piano and winds, including the flute, which is used here for the first time in a concerto finale. In the second theme area and the central developmental section, Mozart sometimes uses the flute to reinforce the sonority of the piano in its upper register; the oboes appear in dialogue with the soloist, as phrases are tossed back and forth. The give-and-take of imitation operates on many levels. Initially, the swinging rondo theme is heard in the solo piano and then answered in the full orchestra in forte. This sturdy pattern is maintained throughout until after the solo cadenza, when the rondo theme is played in the piano for the last time. Then, surprisingly, the soloist hammers out in double octaves a hunting fanfare-type figure—an orchestral motive that had not been heard since the first section of the rondo. This large-scale exchange ushers in a dissolving coda based on the primary rhythm, before four vigorous measures close the door on this delightful work.

48. This score is held at the Thüringische Landesbibliothek in Weimar; a facsimile of the first page of the Andante, showing Mozart's revisions, is contained in the introduction of the edition of the concerto in the Neue Mozart Ausgabe, Serie V, Supplement 4, ed. Marius Flothuis, *Konzerte* (Kassel: Bärenreiter).

49. Elaine Sisman suggests that Mozart changed his theme on account of a resemblance to the theme of the slow movement of Haydn's Symphony no. 75 in D Major, but this seems unlikely to have been the only factor. See Sisman, "Form, Character, and Genre," 339–42.

Ex. 7.7a Concerto in B flat, K. 450, II, original version of melody, mm. 1–8

sempre piano

Ex. 7.7b Concerto in B flat, K. 450, II, final version of melody, mm. 1–8

*sempre **p***

Mozart composed his Concerto in D, K. 451, during the single week ending 22 March 1784. The powerful opening Allegro, in particular, aspires to a symphonic brilliance and grandeur new to the form and also employs a larger orchestra than any of the preceding concertos, with flute employed in addition to oboes, trumpets, and drums. The control of dynamic shading and juxtaposition of diatonic and chromatic phrases is masterful; and even if much of the material seems conventional, each of the three movements introduces unexpected complications or surprises, such as the piano passage after the recapitulation in the first movement. In the Andante, the chromaticism and pedal points of the first movement are transformed in the sinuous main subject, as Girdlestone observed.[50] The bareness of texture in certain passages of the solo part in the Andante demands some elaboration of the written notes, as Mozart himself stated in a letter to his sister, Nannerl. Especially noteworthy in the rondo finale is the substantial development section, where the head of the principal theme is exchanged between the piano and winds and finally stated on C-sharp major and minor before pitches from this harmony are reinterpreted to become the dominant of D, opening a path for reentry of the refrain in the tonic.

Immediately after composing K. 449–51, Mozart wrote his Quintet for Piano and Winds, K. 452, the Piano Concerto in G, K. 453, and the Violin Sonata in B-flat, K. 454, completing all six major works in just ten weeks. He entered the quintet into his catalogue on 30 March 1784 and performed the piece to enthusiastic acclaim in the Vienna Burgtheater on 1 April. To his father, he proudly described K. 452 as "the best work I have ever composed."[51] It does not seem coincidental that this composition is sandwiched between his impressive piano concertos, and it shows some concerto-like features, such as the extended "Cadenza in tempo" for all five instruments beginning at m. 159 in the finale. The colorful sonorities, lively dialogue, and masterful balance in the handling of the wind instruments that characterizes K. 452 is felt in the concertos beginning with K. 450, as we have seen; but new dimensions surface in K. 453 and later works. More than ever, Mozart exploits a great variety of dialogical possibilities between parts of the orchestra, with the winds often assuming prominence, entirely

50. Girdlestone, *Mozart's Piano Concertos,* 237.
51. *Letters,* L. 508 (10 April 1784).

apart from his blending of the piano with changing groups of instruments. A sensitive layering and gradual building up of sonority can be observed at the outset of the opening Allegro of the G-Major Concerto, K. 453. The first measure is given to the unaccompanied first violins, who play softly a head motive with prominent repeated notes—a feature of the themes of later movements as well (example 7.8).

In m. 2, a soft tonic pedal point is sounded in the horns, and the second violins and violas enter with a steady figurative accompaniment, while the basses punctuate the downbeats. In mm. 4–5, the entry of the flutes, oboes, and bassoons supplies vivid contrast and lends weight to the end of the first phrase, while serving as bridge to the sequential repetition in the first violins in mm. 5–8. The restatement of this gesture in the woodwinds in mm. 8–9 makes clear its formal role in extending by one measure the four-measure phrases of the violin melody. Only in the pair of two-measure phrases that follow is the full orchestra sounded for the first time, yet the anacrusis to each of these accented chords in the tutti is also varied in sonority, since it is heard in the strings and then in the winds.

Like the opening movements of K 451 and the two following concertos, K. 456 and K. 459, the Allegro of K. 453 employs the seminal march rhythm ♩♪♫♩♩, yet the character of each work remains distinct. The delicate transparency of the orchestration in K. 453 contributes to a quality of intimacy, and its touches of the ethereal and pastoral may well have influenced Beethoven's conception of this key in works like his Concerto in G, op. 58, and his Violin Sonata in this key, op. 96. Great energy lurks just beneath its surface, however, as is revealed by the deceptive cadences in the ritornello, which take the music momentarily to E-flat major, reinforced by sudden forte interjections with wind support. Not merely an isolated effect, this deceptive cadence returns to introduce the fantasy-like development and also marks the tutti preceding the cadenza.

The slow movement in C major explores a surprising disjunction between the opening thematic statement for strings in the ritornello, which is set off by a fermata, and the contrasting continuation featuring the oboes and other winds. This beginning of the Andante features a calm five-measure phrase suggestive of a motto, which is heard over a stepwise falling bass (example 7.9).

In the solo exposition, the piano pauses at the fermata and then fills in this structural gap with a passionate and highly chromatic continuation in the dominant minor, whose pathos is heightened by leaps in register; at the recapitulation, the passage is rewritten to go to E-flat major. After the cadenza, Mozart goes further to reveal new possibilities hidden within the opening phrase, whose descending bass now falls chromatically in a vivid orchestration of winds alone, heightened through suspensions and exploitation of the higher pitch registers. Here, unlike earlier passages, the fermata is dropped and the sense of disjunction overcome, as the pianist supplies a firm resolving phrase leading to a cadence in C major, whereupon the sonorities of the piano, winds, and strings are integrated in the final passage. For McClary, in her discussion of K. 453, this is a case of "the *individual* (not the group) that utters the full acceptance of faith, that is able to follow the implications of the motto so as to ren-

Ex. 7.8 Concerto in G major, K. 453, I, mm. 1–12

der, in the final measures of the movement, its consequent that gives closure to its perennially open-ended challenge. The group in this instance follows, is shown the way to transcendence by the individual, by the self-indulgent artist."[52] In this view, the opening motto is identified with a "transcendental principle" within which lurk "serpents of dissent, coercion, and even what appears to be a kind of closet theology."[53] This interpretative framework is too blunt or predetermined to do justice to Mozart's calm, open-ended theme, diverse continuations, and the eventual serene reso-

52. McClary, "A Musical Dialectic," 159.
53. McClary, "A Musical Dialectic," 159, 160.

Ex. 7.9 Concerto in G major, K. 453, II, mm. 1–7

lution. More convincing is Simon P. Keefe's sober assessment that "the piano and the orchestra progress systematically in their interaction over the course of the movement, presenting the theme together (i.e., without dialogue), later engaging in confrontational dialogue, and finally producing co-operative dialogue."[54]

Mozart indulged in "co-operative dialogue" of a rather different kind after he purchased a pet starling for 34 kreuzer on 27 May 1784. He felt inspired to teach his pet bird the theme of the variation finale of K. 453, and he even wrote out in a notebook the starling's version of the first five measures, labeling it "The Starling's Tune" (example 7.10a).[55] This version includes a fermata over the G in m. 2; in the following measure the bird alters Mozart's G to G-sharp, introducing an audacious harmonic nuance lacking in the original theme (example 7.10b).

Mozart's playful interaction with his starling is fascinating in light of the affinity of this delightful movement to the music for the bird-catcher Papageno in *The Magic Flute*, a work composed seven years later.[56] The notes attempted by the bird outline the rising fourths D–G and F-sharp–B, a configuration that Mozart inverts in his second phrase and decorates with grace notes and wind interjections on the closing turn figure. In K. 453, the whole melody is played in the first violins together with the flute. If we are to believe Mozart's entry in his notebook, the turn figure was also mastered

54. Keefe, *Mozart's Piano Concertos: Dramatic Dialogue in the Age of Enlightenment* (Woodbridge: Boydell, 2001), 160.
55. See Robert L. Marshall, *Mozart Speaks: Views on Music, Musicians, and the World* (New York: Schirmer, 1991), 142–43.
56. Papageno's music displays similarity to K. 453 in its frequent use of G major as well as in some motivic aspects, such as the prevalence of turn figures in his first number, "Der Vogelfänger bin ich ja."

Ex. 7.10a "The Starling's Tune"

Ex. 7.10b Melody from Concerto in G major, K. 453, III

by his feathered friend. The opening variations gradually increase the rhythmic speed, with duplet and then triplet figuration in the piano. The heart of the movement is a mysterious minor variation heard pianissimo, characterized by syncopations and strange leaps in register. After this contrast, the unbridled high spirits of the reprise carry the day, and a "presto finale" in *opera buffa* style caps the concerto. Yet even here, soft dark shadows reminiscent of the minor variation reappear before the triumphant close based on elaboration of the turn figure from the starling's song.

Mozart's next concerto, K. 456, in B-flat major, shows the sunny disposition of his other works in this key, but not without darker and mysterious regions akin to the shadows in the finale of the G-Major Concerto. Between the first and second thematic group of the ritornello, for example, the strings repeatedly stress the dark sonority of E-flat minor, with a chromatic continuation that effectively sets off the playful and purely diatonic themes to follow. The large-scale expressive contrast in this work comes in the slow movement, however—a set of poignant variations on an Andante theme in G minor suggestive of a gavotte. The third variation is fiery and passionate, full of dark chromaticism and stern rhetoric akin to *opera seria*. This sets into sharp relief the fourth variation, a beautifully luminous *maggiore*, featuring the flutes, oboes, bassoons, and horns.

The sonata rondo finale is in 6/8 meter, like Mozart's other Viennese concerto finales in B-flat major, and its main theme has a thematic profile strangely similar to the Andante theme and yet completely transformed and transported into the world of *opera buffa*. Yet even here a darker, contrasting, and heavily chromatic region is placed at the center of the design, bringing departure to the remote key of B minor and a conflict in meter between 2/4 and 6/8.

The work in F major, K. 459, is the last of the series of six concertos from 1784. As we have seen, it is the fourth consecutive concerto that is launched by the characteristic march rhythm with repeated notes and a dotted figure on the second beat of the 4/4 meter. In this context, it seems likely that Mozart's unusual use of the solo recapitulation in K. 459 was one by-product of a general concern to differentiate this piece from its sister concertos. It is remarkable, however, how thoroughly Mozart engages with the structural implications of the opening motivic material. This is displayed not only through the many imitations and permutations of the initial dotted figure, but in the new theme in C major that is positioned at the threshold to the second thematic group in the piano exposition (example 7.11).

Ex. 7.11 Concerto in F major, K. 459, I, mm. 128–142

Its audible relation to the opening motive relies upon pitch repetitions of a figure emphasizing the tonic, followed by an upward pivot to the fifth degree and a stepwise fall. This contour also characterizes the new theme, with its threefold motive of a falling third E–C, followed by its rise to the dominant note, G, which is emphasized by the change in orchestration, as the melody shifts from the first violins to the oboes. An upward sequence of the first phrase in the violins and an answering phrase in the winds rounds off the theme as an eight-measure period, but Mozart now gives the piano its own decorated version of the theme, uniting the pairs of antiphonal phrases of the strings and winds. Not only that: the piano now elaborates the second half of the theme using sixteenth notes, with string support, and it then departs from the orchestral model, expanding the theme from within. The rising triadic figure, which is derived from the ascending fifth in mm. 1–2 of the movement, is altered by the pianist to reach B-flat and harmonized by a diminished chord. The triadic motive is then restated twice, as the music veers momentarily toward D minor, and the whole thematic statement is expanded from eight to eleven measures. This developmental passage contains a brief but startling glimpse of the idiom of the first movement of the G-Minor Symphony, K. 550, from 1788.

The Allegretto in C major has a binary form—or a sonata design without development—yet is richly endowed with development of its main theme. As in the slow movement of K. 453, Mozart initially presents an isolated but important thematic idea, which is here concentrated into the single, short phrase marked by a crescendo in mm. 1–2 that is followed by a pause. In later passages in both exposition and recapitulation, this idea grows in length and breadth. In mm. 44–51, the idea is developed into a fresh four-measure variant, in which the melody is extended to bridge the rests of the original theme, while the following rising scale segment is changed from eighth notes to sixteenths. With canonic entries of this tune placed in the flute and bassoon, and then in the two hands of the pianist, a vast range of register is opened up. Yet even more miraculous is the corresponding passage in the recapitulation (mm. 103–10), in which Mozart places appearances of this subject in eight successive measures, with each entry paired with an answer two octaves lower. That this is the definitive version of the theme is shown at the conclusion, as a final statement of the head motive in the piano is answered pianissimo by the stepwise ascending sixteenths of the flute, leading to the cadence on lofty high C, supported by a soft reiteration of the main rhythmic motive in the strings. Here, as in the slow movement of K. 453, the soloist and orchestra merge together at the close, without any hint of force or coercion.

Mozart's impressive mastery of counterpoint, which owed much to his study of the music of Johann Sebastian Bach during the immediately preceding years, is perhaps most obvious in the great finale of K. 459. After the exposition of a comic rondo theme, whose two halves are heard from the piano and orchestra in turn, the tutti launches into a dense and elaborate fugal exposition on a different subject before again picking up the thread of the rondo theme and developing its rhythmic components. This massive orchestral passage is balanced, in the development, by a double fugue for orchestra combining the contrasted subjects; even after the reentry of the piano, the texture remains contrapuntal. As Charles Rosen has pointed out, the recapitulation is in "mirror form, with the first theme last—held back, in fact, until after the cadenza."[57] The presence of such orchestral developments with their brilliance of texture makes this finale more weighty than the first movement and an excellent example of Mozart's formidable powers of stylistic synthesis. In this closing Allegro assai of K. 459, rondo is merged with sonata and fugue, and learned counterpoint blended with

57. Rosen, *The Classical Style*, 227.

comic operatic effects. The *opera buffa* character prevails at the conclusion in the rhythmic echoes tossed between tutti and solo in the final moments.

The Viennese Concertos of 1785–86: K. 466 to K. 503

Mozart's wrote two celebrated concertos in early 1785: the Concertos in D Minor, K. 466, and C Major, K. 467. This is a contrasting work-pair, like Mozart's last two symphonies or Beethoven's Fifth and Sixth Symphonies. In Mozart's aesthetics, the use of the minor mode was striking and unusual and aroused special expectations. D minor is generally associated in his dramatic works with ideas of vengeance or terror, and the music of the D-Minor Concerto indeed foreshadows something of the idiom of the so-called *ombra* music in this key in *Don Giovanni,* written two years later.[58] The forte statement of the opening theme when heard in the full tutti, for example, resembles the music for the Don's slaying of the Commendatore, early in the opera, and the persistent syncopations so characteristic of the concerto are heard at the cadence marking Don Giovanni's descent into hell. The analogy should not be stretched, but there is no doubt but that the foreboding character and dark intensity of K. 466 impose new conditions on the concerto form.

The beginning of the ritornello in the Allegro shows how Mozart increases the musical tension through controlled gradation while preserving distinct levels of intensity (example 7.12).

The quiet opening is for strings alone, but the violins and violas are given long chains of syncopations, so that they scarcely play on strong beats of the measures. The downbeats are articulated by the lowest instruments, the basses and cellos, and these points of emphasis are punctuated through upbeat motives, usually a triplet figure outlining a rising fourth. Very gradually, the musical density increases: the low triplet motives ascend and multiply, as pedal points emerge in the horns, bassoons, and oboes. Finally, at the approach to the first cadence in D minor in m. 16, the flute and oboes reinforce the syncopated strings while the basses and cellos play steady quarter notes. All of these devices contribute to the constant intensification of the music, yet the arrival of the full orchestra forte in m. 16 is a threshold that carries us to another level, transforming the subdued foreboding of the beginning into dramatic action. This event is embodied in the emancipation of the triplet upbeat motive, which invades the higher pitch registers in the first violins. The motive is melodically extended into a sinuous descending triadic figure played in the violins and winds, and it gains the power to generate changes in harmony as well. Beginning in m. 16, the full orchestra plays a theme of raging force that had been subtly foreshadowed already in the quiet syncopations and upbeat figure of the very first measure.[59]

58. A discussion of the *ombra* music in *Don Giovanni* is offered by Wye Jamison Allanbrook in her book *Rhythmic Gesture in Mozart's* Le Nozze di Figaro *and* Don Giovanni (Chicago: University of Chicago Press, 1983), 292–319.

59. Here is one of the models for the celebrated opening of Beethoven's Ninth Symphony, which is set in the same key, D minor.

Ex. 7.12 Concerto in D minor, K. 466, I, mm. 1–15

continued

Under such circumstances, the soloist cannot effectively restate the main theme by himself and is instead given a new theme of plaintive character that seems to embody a response to the drama of the ritornello (example 7.13).

This solo theme is a kind of recitative *in tempo,* an utterance of great expressive range, which eventually dissolves into running passagework in sixteenths coordinated with the woodwinds (mm. 88–91). This opening solo theme in K. 466 is never heard in the orchestra, although it is linked in subtle ways with the material of the ritornello. The piano's melody bears some motivic similarity to the flute phrases in the

subordinate theme (mm. 34, 36, 38),[60] and the accompaniment in the left hand recalls the string accompaniment in these same measures. As in Mozart's other concerto in the minor, K. 491, the initial solo theme is positioned as a large-scale upbeat or anacrusis preceding the beginning of the second exposition, which starts at the reemergence in the strings of the music of mysterious, subdued agitation (m. 91).

60. Significantly, these phrases are played in the piano in the solo exposition and the recapitulation.

Ex. 7.13 Concerto in D minor, K. 466, I, first solo piano passage

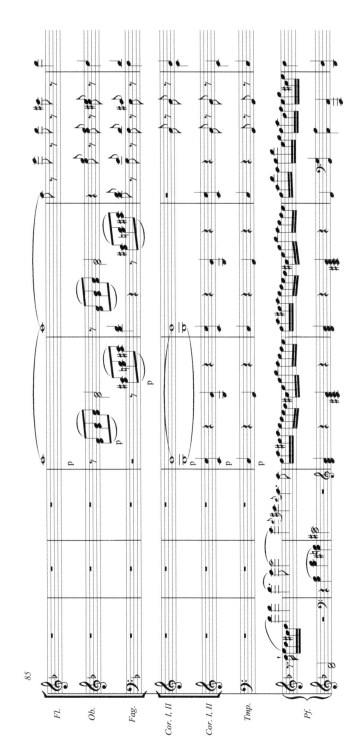

The expressive power of this opening piano statement is lodged, in part, in its treatment of the sigh-figures E–D (m. 78), A–G (m. 80), D–C-sharp (m 82), G–F (m. 82), and F–E (m. 86). Each of these gestures is echoed in the left hand.[61] The melodic climax is reached in m. 85, which is a variant of the motive in m. 79. Here, the passion of the music overreaches itself, and a turn figure generates a leap of a tenth to F in the high register. An effect of lyrical, inward climax is expressed as well through the expansion of the phrase member to three bars (mm. 85–87) following a series of two-bar units. Then, at the entrance of the orchestra in m. 88, Mozart compresses his rhythmic units to two per measure in bars 88–89 and then to four per measure in bar 90, leading to the D-minor cadence, marking the beginning of the second exposition.

This same lyrical subject is played three times by the soloist at the outset of the development, where it is juxtaposed with the music of foreboding drawn from the ritornello. Each of these statements brings changes in key, from F major, to G minor, to E-flat major, whereupon the impassioned *ombra* music turns to C minor and unfolds into a falling circle-of-fifths progression leading to the dominant of D minor preceding the recapitulation. The final tutti passages following the recapitulation and cadenza also reaffirm the characteristic *ombra* idiom, with its rising fourths in triplets and persistent syncopations, and the movement closes pianissimo, in the same hushed mood in which it had begun.

The rondo finale of K. 466 is closely associated with the first movement, and its main themes also share textural features, such as the use of parallel thirds, with the themes of the opening Allegro. The central Romanze movement in B-flat major, on the other hand, represents a serene oasis from the turbulence of the outer movements, and the passivity of its character is emphasized by the many repetitions of its initial phrase. Even here, however, the middle section of its form reverts to the minor mode and to the passionate tone, dissonances, and even syncopations characteristic of the first movement.[62] The finale reaches peaks of intensity that surpass anything in Mozart's previous concertos, particularly in the fiery orchestral tutti near the beginning of the movement. This impassioned idiom returns in later passages, such as the short tutti leading to the solo cadenza, where the orchestra breaks off the piano cadence with a powerful deceptive harmonic shift.

The coda in major has often provoked disapproval, which may be due to misunderstanding its true character. It has been regarded as merely gay, or even sassy, and hence as out of keeping with the spirit of the whole. This is the impression conveyed by many performances as well. One key to the passage lies in the cadenza that is offered, Mozart's own cadenzas for K. 466 unfortunately not having been preserved. If the cadenza builds to a high peak of tension, leading to the final open-ended thematic state-

---

61. A similar technique is employed in mm. 5–7 in the first movement of the "Paris" Sonata, as we have seen in chapter 3 of this volume.

62. Another example of a Romanze movement involving a slow expressive section in the major followed by a brooding, contrasting section in the minor is found in the fifth movement of the "Gran Partita," K. 361 (370a).

ment in the solo as notated by Mozart, the overwhelming need for resolution can seem to motivate the surprising change of mode to major in the coda.[63] Heard in this context, the coda of the D-Minor Concerto can sound not at all harmless, but logical, compelling, and powerful.

Beethoven's cadenzas for the outer movements of this concerto shed a revealing light on his perspective of the piece. At the heart of his first-movement cadenza, Beethoven recalls the opening solo theme over a triplet accompaniment in the left hand. He restates the theme up to the dominant-seventh harmony corresponding to Mozart's m. 83 and then elaborates this harmony in a brilliant più presto passage. In the last moments of the cadenza, the left hand once more plays the opening solo motive, under a trill. Thus the rising octave A and falling sixth to C-sharp—the first three notes for the pianist in Mozart's concerto—become the focal point of Beethoven's cadenza. The same basic motive is highlighted again in the cadenza to the finale. In the culminating passage, Beethoven transforms the falling sixth A–C-sharp by setting these notes ablaze through trills. Acceleration of the trilled figure liquidates the motive as the music ascends to high E, the supertonic, and nine bars later the sustained trill is resolved at last at the entrance of the orchestral tutti.

Whereas Mozart never leaves the basic tonality in his own cadenzas, Beethoven opens the floodgates. Already in the opening moments of his first-movement cadenza to Mozart's K. 466, the music modulates extensively, reaching the major mediant— B major—by the time the second subject is played *pianissimo* beginning in m. 18. A change of mode to B minor coincides with an increase in rhythmic animation in the accompaniment, and the music soon resumes a modulatory path, ultimately leading to the dominant of D minor when the opening solo theme is recalled. A comparison of the cadenzas of these two composers reveals fundamental differences in their attitudes toward modulation.

Mozart's next masterpiece, the Concerto in C, K. 467, from March 1785, again illustrates his virtuosity in handling the wind parts, which take on an independence and a brilliance scarcely matched by any other composer. By this point in his career, Mozart's orchestration has become inseparable from his counterpoint and form. The opening theme of the first movement is deliberately spare, since it represents only one part of the contrapuntal texture of the ensuing tutti continuation. Its initial unharmonized triadic figures on tonic and dominant are given to the strings, piano, with a fully harmonized phrase soon interpolated by the winds, with their contrasting tonal colors. The basic character, in spite of the marking Allegro maestoso that Mozart added in his thematic catalogue, is that of the *opera buffa*. Following the second of these interpolations in the winds, the full tutti enters forte, combining a counterstatement of the triadic subject in the lower strings with a new melodic counterpoint in the winds

---

63. Impressive in its powerful rhythmic drive is the cadenza offered by Alfred Brendel in his excellent recordings with Neville Mariner and the Academy of St. Martin in the Fields (as part of Brendel's collected set of recordings of the concertos [Philips 422 507–2]) and with Charles Mackerras and the Scottish Chamber Orchestra (Philips 462 622–2).

and violins, reinforced by the horns and trumpets. The opening moments of the piece thus expose three distinctly different qualities of sonority, which are treated consistently and with far-reaching implications in the remainder of the work.

Near the end of the opening ritornello, for example, the alternation of wind and string sonority returns unforgettably: chromatically ascending scales in the flute, supported harmonically by the oboes and bassoons, are answered by descending diatonic phrases in the strings. The wind phrase, in particular, is so colorful and distinctive that it lingers in the memory, and listeners will note with pleasure its return in the tutti closing the solo exposition and at the end of the movement. Its full significance, however, goes far deeper and is most clearly exposed at the climax of the development section, which is generated by a long, rhythmically augmented version of this ascending chromatic configuration in the flute, now expanded into half notes instead of quarters. The ascent leads to high E-flat and a short piano cadenza, before an exquisite stepwise descent leads delicately to the recapitulation. Here, as elsewhere in Mozart, a conspicuous detail in the orchestral texture assumes a much broader significance in the work as a whole.

The opening triadic figure, on the other hand, lends itself easily to imitative counterpoint, as near the beginning of the recapitulation, where the motive is exchanged between the violins, solo piano, and flute. What is easily overlooked, however, is that this triadic march-like figure is not confined to the first movement, providing the bass part throughout the exquisite slow movement, an Andante in F major of a reflective, dream-like character. The broad lyric expression of this Andante is operatic in feeling, akin to a "contemplative ensemble" such as "Di scrivermi ogni giorno!" (Promise to write me every day!) in the first act of Così fan tutte, K. 588, from 1790. This quintet of departure for two pairs of lovers, Fiordiligi/Guglielmo and Dorabella/Ferrando, with Don Alfonso as the fifth member, shows some conspicuous stylistic parallels to the slow movement of K. 467. Like the earlier concerto movement, the quintet is an Andante in F major, in duple time, and it superimposes the melody over a pulsating accompaniment in the strings and a pizzicato bass.[64] As so often with Mozart, however, the operatic example did not precede the concerto movement, but followed it several years later. Mozart's profound experience with concerto composition enriched all of his later operatic masterpieces, but there is something about the Andante of K. 467 that is sui generis. A soaring quality is created through irregularities of phrasing,[65] an imaginative treatment of register with vast melodic leaps, and remarkable subtle-

64. See Marion Brück, "Kontemplation und Abschied in den langsamen Sätzen von Mozarts Klavierkonzerten," *Mozart Jahrbuch 1991* (Teilband 1): 165. This parallel deserves mention in the context of discussions of the Andante's operatic features, as in James Webster's study "Are Mozart's Concertos 'Dramatic'? Concerto Ritornellos versus Aria Introductions in the 1780s," in Zaslaw, *Mozart's Piano Concertos,* 123–29. Webster draws attention to a resemblance between the Andante of K. 467 and Cherubino's "Voi che sapete" in *Le Nozze di Figaro.*

65. Following the initial measure of accompaniment, the melody unfolds in two phrases of three bars each, followed by two phrases of two bars each, followed by a series of one-bar units with suspensions over a dominant pedal point.

ties in orchestration. One of Mozart's favorite methods of sustaining long notes, for example, is to transfer them from the strings or piano to the winds, so that the timbre of the prolonged pitches is transformed as the music unfolds. The piano part, on the other hand, is unusual in that after the solo entrance in m. 23 that piano is never silent for longer than a couple of bars. This movement largely suspends the principle of alternation between tutti and solo while creating textures and sonorities that music had never known before.[66]

A diagram of the formal design, an aspect that has stimulated debate, is shown in table 7.1.

Charles Rosen states that "if a description is to correspond to what is actually heard, this is not a sonata movement at all, in spite of our being able to fit it neatly into that category," and he finds aspects of the movement similar to a rondo.[67] On the other hand, Carl Schachter notes "the movement's tendency to project a strongly sectionalized design on the surface of a ceaselessly moving tonal fabric."[68] The formal balance as lodged in the sonata design is precariously maintained in a movement that partakes of several genre types simultaneously, suggesting an instrumental aria that is spun out in the manner of an extended improvisation. The Andante has four main parts, which may be described as the orchestral exposition, the solo exposition, the developmental middle section, and the recapitulation with coda. Although the soaring lyricism and continuous textures blur formal demarcations, Mozart retains the ritornello character of the last section of the second thematic area, with this section assuming a cadential, articulating function at each of its three appearances, in mm. 17–22, 50–55, and 88–93. This cadential theme concludes both the orchestral and solo expositions; at its last appearance in the coda, it undergoes a change in orchestration, with all of the strings pizzicato, a texture that continues until the end of the movement.

No discussion of this Andante should pass over the undercurrent of agitation that coexists with its dream-like melodic unfolding.[69] This is evident already from the first measure, in which the accompaniment of repeated notes in triplets is heard even before the melody begins. All of the sensuous sound-textures involving muted strings as well as the sensitive echo effects, in which the winds reinforce the strings or otherwise enhance or decorate the melodic flow, are superimposed upon the overriding rhythmic continuity of this continuous triplet pattern. In this context, the sudden cessation of the triplet accompaniment in mm. 70–72 is strangely unsettling (example 7.14).

66. Simon P. Keefe stresses the "dialogic interaction between piano and orchestra" in this movement, citing the continuation at the piano entrance of material from the ritornello; yet in some important ways, this kind of dialogue seems to be supplanted by another paradigm. See Keefe, "The Concertos in Aesthetic and Stylistic Context," *The Cambridge Companion to Mozart* (Cambridge: Cambridge University Press, 2003), 81–83.

67. Rosen, *The Classical Style,* 239.

68. Schachter, "Idiosyncratic Features of Three Mozart Slow Movements: The Piano Concertos K. 449, K. 453, and K. 467," in Zaslaw, *Mozart's Piano Concertos,* 331.

69. This aspect of the movement is overlooked in its frequent inclusion in commercial recordings marketed as music for relaxation, one of which is entitled *The Most Relaxing Classical Album in the World—Ever!*

Table 7.1. Formal Design of the Andante in the Concerto in C Major, K. 467

MEASURES	SECTION
1–22 (22)	Orchestral exposition
1–11 (11)	First theme
	1 measure accompaniment alone; 3 + 3 mm.; then 2 + 2 mm.
12–22 (11)	Second theme
	Begins with upbeat; mm. 17–22 are treated like a ritornello, with cadence in m. 22 overlapping with transition
22 (1)	Transition
	Woodwinds
23–55 (33)	Solo exposition
23–35 (13)	First theme (with cadence)
36–44 (9)	Episode
45–55 (11)	Second theme
	Closes in C major, mm. 55; mm. 50–55 are treated like a ritornello
56–72 (17)	Middle section
56–61 (6)	First part
	G minor; D minor
62–72 (11)	Second part
	B flat major, modulatory
73–104 (32)	Recapitulation/coda
73–82 (10)	First theme (begins in A flat major!)
83–93 (11)	Second theme
	Mm. 88–93 are treated like a ritornello (all strings pizzicato!)
94–104 (11)	Coda
	New idea in mm. 100–104

These measures belong mainly to the piano solo, whose gestures lead into the re-capitulation beginning in m. 73. Yet the stabilizing tonal function of a return to the tonic key is completely avoided: instead, the reprise of the main theme is heard in the lowered mediant, A-flat major! This evasion of the tonic key sustains the ungrounded, floating character of the music, conveying its unsatisfied striving toward new regions while defamiliarizing formal landmarks, such as the arrival of the recapitulation.

As Levin has observed, Mozart's use in this slow movement of the texture of repeated triplets in conjunction with chains of suspensions finds a precedent already in his pastiche Concerto in B-flat, K. 39, from 1767, based on Johann Schobert's Sonata in F Major, op. 17, no. 2. Another slow movement employing related material is in the

Ex. 7.14 Concerto in C major, K. 467, II, mm. 68–73

"Paris" Sonata in A Minor, K. 310, from 1778.[70] The exquisite realization of layers of sonority in K. 467 is unique, however, and it is intensified by acute dissonances, such as in m. 15, as A-flat in the melody sounds against B-natural, B-flat, and D-natural in other voices.

The use of music from this Andante in the 1967 Swedish film *Elvira Madigan*, directed by Bo Widerberg, represents a notable station in its reception history. David Grayson has commented that in this Andante, "the surface serenity cannot conceal the turmoil that lies beneath" and that "as the lovers in *Elvira Madigan* sadly discover, the escape to a dream world is consummated only in the imagination."[71] The theme of dangerous beauty, or forbidden pleasure, is indeed effectively conveyed in this film, based on a true story about outcast lovers in Denmark. The lovers in the film are the deserter Lieutenant Spare and the rope dancer Elvira Madigan, who has fled from the circus. Widerberg employs excerpts from Mozart's Andante not just to convey the shared erotic bliss of the pair, but also to help portray their social isolation and foreshadow their eventual joint suicide. During one of these sequences, Spare cuts himself while shaving away his beard; on another occasion, a wine bottle topples, spilling red liquid and suggesting the flow of blood. The use as a framing device of a stern church chorale with no corresponding visual image signals the heartlessness of the puritanical society in which the lovers will find no refuge. Yet their love is richly consummated, in the imagination and in fact. Mozart's music is identified here with the unbroken, blissful shared experience of the lovers, which finds no place in the closed society. The film thus exploits both the shockingly voluptuous beauty of the music and its disturbing undercurrents, which remind us of the precarious dilemma of the lovers in their social context. Their exalted happiness as embodied in the music brooks no compromise, leading with quiet inevitability to the outcome of their love in death.

In *Elvira Madigan,* the excerpts from the Andante are drawn mainly from the opening orchestral exposition. In assessing the movement as a whole, one can concur with H. C. Robbins Landon that "seldom has Mozart presented a more complicated emotional pattern. . . . [T]he strong, conflicting currents are hidden far under the gently ebbing and flowing surface."[72] Girdlestone described the first two movements of Mozart's K. 467 as "movements which he never surpassed," a convincing claim, although his opinion of the finale, that "there are a dozen finales in his concertos more interesting and attractive than this one,"[73] seems too severe. This Allegro vivace assai is a rondo-sonata design, whose character shows a distinct bent toward a comic idiom once more reminiscent of the *opera buffa.* The playful main theme is initially given to the violins, with the closing accents of each four-measure phrase articulated by the full orchestra, including trumpets and drums, which had been silent in the slow

70. Levin, "Mozart's Solo Keyboard Music," 319–20. The relevant passage in the slow movement of the "Paris" Sonata is mm. 43–51.

71. Grayson, *Mozart: Piano Concertos Nos. 20 and 21* (Cambridge: Cambridge University Press, 1998), 72.

72. Landon, "The Concertos: Their Musical Origin and Development," in *The Mozart Companion,* ed. H. C. Robbins Landon and Donald Mitchell (London: Faber and Faber, 1956), 270.

73. Girdlestone, *Mozart's Piano Concertos,* 345.

movement. There are a number of innovative features in this vivacious finale, beginning with the surprise entrance of the soloist to play the last phrases of the opening theme.[74] This early exchange sets up a particularly lively environment for dialogue, which reaches its climax in the development section, as the head of the main theme is tossed back and forth between the woodwinds and piano. As the dialogue unfolds, Mozart foreshortens his theme, which is curtailed to six notes in the piano, oboes, and bassoons, then to four notes, and finally to three notes in the piano and bassoons in the passage leading to the dominant pedal point preceding the recapitulation.

Mozart makes an important reference back to the first movement at the beginning of the second solo entrance, which begins with a rising triadic figure marked by grace notes. This gesture unmistakably recalls the ascending triadic motive on G minor at a roughly analogous point in the *first* movement, forging another link between the movements of the concerto. The two passages are shown as example 7.15a–b.

This motivic plunge into the minor with its extended continuation occurred only once in the first movement; it is absent from the recapitulation. In the finale, by contrast, the dark chromaticism of the earlier passage is purged, as the head motive is resolved into C major, leading into the unbridled gaiety of this delightful rondo. Following the cadenza, a final statement of the rondo theme brings this lively movement to a close with echoes, in the strings and winds in turn, of the cadential figure from the theme heard over the rising scales of the soloist.

We pause at this point in our discussion to consider a work in a related genre: Mozart's Quartet for Piano and Strings in G Minor, K. 478, which was completed on 16 October 1785. Mozart originally intended to write three such works for the firm of Franz Anton Hoffmeister, but the publisher, complaining that the public found the quartet too difficult, abandoned plans for a series. Mozart's second and final piano quartet, the masterly work in E-flat major, K. 493, was issued in 1787 by a different publisher, Artaria and Co. With his G-Minor Quartet, Mozart essentially created a new genre of chamber music, departing for the most part from the *concertante* style of keyboard writing in favor of a balanced dramatic dialogue between the piano and strings.

Here, as in Mozart's two symphonies and the string quintet in this key, G minor is associated with a character of passion, with hints of anguish and fatalism. The opening Allegro is haunted by a dark and defiant unison theme, which continues to lurk ominously in the background before being powerfully reasserted in the coda. As in Mozart's G-Minor Symphony, K. 550, there is an initial emphasis on the dissonant semitone E-flat–D, a motivic relation heard prominently in the transition and second subject group of the Allegro. The development section intensifies this motive with expressive chromaticism and modulations to new keys. Tragic overtones emerge in the recapitulation and coda. The secondary themes are resolved to G minor before the pathos of that key is most vehemently conveyed in the final moments. In the coda,

---

74. This entrance at m. 21 should be preceded by a "lead-in" by the soloist, as is implied by the fermatas placed on the orchestral parts in m. 20.

Ex. 7.15a Concerto in C major, K. 467, I, mm. 109–136

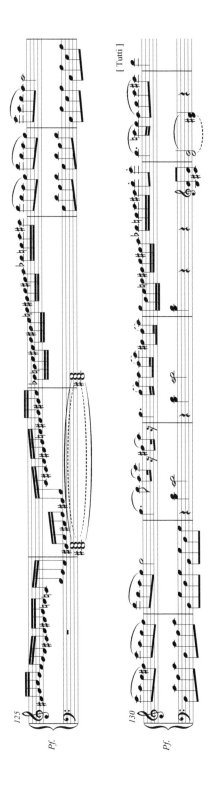

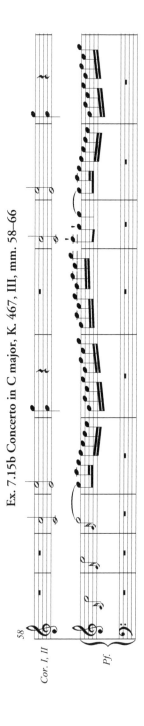

Ex. 7.15b Concerto in C major, K. 467, III, mm. 58–66

Mozart first recaptures the modulatory sequences from the development before leading the music into a forceful reassertion of the initial unison theme, a close in grim resignation.

The following Andante in B-flat major offers a lyrical contrast, featuring a graceful cantabile melody that is treated in dialogue between the piano and strings. The rondo finale does not return to the G minor pathos of the opening Allegro, but is dominated by a vivacious theme in G major, whose broad structure is crowned by a vigorous ascending scale leading to a tonic cadence. The character is cheerful and confident. Still, Mozart makes room for a reference to the first movement in the central developmental episode of the rondo, whose emphatic unison motive is exchanged in dialogue between the piano and strings, carrying the music through minor keys. Here, and elsewhere in the rondo, passages of concerto-like virtuosity enrich the piano's role. Cadenzas and trills preface the return to the principal theme at the main junctures of the rondo form. As in some of the concertos, Mozart absorbs a rich diversity of thematic material into this rondo, even incorporating a charming theme that he borrowed from Johann Christian Bach and used as well in his Rondo for Piano in D Major, K. 485.[75]

The review that appeared of this quartet in 1788 in the Weimar *Journal des Luxus und der Moden* indicates that Mozart had strained the expectations of his audience. According to the Vienna correspondent to the journal, the composition is "very intricate, requiring the greatest precision in all four parts; but even in a very lucky performance, this 'musica di camera' can and should please only musical connoisseurs." After claiming that the music was "scarcely bearable" if performed by amateurs, the reviewer declared the work unsuitable for public performance: "What a difference, when his much-discussed work of art was played in a quiet room by four skilled musicians who have studied it well, where the suspense of each and every note did not escape the attentive, listening ear, and which was played with the greatest precision in the presence of only two or three attentive persons. But then there would be no *éclat*, no brilliant and modish applause to be reaped, no conventional praise to be culled."[76] To judge from this critical response, Mozart's effort to appeal to both connoisseurs and amateurs had become hard to sustain; a challenging concerto like K. 491, in C minor, would surely have met with similar resistance.

Mozart's next concerto, K. 482, in E-flat, dates from the end of 1785 and was written for the following concert season, together with K. 488 and K. 491, both of which date from the first months of 1786. All three of these concertos employ clarinets, which in K. 482 and K. 488 are substituted for oboes and in K. 491 combined with them. Of all the concertos, K. 482 shows perhaps Mozart's greatest luxuriance of tonal coloring, with his favorite clarinets given special prominence from the outset. Like many of Mozart's earlier E-flat works, the first movement begins with a majestic and forthright assertion of the tonic triad in the tutti, followed by a quiet, answering phrase,

75. This thematic borrowing is discussed by Einstein in *Mozart, His Character, His Work,* 118–19.
76. H. C. Robbins Landon, *The Mozart Essays* (London: Thames and Hudson, 1995), 138.

which is here given first to the bassoons and horns, and then in a higher register to the solo clarinets, with the violins providing bass support. Then we hear the flute, clarinets, and bassoons in turn, blended with the strings and horns in piano; only in m. 29 does the full tutti return in forte with a gesture rising stepwise from E-flat to G.

At the soloist's entrance, Mozart recalls this motivic stepwise ascent of a third, assimilating it into an extended and well-profiled thematic statement. Register plays a key role in the passage: sequences of the initial rising figure lead to an expressive two-note figure spanning a falling seventh, C–D, with this interval then framing the ensuing variant of the opening phrase, beginning on D and ascending to C, and leading to a deceptive harmonic shift on the submediant harmony. The continuation of the passage juxtaposes motivic figures involving extreme registral contrasts, with two-octave leaps in the right hand, and the gap is filled through brilliant sixteenth-note figuration as the piano drives toward the cadence in E-flat that brings the return of the opening theme in the orchestra, marking the beginning of the second exposition.

As in the first movement of K. 467, Mozart later gives to the piano a singular passage that responds impatiently to a rather conventional gesture in the orchestra, and veers to the dominant minor (in this case, B-flat minor), preceding the main group of secondary themes in B-flat major. In K. 482, this episode is marked by thick, dark chords, with strong emphasis in both hands on the dissonant semitone G-flat–F, as appears in mm. 129, 130, 136, and 137 (example 7.16).

What is the meaning of this passage, which stands so clearly apart from the surrounding orchestral discourse? One is tempted to regard it as a foreshadowing of the second movement, in which stress on the analogous scale degrees A-flat–G in C minor is so prominent.

The center of gravity in this concerto lies in this Andante, a series of variations with episodes on a mournful tune in 3/8 meter in C minor. The form and expression of the music are closely bound up with its orchestration. The theme is presented in the strings alone, with muted violins, whereas the first and second variations are assigned to the piano, with string accompaniment. Following each variation, we hear consoling episodes in the contrasting tone colors of the winds, in brighter major keys. The second episode, in C major, features much sensitive writing for the solo flute and bassoon. The music reaches a climax in the third variation, with intense dialogue between the full orchestra, forte, and the soloist's restrained answers, often employing trills, in piano. At the end of this variation, the passionate chromatic intensity of the solo piano yields to a cadence in C minor, and poignant, syncopated inflections in the flute and clarinet mark the beginning of the coda. In the final moments, quietly rising chromatic scales are heard in the piano, and the movement closes pianissimo, with a soft reiteration of a rhythmic motive drawn from the main subject.

The rondo finale of K. 482 is based on a swinging, hunting-type theme in 6/8 meter. The two-bar phrases of this theme outline a rising contour, so that the upward shift from B-flat to E-flat reaches G in m. 2, while a sequence of this phrase moving from B-flat through F reaches A-flat in m. 4. The overall melodic peak is reached in the third phrase, which passes from B-flat through G to the B-flat an octave higher, before the

final two-bar unit brings a balancing melodic descent to a tonic cadence. Beethoven imitated this theme in devising the finale of his Quintet for Piano and Winds, op. 16, a work that is otherwise modeled in several respects on Mozart's quintet K. 452. All three pieces are in E-flat major, and the two quintets are written for the same configuration of instruments. Like Mozart in K. 482, Beethoven initially gives the rondo Allegro theme in the finale of op. 16 to the pianist, and its opening pair of two-bar phrases outlines the same basic ascending pattern from B-flat through E-flat to G, and then from F to A-flat. The third two-bar phrase departs from its model, as Beethoven intensifies the ascent to reach C, a melodic peak underscored by a crescendo and a shift to subdominant harmony. Beethoven composed his main theme as a kind of variation on the rondo theme of K. 482, but the rest of the movement shows limited contact with Mozart's model.

Mozart resorts in the rondo of K. 482 to the practice of replacing a central developmental section with a minuet-like Andantino cantabile in the subdominant key, A-flat major. This is similar to his treatment of the rondo finale in his earlier concerto in this key, K. 271, a work that displays several parallels to K. 482, including the presence of a serious slow movement in C minor. In its final passages, the rondo of K. 482 seems reluctant to close. Although forceful tutti passages bring cadences in the tonic, suave phrases in the clarinet and later in the piano prolong the music until yet another outburst from the full orchestra brings the work to a decisive ending.

By 1786, Mozart's works in even his radiant key of A major can take on darker shadows and tragic depths. In K. 488 he places the touching slow movement in the unusual key of F-sharp minor, the only time he ever employed that tonality as tonic for an entire movement. The latent polyphonic richness of the theme, its intervallic and harmonic kinship with the other subjects, and Mozart's consummate control of register and orchestration contribute to its spell. The theme itself suggests a siciliano, that slow dance type that Mozart later used in his Rondo in A Minor, K. 511, for solo piano. One possible source of inspiration for this movement may be the Prelude in F-sharp minor from book 2 of *The Well-Tempered Clavier* by J. S. Bach. Mozart made string quartet arrangements of five fugues from book 2 for Baron Gottfried van Swieten, and we can presume his familiarity with this piece, which like Mozart's Adagio of K. 488, displays a remarkable use of the Neapolitan harmony of G major.[77]

As Charles Rosen has observed, Mozart's treatment of the descending lines from A in the opening subject and subsequent themes has an unusual concentration and poignancy.[78] Each upward striving in the melody inevitably yields to descent, and Mozart rearranges motivic elements from the opening piano theme as the movement progresses. Already in m. 2, the fall of a seventh from A to B signals a tensional treatment of register, and the gap begins to be filled already with the next note, G-sharp (example 7.17a). In the following bar, F-sharp is sounded, but its linear fall through E to D and C-sharp occurs only in mm. 5–6. In m. 7, the upward leap to A and stepwise fall from that pitch seem to be compressed into a single momentous gesture. The ensuing orchestral phrase, on the other hand, has the effect of an enlargement or augmentation of the descending phrase from A heard in the piano.

The second piano statement returns with a vengeance to the melodic leap C-sharp to A followed by a stepwise descent (example 7.17b). Mozart inverts the turn figure from m. 4 and provides yet another version of the falling melody, in which the dotted siciliano rhythm adorns the descending third A–G-sharp–F-sharp. The music seems obsessed with these motivic elements, almost to the exclusion of everything else. It is revealing that these measures—based on a turn figure, an upward leap of a minor sixth, and a stepwise descent employing chromaticism—represent a structural inversion of the main theme of the A-Minor Rondo, with its turn leading to a fall of a fifth, followed by a rising chromatic line.

Despite the utter contrast between this Adagio and the opening Allegro, Mozart nevertheless hints at a somber background within the joyous opening movement through a striking repeated phrase on the harmony of F-sharp minor, but heard within the key of A major. This important gesture first appears in the opening ritornello in mm. 52–54; it gives special prominence to the woodwinds, including the clarinets. The tone color of the clarinets contributes generally to the dark mellow tim-

77. As in mm. 9–10 of Mozart's Adagio and m. 34 of Bach's prelude.
78. Rosen, *The Classical Style*, 244–45.

Ex. 7.17a Concerto in A major, K. 488, II, beginning

Ex. 7.17b Concerto in A major, K. 488, II, mm. 20–25

bre of the work, reminding us of Mozart's great A-major works for this instrument, the Quintet, K. 581, and Concerto, K. 622.

If Mozart's Adagio was focused on the poignant inwardness of an upward melodic leap and a dying chromatic fall, the Presto finale transforms this basic idea into a vivacious but straightforward rondo theme (example 7.18). The upward jump of an octave at m. 2 reaches the same A that was given such emphasis in the Adagio in F-sharp minor. Now, however, the A serves as crux for a swift diatonic descent, played legato. This joyous resolution of tensions from the Andante launches one of Mozart's most exhilarating finales, a movement enhanced by rich melodic diversity and rhythmic energy. One of the most memorable of the tunes in this rondo sonata finale seems to celebrate the very idea of scalar continuity; the piano and then the winds scurry up and down, while the horns and basses sound a pedal point. When this theme appears for the last time, the work is nearly over, but the final measures are significantly grounded in a rhythm of two quarter notes and one longer note, set off by rests, corresponding to that rhythm that had begun the entire movement.

Four concerto fragments exist on a type of paper also found in the autograph score of K. 488; these sources afford glimpses into Mozart's compositional process.[79] Of particular interest is a fragmentary draft that was presumably intended for the finale of K. 488, a manuscript that is catalogued as K. 488c (Anh. 64).[80] Instead of the duple meter of the finale in the finished work, this music is written in 6/8 time; the opening rondo theme shifts between the piano and clarinets in four-measure phrases. Remarkably, this theme has a siciliano rhythm, clearly reminiscent of the slow movement

79. See Alan Tyson, "Mozart's Piano Concerto Fragments," in Zaslaw, *Mozart's Piano Concertos,* 67–69.

80. A facsimile of this manuscript is reproduced in the volume *Fragmente* in Konrad, Neue Mozart Ausgabe, Serie X, Supplement 30/4, 121–22.

Ex. 7.18 Concerto in A major, K. 488, III, beginning

as we know it. In the end, Mozart confined the siciliano idiom to the slow middle movement, while devising thematic connections of a rather different kind between the two last movements of the concerto.

Most remote of all the concertos from the social, *galant* origins of the genre is the work in C minor, K. 491, written immediately after K. 488 in March 1786. The C-Minor Concerto uses the largest orchestra of any of the concertos, since it retains oboes with the clarinets and employs trumpets and drums as well. The trumpets and timpani are often employed, as in the D-Minor Concerto, in the veiled, ominous manner of the D-minor music from *Don Giovanni,* and there are other parallels as well to the opera, which dates from the autumn of 1787, one-and-a-half years after the concerto.

The first movement of K. 491 shows a deepened contrast between the orchestra and soloist, which gives rise to the expressive atmosphere of elegiac resignation or grim passion perceived by various commentators. Alfred Einstein wrote that the affirmations of the principal key in this movement are "more inevitable, more inexorable" than in the D-Minor Concerto,[81] and Charles Rosen, commenting on the developmental episode in the solo exposition, wrote of "a passion, even a kind of terror, that is central to the work."[82] For Eva Badura-Skoda, it is perhaps "Mozart's most personal work," surpassing even the D-Minor Concerto or G-Minor Symphony in its "abysmal depth and tragic quality."[83] Simon Keefe, in his study of dramatic dialogue in the concertos, finds an "apotheosis of relational development in the first movement of K. 491" that amounts to a "*tour de force* of dialogic technique."[84]

Because of these extraordinary features of K. 491, we shall give especially detailed attention to this work, and particularly to the opening Allegro.[85] A somber yet passionate tone is established at once by the opening theme, which appears three times in varied form in the orchestral ritornello alone. In the mysterious introductory state-

81. Einstein, *Mozart, His Character His Work,* 311.
82. Rosen, *The Classical Style,* 249.
83. Badura-Skoda, *Wolfgang Amadeus Mozart. Klavierkonzert C Moll KV 491* (Munich: Wilhelm Fink, 1972), 3.
84. Keefe, *Mozart's Piano Concertos,* 100.
85. The following discussion of K. 491 draws on material that first appeared in my article "Dramatic Development and Narrative Design in the First Movement of Mozart's Piano Concerto in C Minor, K. 491," in Zaslaw, *Mozart's Piano Concertos,* 285–301.

Ex. 7.19 Concerto in C minor, K. 491, I, beginning

Vollendet Wien, 24. März 1786

continued

ment of this theme, heard in unison octaves in the strings and bassoons, Mozart avoids straightforward assertion of the tonic triad by stressing the semitones adjacent to the dominant, in a manner not unlike the beginning of his fantasia for piano in the same key, K. 475 (example 7.19).

It is almost as if Mozart had reshaped the basic idea from the outset of K. 475 to form the beginning of the concerto. The opening of the concerto is more ambiguous harmonically than that of the fantasia, as the dominant note, G, is treated as a passing note to F-sharp, and this pitch is joined motivically to E-flat in a striking upward leap of a diminished seventh, a gesture repeated in sequence by Mozart in the following measures. The sequences lead through the three possible diminished-seventh chords, each outlined by the rising motivic leaps in mm. 4, 6, and 8, and great harmonic tension is consequently pitted against the tonic. As Eva Badura-Skoda has pointed out, it is Mozart's enharmonic reinterpretation of the last diminished-seventh D–C-flat in m. 8 as D–B-natural, together with the harmonically stabilizing entrance of the oboe and other voices, that constitutes the structural turning point of the theme.[86] Strict continuation of the sequential pattern would have led the music into

86. Badura-Skoda, *Wolfgang Amadeus Mozart*, 15–18.

foreign keys, but Mozart's theme converges onto the tonic at this point, as the first vertical sonority of C minor is heard at last in m. 9.

The controlling linear motion of the theme traces a descent through a tritone, from the A-flat in m. 3 to D in m. 8, and it is this same configuration that Mozart varies in the descending oboe line an octave higher beginning on A-flat. The oboe melody also passes through a tritone from A-flat to D, but unlike the initial descent in the strings and bassoons, its final bars are adjusted to lead into the firm C-minor cadence marking the restatement of the entire theme forte beginning in m. 13. The entire theme is an example of the remarkable symmetry so characteristic of Mozart, a symmetry that allows for a gradual, and seemingly inevitable, intensification of the music from within. A fundamental basis for its structure are the two six-measure units outlining first the descent from A-flat to D and then, as a varied, contrapuntal imitation in the oboe, from A-flat to the C, marking the cadence in m. 13. Elements of periodic phrasing are thereby imposed here nevertheless onto the unstable, dissonant thematic material. At the same time, the continuation of the line in the strings and bassoons in the bass after m. 8 stresses the inversion of this A-flat–C relationship in mm. 10–11, outlining the *ascending* chromatic steps from A-flat to C and introducing thereby a motive that later assumes much importance in rhythmic diminution.

We have examined the opening theme closely because of the importance this material assumes throughout the movement. In a sense, however, the definitive exposition of this theme comes only in its ensuing restatement forte in the full orchestra. Here, the sequences passing through diminished sevenths are combined with a bass line descending chromatically through the tetrachord from C to G and outlining together with the treble the series of falling tritones C–F-sharp, B–F, B-flat–E, A–E-flat, and A-flat–D in mm. 16–20 (example 7.19). The theme is now fully harmonized, heard in the richest orchestration Mozart ever used in a concerto. Expanded here, the theme is then given further weight through yet another restatement later in the ritornello; but even more significant is its role in later passages where this theme is pitted against the piano solo. The head of the theme, in its forte version with trumpets and timpani, is asserted three times after the opening ritornello and always in close relationship to important piano passages—namely at the conclusion of the initial solo theme and at the beginning and end of the recapitulation—whereas at the conclusion of the cadenza Mozart draws upon related material from the end of the orchestral ritornello. These appearances of the theme display what Einstein described as an "inevitable" or "inexorable" quality not only on account of their striking thematic material and distinctive orchestration—and their cadential importance, marking structural downbeats in the musical form—but also because of their tonal fixation on the tonic key of C minor.

Mozart's tendency in the D-minor concerto to resolve his main themes into the major is absent from the C-minor concerto. Even in the tutti passage following the solo exposition, where we might expect to hear a transposition of the opening theme to E-flat major, Mozart deletes its first three measures and thoroughly transforms the rest. Only twice does the head of the theme appear in secondary keys, in E-flat minor in the developmental episode in the solo exposition and in F minor at the threshold of the development; both of these passages involve changes in orchestration and an absence of the trumpets and drums. But Mozart also alludes repeatedly to the chromaticism of his main theme in other passages of cadential character, using the trumpets and drums with mysterious, muted effect in C minor. One is reminded in this connection of his treatment of the key of D minor in *Don Giovanni*. The expressive associations of that key with vengeance and divine retribution are prefigured already in the music beginning the overture and in the setting of Don Giovanni's slaying of the Commendatore. Mozart exploits these associations by calling up the key of D minor in connection with Donna Anna in widely separated passages whose inner dramatic connection is made clear in part through similarities in orchestration, such as the use of trumpets and drums. Rosen has described the "strange, veiled effect" of the trumpets and timpani in the C-minor concerto as comparable to parts of *Don Giovanni*.[87] The parallel emerges most clearly when we consider the larger musical context of this movement, focusing on the relationship between the tutti and solo, as well as on some unusual formal and expressive features centered around the climax of the development. (We should note here that whereas D minor tends to be associated in Mozart's operas with ideas of vengeance, C minor is typically connected with pain or despair.)

The plaintive character of the new theme with which the piano enters arises in part from its strict dependence on musical relationships exposed in the preceding tutti and especially from the stress on the pitch A-flat (example 7.20). Again and again, the interval G–A-flat or A-flat–G is heard on different levels of structure. It is embodied in the sustained initial pitches of the opening four-measure gestures, where grace notes ensure that it is played in both upper and middle registers. These initial sustained notes in the piano should in no way seem rushed or strictly confined to the temporal momentum from the orchestral ritornello; they signal a more personal, vulnerable voice. The A-flat is stressed as well in an inner voice in the left hand in m. 103 and in the treble in m. 106; subsequently, it is sounded no less than three times in the upper register in the treble. But most subtle is the emphasis on A-flat in the bass, which is combined with an allusion to the rhythm of the principal theme of the tutti in bars 112–16. This A-flat in the bass should be given more prominence than it usually receives from performers, since it embodies the expressive crux of the progression and foreshadows the imminent return of the main subject in the full orchestra two bars later, in m. 118.

This opening theme of the solo already assumes a less chromatic and more diatonic character than the principal orchestral subject, and this tendency continues in the shared restatement of the main theme, which departs almost immediately from C minor in a transition to the contrasting secondary key of E-flat major. The second subject material in E-flat, in turn, generally remains aloof from and untouched by the pervasive chromaticism of the principal theme, and it is perhaps for that reason that

87. Rosen, *The Classical Style*, 250.

Ex. 7.20 Concerto in C minor, K. 491, I, first solo piano passage

continued

Ex. 7.20 *continued*

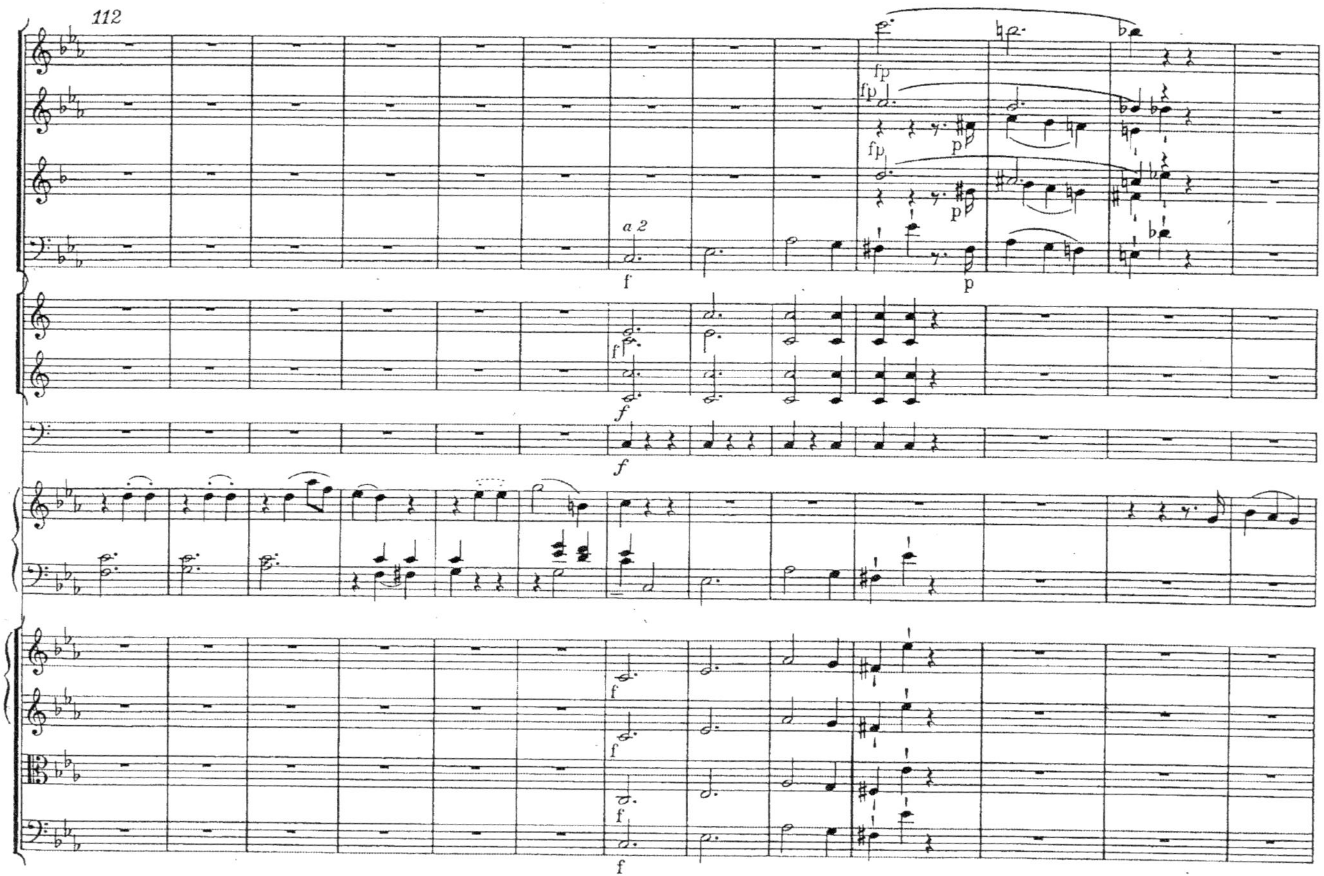

Mozart took the unusual step of reintroducing the opening orchestral subject into the middle of the solo exposition. This is the developmental episode mentioned by Rosen, in which the main theme is heard in the flute, bringing a change of mode to minor and reintroducing the chromaticism from the orchestral ritornello. The serenity and consonance of this part of the form is thereby belied, while at the same time Mozart foreshadows here a climactic passage to come at the end of the development, a passage we shall analyze in detail. The chromatic subject breaks through here, as it were, into the more stable and conventional fabric of the surrounding passages, anchored by the two piano cadences in E-flat major. Even this destabilizing episode conforms to its context, however, inasmuch as the passage remains not in E-flat minor, but turns, at least momentarily, to the relative major, just as had occurred in the earlier statement of this theme in the solo exposition, with its progression from C minor to E-flat. The solo exposition of this concerto movement, then, bears only a tenuous relationship to the ritornello, and its themes in E-flat major are not prepared in the ritornello. And though the orchestra is present throughout the solo exposition, its basic character is softened here and temporarily allied with that of the soloist.

The development of this movement is one of the most powerfully dramatic and broadly architectural in all Mozart's concertos. Mozart begins this section with echo effects, as the winds comment on the piano solo,[88] and he then demonstrates the close kinship between the opening piano and tutti themes in the context of F minor, whereby the play on C and D-flat in the piano resolves with dramatic force into a return of the orchestral tutti in that key. He then develops the descending sequential motive from the main theme in the orchestra, now in a diatonic context beginning in G minor and leading in an extended progression falling through the circle of fifths, while the piano embroiders the texture with figures in sixteenth notes. This passage, which spans more than twenty measures, brings us to a brief but agitated piano solo, whose figuration falls rapidly through two octaves, while coming to the threshold of a cadence in G minor. Here the full orchestra intervenes, breaking off the cadence and initiating a passage described by Badura-Skoda as probably the greatest *Sturmausbruch* (stormy outbreak) in all the concertos (example 7.21).[89]

The thematic link between the main theme of the movement and these sixteen measures of alternation between the full tutti and piano solo consists in the isolation and intensification of the crucial semitone relationship, which is heard here at its original pitch level A-flat–G, as in the earlier C-minor passages. This semitone is repeated fivefold in close succession in the flute and violins, while being reinforced a sixth lower by the lower strings; and the piano arpeggios seem to spring from the tension generated by these expressive upper neighbor-notes. The undulating sixths, A-flat–C resolving to G–B on the dominant of C minor, recall the intervallic structure of the

88. The passage at the beginning of the development, in which the piano's repeated C-flats falling to B-flat are echoed in the flute and clarinets as D-flats falling to C, recalls the dialogue between piano and winds at the outset of the development of the first movement of the Quintet in E-flat, K. 452, in which two such echoes in the winds facilitate modulations to new keys.

89. Badura-Skoda, *Wolfgang Amadeus Mozart*, 23.

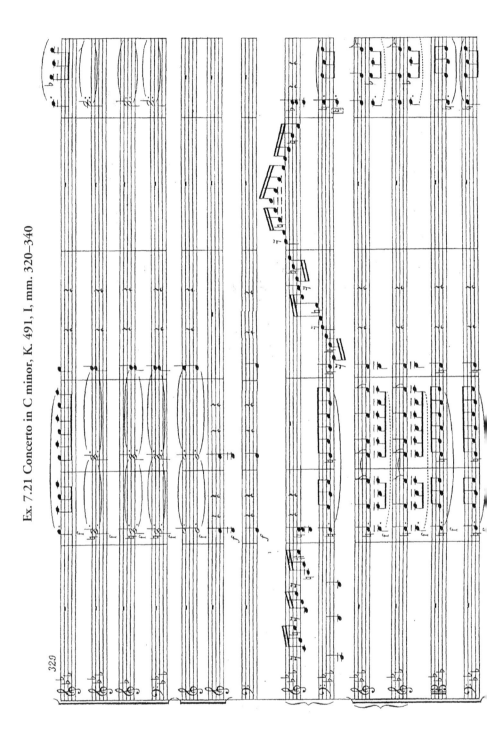

Ex. 7.21 Concerto in C minor, K. 491, I, mm. 320–340

Ex. 7.21 continued

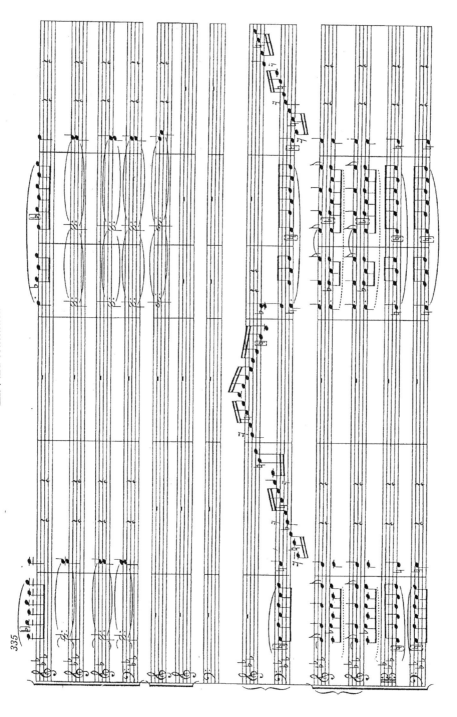

335

main theme, albeit with a difference in harmony, with the A-flat now heard as a dominant ninth. The impact of this gesture is enhanced by the forte dynamic level and the orchestration, including trumpets and timpani in mm. 330–32.[90] The dramatic opposition of tutti and solo in this four-measure unit is then treated three times in sequence, producing a majestic broadening of the harmonic rhythm, and the music passes through the circle of fifths, from the dominant of C minor to the dominants of F, B-flat, and E-flat. This enables Mozart to reinforce in his transpositions the semitone relationships at pitch levels heard in earlier passages, such as in the developmental episode of the solo exposition.

Rosen has written about this movement, "Not only the despair of the music but its energy is introverted, turned away from all that was theatrical, even in Mozart himself"[91]; but although this description indeed applies well to the remainder of the movement, after the beginning of the recapitulation, it does not apply to this climax of the development. These stormy gestures, juxtaposing tutti and solo, seem to break through the more reserved atmosphere of the movement as a whole to encapsulate its central harmonic and dramatic conflict, a conflict that spills over, as it were, into the pervasive chromaticism of the principal orchestral complex and the more introverted transformation of these tensions in other passages, such as the opening solo theme.

In the ensuing and final sixteen-measure segment of the development, Mozart ingeniously blends motivic elements drawn from the principal theme into a new synthesis (example 7.22). The intervallic contour of the head of the theme, with its rising third and fourth, is now combined with the rhythm of the falling sequences from the middle of the theme, producing a rhythmic diminution of the head of the theme in quarter notes instead of dotted halves. At the same time, a high melodic continuation in the flute descends from E-flat in a series of syncopations, while the descending sequential motive from the main theme is heard in diminution in the oboes. This new motivic combination is treated in a threefold descending sequence corresponding to the familiar threefold falling sequence from the principal theme, but the descent is now by thirds, through E-flat, C, and A-flat, a harmonic configuration leading to a dominant pedal point and, eight measures later, to a tonic resolution of unusual strength, owing to its lengthy and powerful preparation. Over the pedal point, the piano now plays the scales that were foreshadowed in the developmental episode of the solo exposition, scales reminiscent, in a way, to those that accompany the Stone Guest in the act 2 finale of *Don Giovanni*. As in *Don Giovanni,* these scales initially creep upward by half step above a pedal point and thereby echo once again the crucial

90. As Badura-Skoda points out (*Wolfgang Amadeus Mozart,* 49 n. 13), the note G in the timpani part in m. 332 was intended by Mozart, but has been omitted in many published editions. The passage in question is found on folio 12v of the autograph score, which has been published in facsimile as *Mozart: Piano Concerto in C minor, K. 491, with a Foreword by Watkins Shaw and a Critical Introduction by Denis Mathews* (Kilkenny, Ireland: Boethius, 1979).

91. Rosen, *The Classical Style,* 250.

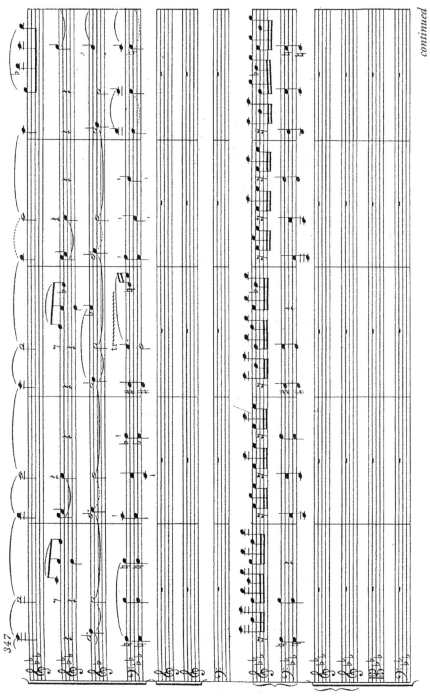

Ex. 7.22 Concerto in C minor, K. 491, I, mm. 347–373

continued

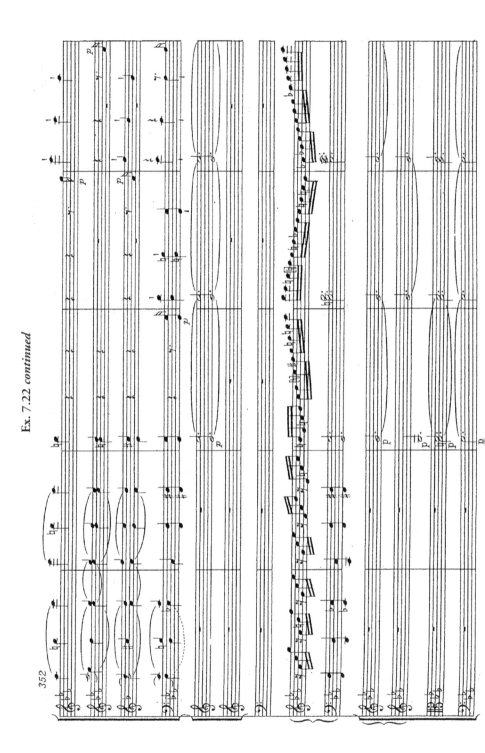

Ex. 7.22 continued

352

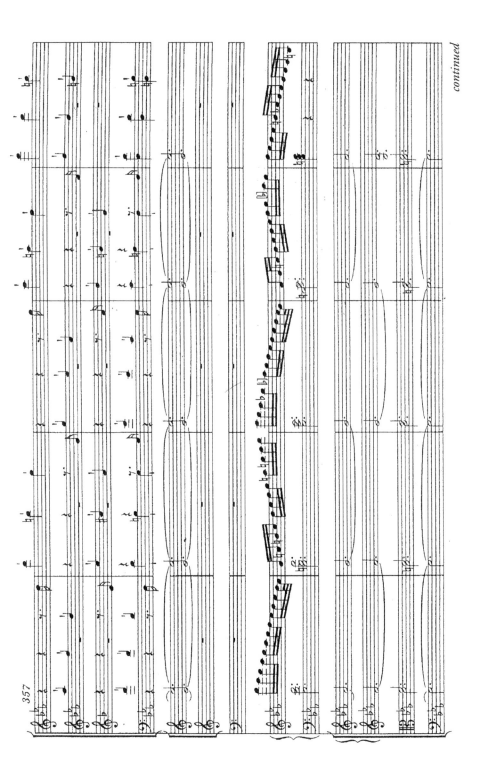

357

Ex. 7.22 *continued*

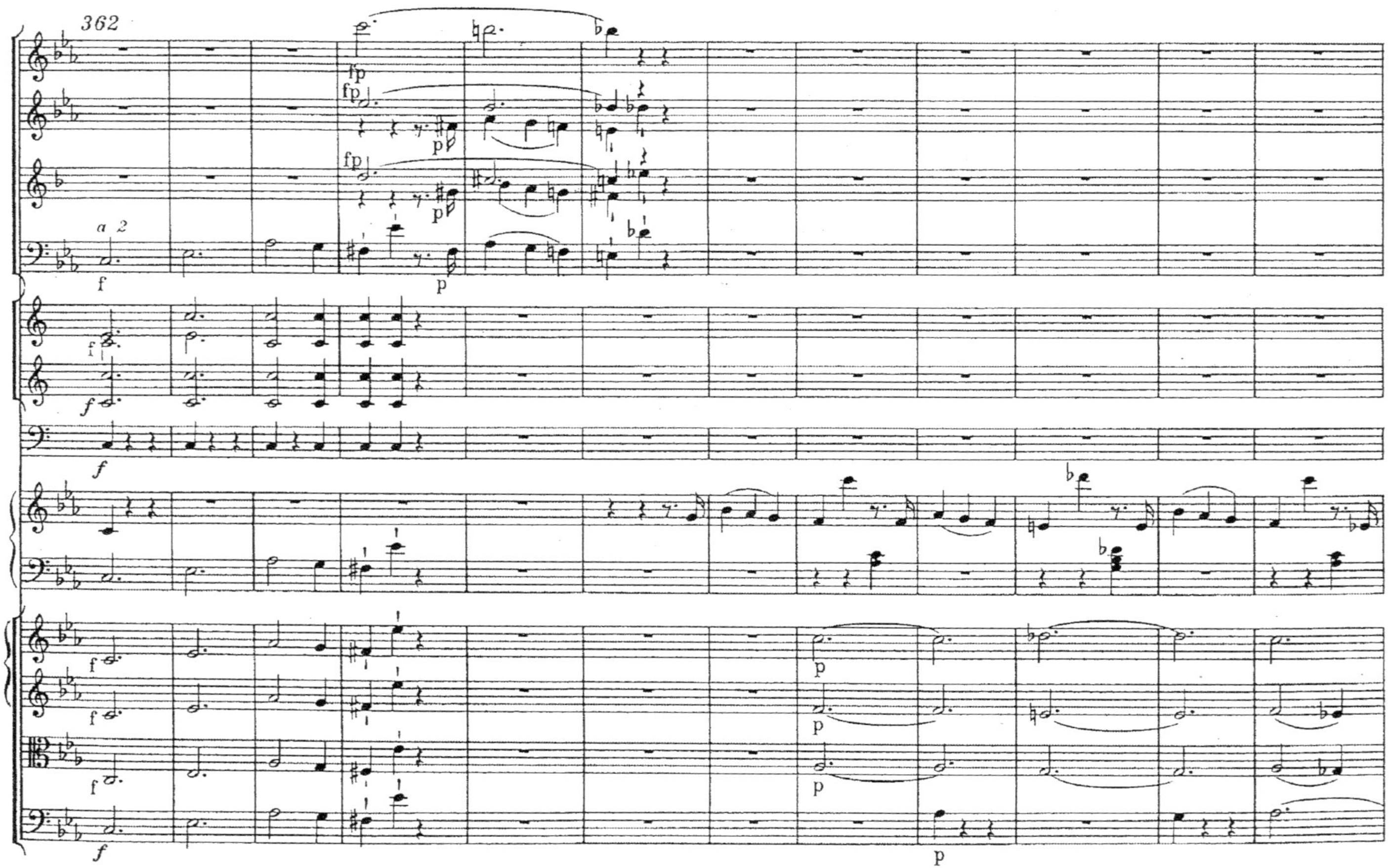

semitone G to A-flat—though, unlike those in the opera, the scales do not continue to rise, but remain rooted on the dominant.

Leonard Meyer observed that the quality of "inevitability" characteristic of this passage leading to the recapitulation is bound up with Mozart's use of two overlapping structural progressions, the circle-of-fifths process beginning in the *Sturmausbruch* passage at m. 330 and a contrapuntal pattern of linear descent beginning at m. 346.[92] Although the circle-of-fifths progression is not actually continued up to the recapitulation, the arrival of the tonic at m. 362 is nevertheless placed precisely where it would have occurred had the original progression been continued. The coordination of these two patterned processes with the same moment of closure thus contributes to the unusual architectural and dramatic weight attached to the moment of recapitulation.

In assessing the larger formal structure of this movement and its apparent narrative implications, it is revealing to consider certain affinities between the D-minor music in *Don Giovanni* and both of Mozart's concertos in minor, the composition of which, of course, preceded the opera.[93] A parallel to the D-Minor Concerto is quite obvious, because of its key, its thematic similarity to the music accompanying the death of the Commendatore, other shared features (such as the prominent use of chains of syncopations), and even the resolution into the major mode at the conclusion. The affinity to the C-Minor Concerto is less direct, but it too shares some characteristics of the so-called *ombra* style in *Don Giovanni,* summarized by Allanbrook, such as the assertion of the Neapolitan half-step in side-slipping chromatic progressions; the use of disconnected "filler" figures such as scales ascending through the octave; and the use of the descending, *chaconne*-type bass, which is present in the C-Minor Concerto in the main theme itself.[94] The triple meter of the concerto, on the other hand, might seem incompatible with this style; but Mozart succeeds in the development of the C-Minor Concerto in combining the faster pacing of an allegro in 3/4 time with a remarkable breadth, solemnity, and grandeur—qualities also reminiscent of that luminous companion to the C-Minor Concerto composed later in 1786, the Concerto in C Major, K. 503.

However, the most suggestive comparison between the opera and this concerto movement probably resides in the dramatic significance of the cadence as a turning-point in the action. One thinks here of the D-minor cadence signaling Don Giovanni's damnation—the cadence that fatefully answers his defiant words "No, No!" set to his falling fourth D–A, with the harmonic support of diminished seventh and dominant, resolving, after a five-measure interpolation by the Stone Guest, to the D-minor Allegro (whose syncopations resemble the first movement of the D-Minor Concerto) (example 7.23).

One could hear the harmonic gesture opening the scene when the statue appears—with its identical falling fourth D–A in the strings and timpani, its identical harmony

92. Meyer, "Process and Morphology in the Music of Mozart," *Journal of Musicology* 1 (1982): 77–79.

93. As we have seen, the D-Minor Concerto, K. 466, was composed the preceding year, at the beginning of 1785, whereas *Don Giovanni* was completed in late October 1787.

94. See Allanbrook, *Rhythmic Gesture in Mozart's* Le Nozze di Figaro *and* Don Giovanni, 292–319.

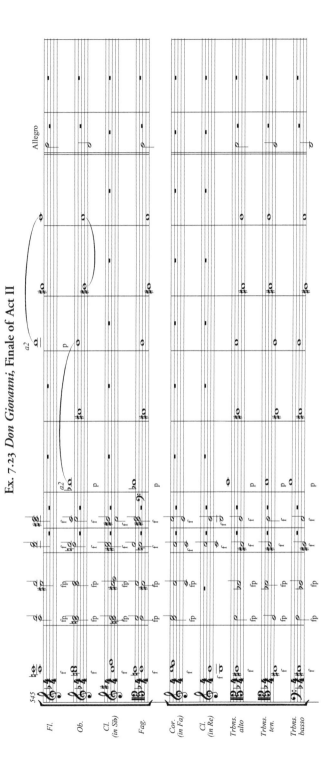

Ex. 7.23 *Don Giovanni*, Finale of Act II

and very similar orchestration, and by extension the chords opening the overture—as a rhythmic augmentation of this setting of Don Giovanni's moment of defiance at his damnation and, hence, as something far more dramatically significant and evocative than the conventional flourish for which these chords are often taken. The climax of the development in the C-Minor Concerto, with its isolation of the crucial semitone relationship, provides a comparable example of dramatic concision in a purely instrumental context. But it is the cadence marking the recapitulation of the movement—with its unusually lengthy and powerful preparation, giving us the sense that it articulates a passage reaching back at least to the *Sturmausbruch*—that presents the dramatic turning point. After this cadence, the previous influence of the soloist in the exposition—in departing from the chromatic sphere of C minor, with its pathetic or tragic associations—seems to be inexorably reversed. The expected resolution of themes from the solo exposition to C minor and incorporation of ritornello themes into the recapitulation contribute to this effect, but Mozart also substantially reinterprets some of this thematic material, darkening its cast so that the solemn or even tragic implications of the development seem to be played out in the recapitulation and coda.

The beginning of the recapitulation is announced forte, with trumpets and drums, and its continuation incorporates a vehement passage stressing the A-flat–G semitone from the end of the orchestral ritornello. All of the themes of the second subject group are in the minor, and the first of them sounds even more somber because of its placement in the subdominant, F minor. Mozart also incorporates a chromatically ascending transitional theme from the ritornello that had been omitted from the solo exposition, and he alters one of the other secondary themes so that its head stresses the minor third degree, darkening its sonority, while the continuation stresses the chromatic ascent from G to C, underlining its relation to the principal theme (mm. 411–19). The remaining orchestral tutti passages reassert the oppressive expressive atmosphere, bringing a return of the rising chromatic cadential figure supported by trumpets and timpani following the cadenza; in the unusual coda the soloist is drawn yet again into the drama in a passage echoing the end of the development section and providing a fitting poetic close in the minor. Mozart sustains a tonic pedal point throughout these fifteen measures of coda and ends the movement with piano arpeggios over the immovable bass, accompanied by the soft, ominously mysterious cadential accents of trumpets and timpani.

This is the concerto about which Beethoven reputedly said to his fellow pianist-composer Johann Baptist Cramer that "we shall never be able to do anything like that."[95] His admiration was surely based both on the work's mastery of form and compelling motivic integration as well as on its emotional force—though ultimately, of course, there is no clear separation between these aspects of a work of art. The chromatic relationships we have considered represent part of the underlying musical structure that Mozart differentiated so strongly in its tutti and solo manifestations. The orchestral discourse often seems unyielding and implacable in relationship to the

95. *Thayer's Life of Beethoven*, ed. Eliot Forbes (Princeton: Princeton University Press, 1970), 1:209.

solo, whose passages in C minor carry an air of resignation and, in the recapitulation, even of depression. Girdlestone described the movement as alternating moods of elegy, in solo passages, with strife and tragedy, as embodied in the modulating flute episode and the development; but the tragic expression emerges not merely from individual passages, but from the design of the whole.[96] Many unusual features of the movement seem to contribute to an overriding narrative pattern in which the apparent autonomy of the soloist in much of the solo exposition is subsequently relinquished as a result of the confrontation and combination of solo and tutti materials in the development and recapitulation. One could, perhaps, even be tempted to compare the role of the piano soloist here in relationship to the tutti to the role of a dramatic protagonist, such as Don Giovanni in relationship to the *ombra* music, with his freedom of action and defiance of constraints finally overcome at the cadence shown in example 7.23.

Discernment of a basic narrative design in the C-Minor Concerto requires no such analogy with Mozart's later opera, however, and the general affinity between these works arises largely from the archetypal human themes of confrontation and defeat or submission implicit in them. This kind of psychological process is richly developed in the first movement of K. 491, where it is effectively embodied in the relationship between the tutti and solo and coordinated with the demands of the large-scale musical form. The narrative pattern we have described is not a "program" imposed on the music from without, but an attempt to account for the unique configuration of elements in this work that creates a whole greater than the sum of its parts.

The instrumental context of the concerto of course sets conditions different from an opera and allows the tensions from one movement to reemerge transformed in another. That the second movement, a serene Larghetto in E-flat major, is by no means untouched by these relationships is reflected in the first wind-and-piano interlude in C minor, with its prominent stress on A-flat.[97] This interlude, which is begun by a pair of oboes, is the first of two related wind-led sections in the Larghetto; the later section in A-flat major is led by the two clarinets. In the coda, Mozart recalls and unifies the contrasting timbral and tonal aspects of the two passages.[98]

The mood of the first movement of K. 491 much more obviously infects the great finale of the concerto, whose march-like variations in C minor exploit their own version of the semitone conflict. The predominantly serious tone of this finale represents a departure from the lighter, playful, or comic spirit that often inspired Mozart's last movements in his concerti. In the theme of the variations, marked "Allegretto," these tensions from the first movement surface in the German-sixth chord of m. 3 and the prominent stress on the G–A-flat semitone in mm. 3–4. Most striking of all, however, is the importance of the linear descent from the high A-flat in mm. 10–11 in the sec-

---

96. See Girdlestone, *Mozart's Piano Concertos*, 392–400.

97. Mozart's strong interest in this C-minor theme is also reflected in his re-use of the material in the same key as the first episode of the Adagio of his penultimate piano sonata, K. 570.

98. An analysis of this process is offered by Jonathan P. J. Stock in "Orchestration as Structural Determinant: Mozart's Deployment of Woodwind Timbre in the Slow Movement of the C Minor Piano Concerto K. 491," *Music and Letters* 78 (1997): 210–19.

ond half of the theme, which corresponds audibly to the descent from this same A-flat in the oboe at the outset of the first movement. However, in his variations, unlike the opening Allegro, Mozart stresses the semitone D-flat–C, repeating it over and over in the coda to the finale. There is no closing resolution here in the major mode, as in the D-Minor Concerto or in *Don Giovanni*. This, too, was music that deeply impressed Beethoven, and it seems to be echoed in one of his very few unremittingly tragic works, the "Appassionata" Sonata, op. 57.

The last of the series of twelve great concertos from 1784 to 1786 is the work in C major, K. 503, completed in December 1786. As we have seen, however, the compositional origins of the opening Allegro maestoso of K. 503 go back to around early 1785, the period of K. 466 and K. 467. The opening movement of K. 503 matches its sister concertos in ambition and originality. Its orchestration includes trumpets and drums, but not clarinets. This Allegro maestoso is one of Mozart's grandest and most symphonic conceptions, inviting comparison with the "Prague" and "Jupiter" Symphonies. No earlier concerto exploits large masses of sound more effectively, and the time-scale of this movement is even broader than the "Jupiter." Here, unlike in many of the preceding concertos, the language of *opera buffa* is largely avoided, and in its first two movements, K. 503 is decidedly a *concerto serio*. Prominent features of the Allegro maestoso include a unifying upbeat figure of repeated notes, similar to the so-called fate motive in Beethoven's Fifth Symphony, and a conspicuous use of modal contrast—the juxtaposition of major and minor.

Beethoven was probably inspired by this movement to use the upbeat figure in the piano at the beginning of the development of the first movement in his G-Major Concerto, since the same rhythmic motive appears very extensively at this point in K. 503 and even serves a similar transitional function at the change in key. This motive of repeated notes is prominent already from the beginning of Beethoven's concerto, and it is with this rhythmic figure that the pianist opens both his initial dolce statement as well as the first extneded solo after the orchestral ritornello. Later, following the climax of the development on C-sharp minor, Beethoven places the motive in the low strings pizzicato (mm. 231–235) before it passes to the woodwinds in the succeeding bars (mm. 235–238).

Quite unlike Beethoven's concerto is the opening of Mozart's K. 503, with two broad and massive eight-measure forte statements, which move from tonic to dominant and then from dominant to tonic, respectively. A foreshortening of rhythm in each statement motivates the shift in harmony, but the last two bars of each unit are given in piano to the bassoons and oboes, which play a motivic flourish with a dotted rhythm. At mm. 17–18, the oboes and bassoons change the mode to C minor, and the ensuing eight-bar phrase is based largely on the upbeat figure of repeated notes in the violins, which is heard in C minor in a rising sequence, moving up the scale. The dynamic level has remained piano, so that in the next eight-bar phrase the full orchestra can reenter forte, in C major, as the violins are given an energetic figure rushing up the scale. The majestic unfolding of rising linear patterns is thus compressed motivically into these upward sweeping scales in sixteenth notes, which in turn are now combined with the upbeat figure of repeated notes, heard in the bassoons and basses. Already in the opening ritornello or orchestral exposition, Mozart displays a contrapuntal virtuosity that is wedded to a masterful control of his orchestral resources. In this context, it is no wonder that he took pains to make the soloist's entrance indirect and almost reluctant. In the Allegro maestoso of K. 503, more than any other Mozart concerto, the soloist cannot compete directly with the full orchestra.[99]

The development section is highly contrapuntal, but Mozart does not set the soloist into opposition with the orchestra, in the manner of the first movement of K. 491. To be sure, the modulatory pivot of repeated notes admired by Beethoven serves as springboard here for the soloist in initiating shifts in key to E minor, and later F major, G minor, and A minor. This is a fine example of Mozart's ability to expand the basic motivic idea of rising scale steps to help shape the *tonal* plan of the movement. An increasing density of contrapuntal voices now embraces the piano and orchestra together in a cooperative endeavor, forging a whole greater than the sum of the parts. The process culminates in a quadruple canon of no less than eight parts, two in the strings, four in the winds, and two in the piano. Tovey observed that "no such polyphony has occurred since in any concerto, except one passage in the middle of the finale of Brahms's D minor."[100]

The main weight of K. 503 lies in its opening movement. One can perceive a sense of retrenchment in Mozart's completion of this ambitious concerto in late 1786, which involved borrowing a preexisting main theme for the finale.[101] Nevertheless, the Andante in F major shows a breadth and dignity in keeping with the character of the whole work, and unlike most of Mozart's slow movements it is in sonata form, with a brief but weighty retransition in place of a development.

The Allegretto finale is a substantial rondo-sonata design, in which a character of playfulness is prominent. Mozart adapted the main subject from the gavotte in the ballet music of *Idomeneo,* from 1781. Like the first movement, this rondo indulges in effective contrasts of major and minor, and its memorable and passionate development contains much felicitous writing for the winds in dialogue with the piano. The melody of the rondo theme profiles the interval of the fourth, with two falling fourths, C–G and A–E, heard in the opening measures. This rondo theme is initially heard in the strings, with answering phrases in the winds, including trumpets and drums, based on a pair of rising fourths: C–F and D–G. The later appearances of the rondo subject are assigned to the soloist, and preceded by cadenza-like passages in the piano that lend weight and emphasis to the main theme. Mozart cleverly develops motivic

99. It is noteworthy that those passages in which the soloist joins with the orchestra in presenting the primary theme are cooperative, not competitive, in character.

100. Tovey, "The Classical Concerto," in *Essays in Musical Analysis: Concertos and Choral Works* (London: Oxford University Press, 1981), 22. This essay was originally published in 1903.

101. Kerman finds K. 503 "strangely cold" and writes that "K. 503 registers a clear change in mood in the sequence of Mozart concertos. It could be said to register a loss of heart" (Kerman, "Mozart's Piano Concertos and Their Audience," 333). It is difficult, however, to associate "loss of heart" with such a uniquely impressive work as the first movement of K. 503.

ideas derived from the rondo theme, and even the furious passagework for the orchestra at the conclusion outlines the contour of fourths that is conspicuous throughout. The heart of the movement lies in the inspired cantabile episode in F major at the middle of the rondo design. The warm lyricism of the subject is felt at once in its motives of falling stepwise movement through a third above shifting harmonies; the theme is soon intensified through expressive chromaticism, with an acceleration of the accompaniment from sixteenth notes to triplet-sixteenths. In this section, the lyrical phrases of the pianist are answered by an increasing number of layered woodwind voices, featuring flute, oboe, and bassoon.

The Last Concertos: K. 537 and K. 595

Only two piano concertos date from Mozart's last years: the "Coronation" Concerto in D Major, K. 537, from 1788, and the final Concerto in B-flat Major, K. 595, completed in January 1791. K. 537 was begun probably by early 1787, and its completion was entered into his catalogue on 24 February 1788. Its first known performance by Mozart was at Dresden on 14 April 1789.[102] The work owes its title to the fact that he played it, along with K. 459, during the coronation festivities of Leopold II at Frankfurt on 15 October 1790. Along with the D-Minor Concerto, the "Coronation" was the best known of all Mozart's concertos during the nineteenth century and into the twentieth, but it is not as fine a work as many of the concertos from the preceding years, and the solo piano part has not survived in a wholly authentic version. Several of Mozart's other concertos, including K. 482 and K. 491, contain passages in which the text of the solo part is not entirely complete, but this problem is most acute with K. 537. Mozart left the solo part in a particularly sketchy state, especially in the second and third movements, and Johann Anton André—who first published the work in parts in 1794—evidently prepared the version of the text that most pianists have accepted without question.

In its orchestration, formal design, and interplay between tutti and solo, the D-Major Concerto is a somewhat regressive work, and if its concessions to the *galant* style were aimed at popular success, the reception history of the piece confirms the success of Mozart's strategy. Einstein wrote of K. 537 that "it is very Mozartean, while at the same time it does not express the whole or even the half of Mozart."[103] But in some respects, such as the brilliant keyboard figuration of the opening Allegro, the "Coronation" Concerto does break new ground. The Larghetto has an air of elegance and gracefulness, but it lacks contrast, and states a theme several times that is itself repetitive. Embellishment cannot compensate for this situation. A sketch for this theme is labeled "Romance," and shows that the chromatic inflection involving D-sharp in m. 19 was an afterthought, since the sketched version is completely diatonic.[104]

102. H. C. Robbins Landon has speculated that K. 537 may have first been performed in a subscription series in Vienna in 1788. See Landon, *1791: Mozart's Last Year* (London, Thames and Hudson, 1988), 32.
103. Einstein, *Mozart, His Character, His Work*, 313.
104. This manuscript is held by the Mayeda Ikotoku Foundation in Tokyo.

The rondo finale returns to the brilliant character of the first movement, featuring showy passagework and audacious modulations. The opening section of this Allegretto includes two main themes introduced by the piano in the tonic D major. In later passages, short but emphatic orchestral interjections trigger rapid passagework in the piano. In the middle of the rondo design, after the opening rondo theme is restated, an abrupt orchestral statement carries the music surprisingly to B-flat major. The soloist takes up the second main theme in this key, then changes the mode to B-flat minor and modulates further to B minor and G major, all within nine bars (mm. 196–204). Even in this rather traditional work, Mozart's innovative shaping of the rondo design is apparent.

Mozart's final Piano Concerto in B-flat Major, K. 595, begins, like the G-Minor Symphony, with a bar of accompanimental introduction in a steady rhythm (example 7.24). A sense of serenity with hints of resignation emanates from this important work, the most introverted of Mozart's concertos in this key. Striking about the opening theme are the differing lengths of its three phrases, and the interjections of the wind instruments setting these phrases apart. Whereas the initial soft phrase in the violins first ascends to open the space of the tonic triad, and then elaborates the corresponding descent with a turn figure and a stepwise fall, the winds firmly interject the higher B-flat and echo the descending third F–D just heard in the violins. The second violin phrase varies the first, while curtailing its length from four to three measures, and is again answered by the winds, in forte. The third violin phrase, on the other hand, reaches up to the B-flat sounded by the winds and carries it onto a subdominant harmony, leading to the cadence of the opening theme in m. 13. At this juncture, a motive in dotted rhythm that is related to the woodwind fanfare is played by both strings and winds—a circumstance that at last unifies the orchestral texture. This Allegro displays a particularly subtle treatment of dialogue between parts of the orchestra as well as between the tutti and soloist.

The development of this movement begins with a passage of harmonic daring. After the cadence in F major that closes the solo exposition and another strong cadence in this key in the orchestra, Mozart employs an arresting four-note motive starting with an accent, a figure drawn from the opening ritornello. After first coupling this figure with a conventional cadential phrase, he chromaticizes the motive, so that the upper line outlines the rising minor third: B-flat, B-natural, C, D-flat. Two sequences of this chromatic variant follow, each a minor third lower. Within seconds, the bottom drops out of the seemingly secure tonal environment of F major, and the soloist then states the opening subject in the remote key of B minor. An ingenious three-part dialogue between piano, strings, and winds ensues, building on the asymmetrical phrases that had opened the concerto.

After the beautiful Larghetto in E-flat major, with a principal melody in a romanza style akin to K. 466, the concerto concludes with a rondo in 6/8 time, Mozart's favorite meter for finales in this key, as we have seen. The gaiety of this movement is more rarefied than in the earlier concerto finales in B-flat, and the themes share a distinct rhythmic profile with prominent use of appoggiaturas. This raises the matter of

Ex. 7.24 Concerto in B flat major, K. 595, I, beginning

Datiert Wien, 5. Januar 1791

Mozart's departure in some later works from that thematic diversity that has always been regarded as characteristic of his style. His contemporary, the composer Carl Dittersdorf von Dittersdorf, already lodged this observation as a complaint, confessing that "I have never yet met with any composer who had such an amazing wealth of ideas; I could almost wish he were not so lavish in using them."[105]

105. Dittersdorf, *The Autobiography of Karl von Dittersdorf,* trans. A. D. Coleridge (London, 1896), 251–52, cited in Malcolm S. Cole, "The Rondo Finale: Evidence for the Mozart-Haydn Exchange?" in *Mozart-Jahrbuch 1968/70: 250.*

Haydn's influence surely contributed to Mozart's quest for thematic integration in works of his last years, such as the finales of the piano sonata, K. 576, and of this concerto, K. 595. Fragments or variants of the main theme are used throughout the rondo, which imparts an uncommon unity to the whole. The opening phrase of the main theme is shown in example 7.25, where it is juxtaposed with three later passages. In the first of these, the theme becomes an agent for upward-ranging modulations (example 7.25b); in the second variant, a striking melodic alteration changes the harmony of the second bar (example 7.25c); in the third example, more pronounced rhythmic emphasis is given to the second bar while the melody is transformed (example 7.25d).[106] On the other hand, the frequent oscillation between major and minor recalls the first movement. Elements of sonata procedure are absorbed here into the rondo, with an incomplete solo statement of the main theme in the unusual subdominant key placed at the center of the design. The piano phrase is answered by the winds in the minor, leading to a developmental continuation with changes in key, and this striking passage substitutes for a normal return of the refrain in the overall form.

Like the main theme of the first movement, the rondo theme begins with an ascent through the notes of the tonic triad. This motivic kinship is strengthened by the parallel between the woodwind fanfare interjections in the opening movement and the contour of the continuation of the rondo subject, which includes a falling arpeggiation from high B-flat. At the beginning of the developmental central episode of the rondo, Mozart incorporates a passage into the solo part that might be heard as a veiled allusion to the outset of the first movement. Following the statement of the rondo theme in the piano and orchestra in mm. 131–146, the soloist echoes the last

106. Discussion of these passages is offered by Cole in "The Rondo Finale," 242–56, esp. 251.

Ex. 7.25a Concerto in B flat major, K. 595, III, beginning of rondo theme

Ex. 7.25b Concerto in B flat major, K. 595, III, mm. 79–83

Ex. 7.25c Concerto in B flat major, K. 595, III, mm. 94–97

Ex. 7.25d Concerto in B flat major, K. 595, III, mm. 108–111

two bars of the tutti phrase while changing the mode to B-flat minor. This passage in mm. 148–150 is based on the melodic flourish in the oboes in m. 146, with a turn figure on the dominant serving as springboard for an upward leap to B-flat, the tonic note. Mozart restates the figure three times, so that the prominent high notes at the end of these motives outline B-flat, D-flat, F—the rising triadic contour from the beginning of the concerto, heard in the minor. The soloist's version of the first-movement theme had included similar turn figures, which enhances the similarity.

The finale of the last piano concerto thus displays the ingenious experimentation so characteristic of Mozart's treatment of the rondo form throughout his career. As the last of his 6/8 rondo finales in B-flat, the movement looks back to K. 450 and K. 456, from 1784. In its thematic organization, the rondo of K. 595 is more tightly integrated than these earlier finales, and it shares with them a superbly imaginative handling of dialogue between the piano and the orchestral instruments. At times, brilliant gestures in the piano are echoed in the woodwinds; the sound of the soloist transcends itself as it passes into the oboes and flute. To the end of the movement, Mozart continues to display an obsession with the head of the theme, which appears in a double statement in the piano, which is then echoed in the oboes. All that remains are six measures for the orchestra, which again stress the beginning of the melody and close the work by reaffirming the basic thematic contour, with a minimum of harmonic support.

As we have seen, a sense of unity or integration in Mozart's works—the thread, or "*il filo*" in Leopold Mozart's formulation—is embodied in the sensuous, audible experience of the music as it unfolds, and not in some abstract mode of perception. One should resist suggestions to the effect that "in Mozart's music, unity lies in the deep structure of the music and is accessible only to analysis, which is superior to mere hearing."[107] Such attitudes can lead us away from rather than into the rich experiences of these works. Analysis should draw upon structure and style, without missing the lively eventfulness and remarkable subtlety that animates pieces such as Mozart's final concerto.

To judge from the manuscript of K. 595, much of this composition dates from the period between the end of 1787 and early 1789; in all probability, Mozart returned to the concerto after putting it aside for an extended period, completing the piece in January 1791.[108] Only for the finale did he use paper that stems from early 1791, when he found another way to employ the theme of the rondo. His continuing preoccupation with this folk-like tune is shown by his use of it in a song written immediately after the concerto and entitled *Sehnsucht nach dem Frühlinge* (Longing for spring), K. 596. This song, beginning with the words "Komm, lieber Mai" (Come, dear May), was one of three children's songs composed for an album of "Spring Songs" commissioned by the bookseller Ignatz Alberti and dedicated to the archduke Franz and his wife. The text of K. 596 begins, "Come, dear May, and clothe the trees in green once more"; the second song, "Im Frühlingsanfang," K. 597, opens "At the beginning of spring, awaken to a new life."

The revival and completion of the concerto in conjunction with these cheerful songs was auspicious. During 1790, Mozart's productivity had virtually collapsed; Maynard Solomon writes that "the deterioration in Mozart's circumstances accelerated and came perilously close to something approaching a total breakdown involving his family, his finances, his career, and his productivity, leaving him in a state of dejection, anxiety, and partial creative paralysis."[109] In early 1791, the composer was no stranger to longing, and the springtime melody "Komm, lieber Mai" lodged deeply in his

---

107. Marie-Agnes Dittrich, "Die Klaviermusik," in *Mozart Handbuch,* ed. Silke Leopold (Kassel: Bärenreiter and Metzler, 2005), p. 484. Dittrich cites in this connection a recent study by Martin Eybl, "Archaeologie der Tonkunst. Mozart-Analysen Heinrich Schenkers," in *Mozartanalyse im 19. und frühen 20. Jahrhundert. Bericht über die Tagung Salzburg 1996* (Laaber: Laaber, 1999), pp. 133–145.

108. For discussion of the chronology of the manuscript of K. 595, see Tyson, *Mozart: Studies of the Autograph Scores,* 153, 156.

109. Solomon, *Mozart: A Life,* 465.

imagination. He entered the three children's songs into his work catalogue directly under K. 595, on 14 January 1791. And although K. 595 was perhaps begun as early as 1788 and was entered into the catalogue on 5 January 1791, Mozart first performed the work on 4 March, at the beginning of his own last spring.[110] That concert was his final public appearance at the keyboard in Vienna, marking the end of an illustrious pianistic career in that city that had begun a decade earlier.

110. This performance was at a benefit concert for a clarinetist named Joseph Bähr, or Beer, at the "Jahnscher Saal" in the Himmelpfortgasse, close to Mozart's lodgings in the Rauhensteingasse. For a discussion of the circumstances, see H. C. Robbins Landon, *1791*, 34–35.

SELECTED BIBLIOGRAPHY

Abbate, Carolyn. *In Search of Opera*. Princeton: Princeton University Press, 2001.
Abert, Hermann. *W. A. Mozart. Neu bearbeitete und erweiterte Ausgabe von Otto Jahns Mozart*. Leipzig: Breitkopf & Härtel, 1919.
Adorno, Theodor W. *Aesthetic Theory*. Trans. Robert Hullot-Kentor. Ed. Gretel Adorno and Rolf Tiedemann. Minneapolis: University of Minnesota Press, 1997.
———. *Gesammelte Schriften*. Ed. Rolf Tiedemann. 20 vols. Frankfurt am Main: Suhrkamp, 1971–86.
Allanbrook, Wye. *Rhythmic Gesture in Mozart's* Le Nozze di Figaro *and* Don Giovanni. Chicago: University of Chicago Press, 1983.
———. "Two Threads through the Labyrinth: Topic and Process in the First Movements of K. 332 and K. 333." In *Convention in Eighteenth- and Nineteenth-Century Music: Essays in Honor of Leonard G. Ratner*, ed. Wye Allanbrook, Janet M. Levy, and William P. Mahrt, 125–71. Stuyvesant, N.Y.: Pendragon Press, 1992.
Ambruster, Richard. "Joseph Sardi—Autor der Klaviervariationen KV 460 (454a). Zum Schaffen eines unbekannt gebliebenen Komponisten in Wien zur Zeit Mozarts." *Mozart-Jahrbuch 1997*: 225–48.
Anderson, Emily, trans. and ed. *The Letters of Mozart and His Family*. London: Macmillan, 1985.
Angermüller, Rudolph, ed. *Wolfgang A. Mozart. Leben und Werk*. Digitale Bibliothek 130. Berlin: Directmedia, 2005.
Badura-Skoda, Eva. *Wolfgang Amadeus Mozart. Klavierkonzert C Moll KV 491*. Munich: Wilhelm Fink, 1972.
Badura-Skoda, Eva, and Paul Badura-Skoda. "Zur Echtheit von Mozarts Sarti-Variationen KV 460." *Mozart-Jahrbuch 1959*: 127–39.
———. *Interpreting Mozart at the Keyboard*. Trans. Leo Black. New York: St. Martin's Press, 1962.
Bilson, Malcolm. "Execution and Expression in the Sonata in E flat, K282." *Early Music* 20 (1992): 237–43.
Bonds, Mark Evan. "Ästhetische Prämissen der musikalischen Analyse im ersten Viertel des 19. Jahrhunderts, anhand von Friedrich August Kannes 'Versuch einer Analyse der Mozart'schen Clavierwerke' (1821)." In *Mozartanalyse im 19. und frühen 20. Jahrhundert*. Ed. Gernot Gruber and Siegfried Mauser, 63–80. Laaber: Laaber, 1999.

Braunbehrens, Volkmar. *Mozart in Vienna, 1781–1791.* Trans. Timothy Bell. New York: Grove Weidenfeld, 1989. Originally published as *Mozart in Wien* (Munich: Piper, 1986).

Brendel, Alfred. *Alfred Brendel on Music: Collected Essays.* Chicago: A Cappella, 2001. This collection contains two essays on Mozart: "A Mozart Player Gives Himself Advice" (1–8) and "Minor Mozart: In Defense of His Solo Works" (9–15).

———. *Me of All People: Alfred Brendel in Conversation with Martin Meyer.* Trans. Richard Stokes. Ithaca, N.Y.: Cornell University Press, 2002.

———. *Music Sounded Out: Essays, Lectures, Interviews, Afterthoughts.* New York: Farrar Straus Giroux, 1990.

Brink, Guido. *Die Finalsätze in Mozarts Konzerten. Aspekte ihrer formalen Gestaltung und ihrer Funktion als Abschluß des Konzerts.* Kassel: Gustav Bosse Verlag, 2000.

Brown, A. Peter. "On the Opening Phrase of Mozart's K. 271: A Singular, Yet Logical, Event." *Mozart-Jahrbuch 1980/83:* 310–18.

Brück, Marion. "Kontemplation und Abschied in den langsamen Sätzen von Mozarts Klavierkonzerten." *Mozart-Jahrbuch 1991* (vol. 1): 164–67.

———. *Die langsamen Sätzen in Mozarts Klavierkonzerten.* Munich: Wilhelm Fink Verlag, 1994.

Budday, Wolfgang. "Das 'Rondeau' im frühen Instrumentalschaffen Mozarts. Anhang: Zur Echtheitsfrage der vierhändigen Klaviersonate KV 19d." In *Mozart Studien,* vol. 8, ed. Manfred Hermann Schmid, 75–102. Schneider: Tutzing, 1998.

Buch, David J. "On the Context of Mozart's Variations to the Aria, 'Ein Weib ist das herrlichste Ding auf der Welt', K. 613." *Mozart-Jahrbuch 1999:* 71–80.

Caplin, William E. *Classical Form: A Theory of Formal Functions for the Instrumental Music of Haydn, Mozart, and Beethoven.* New York: Oxford University Press, 1998.

Cole, Malcolm S. "The Rondo Finale: Evidence for the Mozart-Haydn Exchange?" *Mozart-Jahrbuch 1968/70:* 242–56.

Cone, Edward T. "The Authority of Music Criticism." *Journal of the American Musicological Society* 34.1 (1981), 1–18.

Cooke, Deryck. *The Language of Music.* Oxford: Clarendon, 1959.

Croll, Gerhard. "Ein Überraschender Mozart-Fund." *Mozart-Jahrbuch 1962/63:* 108–10.

———. Zu Mozarts Larghetto und Allegro Es-Dur für zwei Klaviere." *Mozart-Jahrbuch 1964:* 28–37.

Dennerlein, Hanns. *Der unbekannte Mozart: Die Welt seiner Klavierwerke.* Leipzig: Breitkopf und Härtel, 1951.

Deutsch, Otto Erich, ed. *Mozart: A Documentary Biography.* Trans. Eric Blom, Peter Branscombe, and Jeremy Noble. London: Black, 1965. Originally published as *Mozart: Die Dokumente seines Lebens* (Kassel: Bärenreiter, 1961).

Dittersdorf, Karl von. *The Autobiography of Karl von Dittersdorf.* Trans. A. D. Coleridge. London: R. Bentley and Son, 1896.

Dittrich, Marie-Agnes. "Die Klaviermusik." In *Mozart Handbuch.* Ed. Silke Leopold, 482–559. Kassel: Bärenreiter and Metzler, 2005.

Edwards, Stephen Perry. "Extremes of Contrast in Mozart's Sonata-Form Movements." Ph.D. diss., University of Texas at Austin, 1997.

Einstein, Alfred. *Mozart, His Character, His Work.* New York: Oxford, 1945.

Eisen, Cliff. "The Salzburg Symphonies: A Biographical Interpretation." In *Wolfgang Amadé Mozart: Essays on His Life and His Music,* ed. Stanley Sadie, 178–212. Oxford: Clarendon, 1996.

———. "The Mozarts' Salzburg Music Library." In *Mozart Studies 2,* ed. Cliff Eisen, 85–138. Oxford: Clarendon, 1997.

———. "Mozart and the Four-Hand Sonata K. 19d." In *Haydn, Mozart, and Beethoven: Studies in the Music of the Classical Period: Essays in Honour of Alan Tyson,* ed. Sieghard Brandenburg, 91–99. Oxford: Clarendon, 1998.

Elias, Norbert. *Mozart: Portrait of a Genius*. Trans. Edmund Jephcott. Berkeley: University of California Press, 1993. Originally published as *Mozart: Zur Soziologie eines Genies*, ed. Michael Schröter (Frankfurt am Main: Suhrkamp, 1991).

Engel, Hans. *Die Entwicklung des Deutschen Klavierkonzertes von Mozart bis Liszt.* 1927. Reprint, Hildesheim: Georg Olms, 1970.

Feldman, Martha. "Staging the Virtuoso: Ritornello Procedure in Mozart, from Aria to Concerto." *Mozart's Piano Concertos: Text, Context, Interpretation*, ed. Neal Zaslaw, 149–86. Ann Arbor: University of Michigan Press, 1996.

Fischer, Kurt von. "Sind die Klaviervariationen über Sartis 'Come un'agnello' von Mozart?" *Mozart-Jahrbuch 1958:* 18–29.

———. "Sind die Klaviervariationen KV 460 von Mozart?" *Mozart-Jahrbuch 1959:* 140–45.

———. "COME UN'AGNELLO—Aria del SIG'SARTI con Variazioni." *Mozart-Jahrbuch 1978/79:* 112–21.

Flothuis, Marius. *Mozart's Piano Concertos.* Amsterdam: Rodopi, 2001.

Forman, Denis. *Mozart's Concerto Form: The First Movements of the Piano Concertos.* New York: Praeger, 1971.

Forte, Allen. "Generative Chromaticism in Mozart's Music: The Rondo in A minor, K. 511." *The Musical Quarterly* 66 (1980): 459–83.

Freeman, Daniel E. "Josef Myslivček and Mozart's Piano Sonatas K. 309 (284b) and 311 (284c)." *Mozart Jahrbuch 1995:* 95–109.

Gale, Patrick. "Mechanical Organ and Armonica." In *The Mozart Compendium: A Guide to Mozart's Life and Music,* ed. H. C. Robbins Landon, 308–10. London: Thames and Hudson, 1990.

Gerstenberg, Walter. "Zum Autograph des Klavierkonzertes KV. 503 (C-Dur). Anmerkung zu Mozarts Schaffensweise." *Mozart-Jahrbuch 1953:* 38–46.

Goehr, Lydia. *The Imaginary Museum of Musical Works: An Essay in the Philosophy of Music.* Oxford: Clarendon, 1992.

Grayson, David. *Mozart's Piano Concertos: No. 20 in D minor, K. 466, and No. 21 in C major, K. 467.* Cambridge: Cambridge University Press, 1998.

Girdlestone, C. M. *Mozart's Piano Concertos.* London: Cassell, 1948.

Gjerdingen, Robert O. *A Classic Turn of Phrase: Music and the Psychology of Convention.* Philadelphia: University of Pennsylvania Press, 1988.

Glock, William. Program notes to the recordings *Mozart: The Complete Music for Piano Solo,* by Walter Gieseking. 2 vols. (Seraphim ID-6047 and ID-6048).

Gülke. Peter. "Die Konzerte." In *Mozart Handbuch.* Ed. Silke Leopold, 328–81. Kassel: Bärenreiter, 2005.

Gutman, Robert W. *Mozart: A Cultural Biography.* New York: Harcourt Brace, 1999.

Halliwell, Ruth. *The Mozart Family: Four Lives in a Social Context.* Oxford: Clarendon, 1998.

Hatten, Robert. *Interpreting Musical Gestures, Topics, and Tropes: Mozart, Beethoven, Schubert.* Bloomington: Indiana University Press, 2004.

Heartz, Daniel. *Haydn, Mozart, and the Viennese School, 1740–1780.* New York: Norton, 1995.

Hildesheimer, Wolfgang. *Mozart.* Trans. Marion Faber. New York: Farrar, Straus and Giroux, 1982. Originally published, 1977.

Hutchings, Arthur. *A Companion to Mozart's Piano Concertos.* London: Oxford University Press, 1948.

———. "The Keyboard Music." In *The Mozart Companion,* ed. H. C. Robbins Landon and Donald Mitchell. London: Faber and Faber, 1956. 32–65.

Ivanovitch, Roman Maximilian. "Mozart and the Environment of Variation." Ph.D. diss., Yale University, 2004.

Irvine, Thomas. "Mozart's KV 475: Fantasie als Utopie?" *Acta Mozartiana* 50 (2003): 37–49.

Irving, John. "A Fresh Look at Mozart's 'Sonatensatz', K. 312 (590d)." *Mozart-Jahrbuch 1995:* 79–94.

————. *Mozart's Piano Concertos*. Aldershot: Ashgate, 2003.

————. *Mozart's Piano Sonatas: Contexts, Sources, Style*. Cambridge: Cambridge University Press, 1997.

Keefe, Simon P. "The Concertos in Aesthetic and Stylistic Context." In *The Cambridge Companion to Mozart*, ed. Simon P. Keefe, 78–91. Cambridge: Cambridge University Press, 2003.

————. *Mozart's Piano Concertos: Dramatic Dialogue in the Age of Enlightenment*. Suffolk: Boydell and Brewer, 2001.

Kecskieméti, István. "Barock-Elemente in den langsamen Instrumentalsätzen Mozarts." *Mozart-Jahrbuch 1967*: 182–92.

Kerman, Joseph. *Concerto Conversations*. Cambridge: Harvard University Press, 1999.

————. "Mozart's Piano Concertos and Their Audience." In *Write All These Down: Essays on Music*, 322–34. Berkeley: University of California Press, 1994.

Kinderman, William. *Beethoven*. Oxford: Clarendon, 1995.

————. "Dramatic Development and Narrative Design in the First Movement of Mozart's Piano Concerto in C Minor, K. 491." In *Mozart's Piano Concertos: Text, Context, Interpretation*, ed. Neal Zaslaw, 285–301. Ann Arbor: University of Michigan Press, 1996.

————. "Subjectivity and Objectivity in Mozart Performance." *Early Music* 19 (1991): 593–600.

King, Hyatt A. *Mozart's Chamber Music*. London: British Broadcasting Corporation, 1968.

Koch, Heinrich Christoph. *Versuch einer Anleitung zur Composition*, iii. Leipzig: A.F. Böhme, 1793. Reprinted Hildesheim: Georg Olms, 1969. Translated by Nancy Kovaleff Baker as *Introductory Essay on Composition: The Mechanical Rules of Melody, Sections 3 and 4*. New Haven: Yale University Press, 1983.

Knepler, Georg. *Wolfgang Amadé Mozart*. Trans. J. Bradford Robinson. Cambridge: Cambridge University Press, 1994. Originally published in German (Berlin: Henschel Verlag, 1991).

Komlós, Katalin. "Fantasia and Sonata, K. 475/457 in Contemporary Context." *Mozart-Jahrbuch 1991*: 816–23.

————. *Fortepianos and Their Music: Germany, Austria and England, 1760–1800*. Oxford: Clarendon, 1995.

————. "'Ich präludirte und spielte Variazionen': Mozart the Fortepianist." In *Perspectives on Mozart Performance*, ed. R. Larry Todd and Peter Williams, 27–54. Cambridge: Cambridge University Press, 1991.

————. "Mozart the Performer." In *The Cambridge Companion to Mozart*, ed. Simon P. Keefe, 215–26. Cambridge: Cambridge University Press, 2003.

Konrad, Ulrich. "'Gruppenkonzerte' aus den letzten Salzburger Jahren. Probleme der Chronologie und Deutung," in *Festschrift Siegfried Kross*, ed. Reinmar Emans and Matthias Wendt, 141–57. Bonn: Gudrun Schröder, 1990.

————, *Mozarts Schaffensweise*. Göttingen: Vandenhoeck and Ruprecht, 1992.

————, "Neuentdecktes und wiedergefundenes Werkstattmaterial Wolfgang Amadeus Mozarts. Erster Nachtrag zum Katalog der Skizzen und Entwürfe." *Mozart-Jahrbuch 1995*: 1–28.

————, ed. Neue Mozart Ausgabe, Serie X, Supplement 30/4: *Fragmente*. Kassel: Bärenreiter, 2002.

————, *Wolfgang Amadé Mozart. Leben – Musik – Werkbestand*. Kassel: Bärenreiter, 2005.

Korsyn, Kevin. "Schenker and Kantian Epistemology." *Theoria: Historical Aspects of Music Theory* 3 (1988): 1–58.

Kramer, Richard. "Ambiguities in *La Malinconia*: What the Sketches Say." In *Beethoven Studies* 3, ed. Alan Tyson, 29–41. Cambridge: Cambridge University Press, 1982.

Krones, Hartmut. "Rhetorik und rhetorische Symbolik in der Musik um 1800. Vom Weiterleben eines Prinzips." *Musiktheorie* 3 (1988), 117–40.

Küster, Konrad. *Formale Aspekte des ersten Allegros in Mozarts Konzerten*. Kassel: Bärenreiter, 1991.

———, *Mozart: A Musical Biography*. Trans. Mary Whitall. Oxford: Clarendon, 1996.

Landon, H. C. Robbins. *1791: Mozart's Last Year*. London: Thames and Hudson, 1988.

———. "The Concertos: Their Musical Origin and Development." In *The Mozart Companion*, ed. H. C. Robbins Landon and Donald Mitchell, 234–82. London: Faber and Faber, 1956.

———. *Mozart and Vienna, Including Selections from Johann Pezzl's 'Sketch of Vienna,' 1786–90*. London: Thames and Hudson, 1991.

———. *The Mozart Essays*. London: Thames and Hudson, 1995.

Leopold, Silke, ed. *Mozart Handbuch*. Kassel: Bärenreiter and Metzler, 2005.

Levey, Michael. *The Life and Death of Mozart*. 1971. Reprint, London: Abacus, 1995.

Levin, Robert D. "Improvisation and Musical Structure in Mozart's Piano Concertos." In *L'interpretation de la Musique Classique de Haydn à Schubert. Colloque international, Evry, 13–15 octobre 1977*, 45–50. Paris: Minkoff, 1980.

———. "Improvised Embellishments in Mozart's Keyboard Music." *Early Music* 20 (1992): 221–33.

———. "Mozart and the Keyboard Culture of His Time." In *Min-Ad: Israel Studies in Musicology Online* 3 (2004): 1–26 [essay adapted from a keynote address delivered at a conference at Cornell University on 28 March 2003].

———. "Mozart's Solo Keyboard Music." In *Eighteenth-Century Keyboard Music*, ed. Robert L. Marshall, 308–49. New York: Routledge, 2003.

———. "Mozart's Keyboard Concertos." In *Eighteenth-Century Keyboard Music*, ed. Robert L. Marshall, 350–93. New York: Routledge, 2003.

———. "Performance Practice in the Music of Mozart." In *The Cambridge Companion to Mozart*, ed. Simon P. Keefe, 227–45. Cambridge: Cambridge University Press, 2003.

Loesser, Arthur. *Men, Women, and Pianos: A Social History*. New York: Simon and Schuster, 1954.

Lorenz, Franz. *Mozart als Clavier-Componist*. Breslau: Leuckart, 1866.

Lorenz, Michael. "The Jenamy Concerto." *Newsletter of the Mozart Society of America* 10.1 (2005): 1–3.

———. "'Mademoiselle Jeunehomme' Zur Lösung eines Mozart-Rätzels." In *Mozart Experiment Aufklärung* (Essays for the Mozart Exhibition 2006), 423–29. Vienna: Da Ponte Institut, 2006.

Lowinsky, Edward. "On Mozart's Rhythm," *The Musical Quarterly* 42 (1956): 162–86.

Marshall, Robert L. "Bach and Mozart's Artistic Maturity." In *Bach Perspectives*, 3:47–49. Lincoln: University of Nebraska Press, 1998.

Maunder, Richard. *Keyboard Instruments in Eighteenth-Century Vienna*. Oxford: Clarendon, 1998.

McClary, Susan. "A Musical Dialectic from the Enlightenment: Mozart's Piano Concerto in G Major, K. 453, Movement 2." *Cultural Critique* 4 (1986): 129–69.

Mercado, Mario R. *The Evolution of Mozart's Pianistic Style*. Carbondale: University of Southern Illinois Press, 1992.

Meyer, John. "Mozart's Pathétique Concerto." *The Music Review* 39 (1978): 196–210.

Meyer, Leonard B. "Process and Morphology in the Music of Mozart." *Journal of Musicology* 1 (1982): 67–94.

Miller, Malcolm. "Leopold Mozart's Formative Influence on Wolfgang Amadeus Mozart's Early Piano Sonatas." *Piano Journal of the European Piano Teachers Association* 17 (1996): 13–15.

Moser, Hans Joachim. "Über Mozarts Chromatik." *Mozart-Jahrbuch 1956*: 167–99.

Müller, August Eberhard. *Anweisung zum genauen Vorträge der Mozartschen Clavier Concerte hauptsächlich in Absicht richtiger Applicatur*. Leipzig: Schmiedt & Rau, 1796.

Nägeli, Hans Georg. *Vorlesungen über Musik*. Stuttgart and Tübingen, 1826.

Neumann, Friedrich. *Ornamentation and Improvisation in Mozart.* Princeton: Princeton University Press, 1986.

Neumann, Hans. "The Two Versions of Mozart's Rondo K. 494." Revised and completed by Carl Schachter. In *The Music Forum,* vol.1, ed. William J. Mitchell and Felix Salzer, 1–34. New York: Columbia University Press, 1967.

Niemetschek, Franz. *W.A. Mozart's Leben.* 1798. Facsimile reprint, including revisions and additions of the second edition from 1808, ed. Ernst Rychnovsky, Prague: T. Taussig, 1905.

Nissen, Georg Nikolaus von. *Biographie W.A. Mozart's. Nach originalbriefen, sammlungen alles über ihn geschriebenen, mit vielen neuen beylagen, steindrücken, musik-blättern und einem fac-simile. Von Georg Nikolaus von Nissen. Nach dessen tode herausgegeben von Constanze, wittwe von Nissen, früher wittwe Mozart.* Leipzig: Breitkopf & Härtel, 1828.

Pesic, Peter. "The Child and the Daemon: Mozart and Deep Play," *19th-Century Music* 25 (2001–02): 91–107.

Plath, Wolfgang. "Zur Datierung der Klaviersonaten KV 279–84." *Acta Mozartiana* 21 (1974): 26–30.

Rampe, Siegbert. *Mozarts Claviermusik. Klangwelt und Aufführungspraxis.* Kassel: Bärenreiter, 1995.

Ratner, Leonard G. "Topical Content in Mozart's Keyboard Sonatas." *Early Music* 19 (1991): 615–19.

Reijen, Paul Willem van. *Vergleichende Studien zur Klaviervariationstechnik von Mozart und seinen Zeitgenossen.* Buren: Frits Knuf, 1988.

Ringer, Alexander L. "Mozart und der Josephinismus. Sozio-ökonomische Anmerkungen zu einem musikalischen Stilwandel." In *Musik als Geschichte,* 55–61. Laaber: Laaber, 1993.

Rosen, Charles. *The Classical Style: Haydn, Mozart, Beethoven.* 1971. Reprint, expanded ed., New York: Norton, 1997.

———. *Sonata Forms.* New York: Norton, 1988.

Rosen, David. "The Composer's 'Standard Operating Procedure' as Evidence of Intention: The Case of a Formal Quirk in Mozart's K. 595." *Journal of Musicology* 5 (1987): 79–90.

———. "'Unexpectedness' and 'Inevitability' in Mozart's Piano Concertos." In *Mozart's Piano Concertos: Text, Context, Interpretation,* ed. Neal Zaslaw, 261–84. Ann Arbor: University of Michigan Press, 1996.

Rosenblum, Sandra P. *Performance Practices in Classic Piano Music: Their Principles and Applications.* Bloomington: Indiana University Press, 1988.

Rothstein, William. *Phrase Rhythm in Tonal Music.* New York: Schirmer, 1989.

Ruile-Dronke, Jutta. *Ritornell und Solo in Mozarts Klavierkonzerten.* Tutzing: Schneider, 1978.

Rushton, Julian. *Mozart.* New York: Oxford University Press, 2006.

Sadie, Stanley. *Mozart: The Early Years 1756–1781.* New York: Norton, 2006.

Schachter, Carl. "Idiosyncratic Features of Three Mozart Slow Movements: The Piano Concertos K. 449, K. 453, and K. 467." In *Mozart's Piano Concertos: Text, Context, Interpretation,* ed. Neal Zaslaw, 315–33. Ann Arbor: University of Michigan Press, 1996.

Schenker, Heinrich. *Das Meisterwerk in der Musik.* Munich, Vienna, and Berlin: Drei Masken Verlag, 1925. Trans. by William Drabkin as *The Masterwork in Music. A Yearbook.* 2 vols. (Cambridge: Cambridge University Press, 1994).

———. *Neue musikalische Theorien und Phantasien,* iii: *Der freie Satz.* Ed. Oswald Jonas. Vienna: Universal, 2nd edition 1956; first published 1935. Edited and translated by Ernst Oster as *Free Composition (Der freie Satz). Volume III of New Musical Theories and Fantasies.* New York: Longman, 1979.

Schiff, András. "Playing Mozart's Piano." Essay accompanying Schiff's compact-disc recording *Mozart: Piano Sonatas K545 and K570, Fantasie K475, Rondos K485 and K511.* Editions de L'Oiseau-Lyre 433 328–2, a coproduction with Internationale Stiftung Mozarteum Salzburg, 1991.

Schmid, Manfred Hermann. *Orchester und Solist in den Konzerten von W.A. Mozart. Mozart Studien.* Vol. 9. Tutzing: Schneider, 1999.

———. "Variation oder Rondo? Zu Mozarts Wiener Finale KV 382 des Klavierkonzerts KV 175." In *Mozart Studien,* 1:59–80. Tutzing: Schneider, 1992.

Simon, Edwin J. "Sonata into Concerto. A Study of Mozart's First Seven Concertos." *Acta musicologica* 30 (1959): 159–85.

Sisman, Elaine. "Form, Character, and Genre in Mozart's Piano Concerto Variations." In *Mozart's Piano Concertos: Text, Context, Interpretation,* ed. Neal Zaslaw, 335–63. Ann Arbor: University of Michigan Press, 1996.

Solomon, Maynard. *Mozart: A Life.* New York: Harper Collins, 1995.

Somfai, László. "Mozart's First Thoughts: The Two Versions of the Sonata in D major, K. 284." *Early Music* 19 (1991): 601–13.

Sponheuer, Bernd. "Zum Problem des doppelten Finales in Mozarts 'erstem' Klavierkonzert KV 175." *Archiv für Musikwissenschaft* 42.2 (1985): 102–20.

Stanley, Glenn. "Einzelwerk als Gattungskritik. Mozarts Klavierrondo in a-Moll KV 511." *Mozart-Jahrbuch 2001:* 257–71.

Steglich, Rudolf. "Das Auszierungswesen in der Musik W. A. Mozarts." *Mozart-Jahrbuch 1955:* 181–237.

———. "Über das melodische Motiv in der Musik Mozarts. Eine Analyse der d-moll-Phantasie für Klavier." *Mozart-Jahrbuch 1953:* 128–42.

Stevens, Jane R. "Theme, Harmony, and Texture in Classic-Romantic Descriptions of Concerto First-Movement Form," *Journal of the American Musicological Society* 27 (1974): 25–60.

———. "The Importance of C. P. E. Bach for Mozart's Piano Concertos." In *Mozart's Piano Concertos: Text, Context, Interpretation,* ed. Neal Zaslaw, 211–36. Ann Arbor: University of Michigan Press, 1996.

Stock, Jonathan P. J. "Orchestration as Structural Determinant: Mozart's Deployment of Woodwind Timbre in the Slow Movement of the C Minor Piano Concerto K. 491." *Music and Letters* 78 (1997): 210–19.

Sutcliffe, Dean W. "The Keyboard Music." In *The Cambridge Companion to Mozart,* ed. Simon P. Keefe, 61–77. Cambridge: Cambridge University Press, 2003.

Taruskin, Richard. *Text and Act: Essays on Music and Performance.* New York: Oxford University Press, 1995.

Tishler, Hans. *A Structural Analysis of Mozart's Piano Concertos.* Brooklyn: Institute of Medieval Music, 1966.

Todd, R. Larry, and Peter Williams. *Perspectives on Mozart Performance.* Cambridge: Cambridge University Press, 1991.

Tovey, Donald Francis. "The Classical Concerto." In *Essays in Musical Analysis: Concertos and Choral Works,* 3–27. London: Oxford University Press, 1981. This essay was originally published in 1903.

Türk, Daniel Gottlob. *Klavierschule, oder Anweisung zum Klavierspielen für Lehrer und Lernende.* Leipzig: Schwickert, 1789. Trans. by R. H. Haagh as *School of Clavier Playing.* Lincoln: University of Nebraska Press, 1982

Tyson, Alan. "Mozart's Piano Concerto Fragments." In *Mozart's Piano Concertos: Text, Context, Interpretation,* ed. Neil Zaslaw, 67–72. Ann Arbor: University of Michigan Press, 1996.

———. *Mozart: Studies of the Autograph Scores.* Cambridge, Mass.: Harvard University Press, 1987.

———. "Proposed New Dates for Many Works and Fragments Written by Mozart from March 1781 to December 1791." In *Mozart Studies,* ed. Cliff Eisen, 213–26. Oxford: Clarendon, 1991.

Uhde, Jürgen, and Renate Wieland. *Denken und Spielen: Studien zu einer Theorie der musikalischen Darstellung.* Kassel: Bärenreiter, 1988.

Valentin, Erich "Zu Mozarts frühesten Werken, Die Klavierstücke von 1761." *Mozart-Jahrbuch 1955:* 238–42.

Webster, James. "Are Mozart's Concertos 'Dramatic'? Concerto Ritornellos versus Aria Introductions in the 1780s." In *Mozart's Piano Concertos: Text, Context, Interpretation,* ed. Neal Zaslaw, 107–37. Ann Arbor: University of Michigan Press, 1996.

Weising, Klaus. *Die Sonatenform in den langsamen Konzertsätzen Mozarts.* Hamburg: Verlag der Musikalienhandlung Karl Dieter Wagner, 1970.

Willis, Andrew S. "Free Variation of Repeated Passages in Mozart's Keyboard Music." DMA diss., Cornell University, 1994.

Winter, Robert. "The Bifocal Close and the Evolution of the Viennese Classical Style." *Journal of the American Musicological Society* 42 (1989): 275–337.

Wolf, Eugene. "The Rediscovered Autograph of Mozart's Fantasy and Sonata in C minor, K. 475/457." *Journal of Musicology* 10 (1992): 3–47.

Wolff, Christoph. "Mozart 1784: Biographische und stilgeschichtliche Überlegungen," *Mozart-Jahrbuch 1986:* 1–10.

Wyzewa, Théodore de, and Georges de Saint-Foix. *Wolfgang Amadé Mozart: Sa vie musicale et son oeuvre. Essai de biographie.* 5 vols. 1936. Reprint, 3rd ed., Bruges: Desclée, De Brouwer et Cie, 1958.

Zaslaw, Neal, ed. *Mozart's Piano Concertos: Text, Context, Interpretation.* Ann Arbor: University of Michigan Press, 1996.

———. "The Adagio in F Major, K3 Anhang 206a + K6 Anhang A 65." In *Haydn, Mozart and Beethoven: Studies in the Music of the Classical Period,* ed. Sieghard Brandenburg, 101–13. Oxford: Clarendon, 1998.

INDEX OF COMPOSITIONS

Works are organized numerically by Köchel number. Those listed as Anh. (Anhang) are found in the appendix to the Köchel catalogue; K. deest. items are not in the catalogue. Page numbers in bold print indicate detailed discussion. For a list of works by categories, see Mozart, works, in the general index.

GENERAL INDEX

Sonata in E-flat major, K. 282 (189g), 27n, **37**, 50
Sonata in G major, K. 283 (189h), **16–27**, **37–40**, 64, 126n, 142n
Sonata in D major ("Dürnitz"), K. 284 (205b), 29, **40–41**, 50, **117–127**
Sonata in C major, K. 309 (284b), **41–42**, 51
Sonata in A minor ("Paris"), K. 310 (300d), 31, 40, **44–47**, 48, 180n
Sonata in D major, K. 311 (384c), **42–44**, 57, 126
Sonata in C major, K. 330, **48–51**
Sonata in A major, K. 331 (300i), 48, **50–51**
Sonata in F major, K. 332 (300k), 27n, 48, **51–54**
Sonata in B-flat major, K. 333 (315c), 27n, 48, **54–57**, 105
Sonata in C minor, K. 457, 6, 57–58, **60–63**, 117
Sonata in F major, K. 533: **63–64**, 88
Sonata in C major, K. 545, 5n, **64–66**, 99
Sonata in B-flat major, K. 570, 5n, 13, **66–67**, 570
Sonata in D major, K. 576, 13, **67–69**, 94, 215
Sonata in G major, K. Anh. q99 (33d), 95n
Sonata in B-flat major, K. Anh. 200 (33e), 95n
Sonata in C major, K. Anh. 201 (33f), 95n
Sonata in F major, K. Anh. 202 (33g), 95n
Sonatas, K. 279–284 (189d–h, 205b), 4, **28–41**, 140, 147
Sonatas for Violin and Piano, K. 301–306, 147
Der Stein der Weisen oder die Zauberinsel, 79
String Quartet in A major, K. 464, 128
String Quartet in A major (fragment), K. 464a, 128
Suite for Piano in C major, K. 399 (385i), 86
Symphony in D major ("Haffner"), K. 385, 154
Symphony in C major ("Linz"), K. 425, 48, 105n
Symphony in D major ("Prague"), K. 504, 88, 105n, 210
Symphony in G minor, K. 550, 169, 181, 190, 214
Symphony in C major ("Jupiter"), K. 551, 9, 41, 148, 153, 210
Variations in G major ("Laat ons Juichen"), K. 24, 70–71
Variations in D major ("Willem van Nassau"), K. 25, 71
Variations in C major, K. 179 (189a), **71–72**
Variations in G major ("Mio caro Adone"), K. 180 (173c), 71
Variations in C major ("Lison dormait"), K. 264 (315d), 72
Variations in C major ("Ah, vous dirai-je Maman"), K. 265 (300e), **72–73**, 141
Variations in F major, K. 352 (374c), 73–74
Variations in E-flat major ("La belle Francoise"), K. 353 (300f), 73
Variations in E-flat major ("Je suis Lindor"), K. 354 (299a), 72
Variations in F major ("Salve tu, Domine"), K. 398 (416e), 70, **74–75**
Variations in G major, K. 455, 70
Variations in A major ("Come un agnello"), K. 460 (454a), **74–76**
Variations in B-flat major, K. 500, 76
Variations in G major, K. 501, **106**
Variations in D major ("Duport"), K. 573, 13, **76–79**
Variations in F major ("Ein Weib ist das herrlichste Ding auf der Welt"), K. 613, **79–80**
Müller, August Eberhard, 87, 138
Müller-Deym, Joseph. *See* Deym, Count Joseph

Nägeli, Hans Georg, 152
Neue Mozart Ausgabe, 13n, 128, 189n
Niemetschek, Franz, 116
Nissen, Georg Nikolaus, 116–117
Notenbuch (of Nannerl Mozart), 4, 80–81, 83
Noverre, Jean Georges, 141, 147

opera *buffa*, 6, 52, 156, 167, 170, 175, 180, 210
opera *seria*, 6, 140, 167, 210

Paisiello, Giovanni, 74
perpetuum mobile, 45–47, 145
Pertl, Maria Anna, 80
Pezzl, Johann, 150
Plath, Wolfgang, 44, 48, 95
Ployer, Barbara ("Babette") von, 87, 156
Pollet, Benoît, 148
Puchberg, Michael, 11, 67

Rampe, Siegbert, 55
Ratner, Leonard G., 20
Raupach, Hermann Friedrich, 10, 139
Realzeitung, 141, 150
Rehm, Wolfgang, 95
Reijen, Paul Willem van, 70n
rhetoric, musical, 5–6, 8, 9, 17, 26–27, 32, 35, 38, 61, 65, 97, 130–131, 143, 158
Richter, Jean Paul, 8
rondo (rondeau), form 36, 40–41, 43–44, 56–57, 64–65, 67, 88–89, 105–106, 147, 153, 154–155, 162, 174, 211–212, 213, 215–217
Rosen, Charles, 9, 67, 125, 141–142, 169, 177, 188, 190, 200
Rosen, David, 129, 142–143
Rutini, Giovanni Marco, 10

Saint-Foix, Georges de, 10n, 79, 88, 141
Salieri, Antonio, 71
Sammartini, Giovanni Battista, 10
Sardi, Joseph/Giuseppe, 76
Sarti, Giuseppe, 74–76, 143
Scarlatti, Giuseppe, 10
Schachter, Carl, 177
Schack, Benedikt, 79
Schenker, Heinrich, 14–15, 53, 217n
Schiff, András, 5
Schikaneder, Emanuel, 79–80
Schlegel, Friedrich, 8
Schmid, Manfred Hermann, 148, 152
Schnabel, Artur, 57
Schobert, Johann, 10, 139, 178
Schubert, Franz Peter, 47
Schuster, Joseph, 148
Scotch snap rhythm, 42, 99
Shaffer, Peter, 116

siciliano, 33–34, 89, 91–92, 188, 189–190
Sisman, Elaine, 148
sketches and manuscripts, 10, 44, 82, 104, 117–129, 132–133, 154, 189, 217
Solomon, Maynard, 11, 45, 47, 217
Somfai, László, 119–121, 127
Sponheuer, Bernd, 147
Stackelberg, Baron Christoph, 112
Stadler, Abbé Maximilian, 86, 87, 94, 104, 127
Steglich, Rudolf, 23n, 87n
Stein, Johann Andreas, 4
Stržitéž, Count Joseph Deym von. *See* Deym, Count Joseph
Sturm und Drang, 52, 88
subscription concert series, 10, 150
Swieten, Baron Gottfried van, 9, 103, 188

Taruskin, Richard, 6
thematic integration, 29, 145, 155–156, 168, 181, 193–200, 215
Tieck, Ludwig, 8
tonal ambiguity, 191–192, 215
topos, musical, 23, 26, 27, 58, 67
Tovey, Donald Francis, 153
Trattner, Johann Thomas von, 57
Trattner, Therese von, 57
Türk, Daniel Gottlob, 15
Turkish style, 51
Tyson, Alan, 44, 48, 127–128, 154, 155

Uchida, Mitsuko, 64n, 87n
Uhde, Jürgen, 45, 58

Wagenseil, Georg Christoph, 10, 81
Wagner, Richard, 93
Walter, Anton, 5, 43
Weber, Aloysia, 44, 84
Weber, Constanze. *See* Mozart, Constanze Weber (wife)
Weber, Sophie, 87
Werkverzeichnis (or *Verzeichnüss*), Mozart's own, 57, 128, 155
Widerberg, Bo, 180
Wiener Zeitung, 112, 148
Winter, Sebastian, 84
Wyzewa, Théodore de, 10n, 141

Zaslaw, Neal, 71n